Lecture Notes in Computer Science 2853

Edited by G. Goos, J. Hartmanis, and J. van Leeuwen

Springer
Berlin
Heidelberg
New York
Hong Kong
London
Milan
Paris
Tokyo

Mario Jeckle   Liang-Jie Zhang (Eds.)

Web Services – ICWS-Europe 2003

International Conference ICWS-Europe 2003
Erfurt, Germany, September 23-24, 2003
Proceedings

Springer

Series Editors

Gerhard Goos, Karlsruhe University, Germany
Juris Hartmanis, Cornell University, NY, USA
Jan van Leeuwen, Utrecht University, The Netherlands

Volume Editors

Mario Jeckle
University of Applied Sciences
Robert-Gerwig-Platz 1, 78120 Furtwangen, Germany
E-mail: mario@jeckle.de

Liang-Jie Zhang
IBM T.J. Watson Research Center
1101 Kitchawan Road, Route 134, Yorktown Heights, NY 10598, USA
E-mail: zhanglj@us.ibm.com

Cataloging-in-Publication Data applied for

A catalog record for this book is available from the Library of Congress.

Bibliographic information published by Die Deutsche Bibliothek
Die Deutsche Bibliothek lists this publication in the Deutsche Nationalbibliografie;
detailed bibliographic data is available in the Internet at <http://dnb.ddb.de>.

CR Subject Classification (1998): H.4, H.3, C.2, H.5, D.2, K.4.4

ISSN 0302-9743
ISBN 3-540-20125-4 Springer-Verlag Berlin Heidelberg New York

This work is subject to copyright. All rights are reserved, whether the whole or part of the material is
concerned, specifically the rights of translation, reprinting, re-use of illustrations, recitation, broadcasting,
reproduction on microfilms or in any other way, and storage in data banks. Duplication of this publication
or parts thereof is permitted only under the provisions of the German Copyright Law of September 9, 1965,
in its current version, and permission for use must always be obtained from Springer-Verlag. Violations are
liable for prosecution under the German Copyright Law.

Springer-Verlag Berlin Heidelberg New York
a member of BertelsmannSpringer Science+Business Media GmbH

http://www.springer.de

© Springer-Verlag Berlin Heidelberg 2003
Printed in Germany

Typesetting: Camera-ready by author, data conversion by PTP-Berlin GmbH
Printed on acid-free paper   SPIN: 10958308   06/3142   5 4 3 2 1 0

Preface

After some time of early experience Web Services are moving themselves from a new highly fragmented technology to a piece of nowadays infrastructures which promise to address various current challenges. These include especially classical issues of integration and data in a heterogeneous environment. The Web Service technology provides an open and technology-agnostic interface, and furthermore propels new usage paradigms in distributed computing infrastructures like Grid Services. Successful adoption of Web Service technology relies on the definition of interoperable architectural building blocks which can be integrated in existing software architectures, like J2EE or CORBA heritage. Interoperability will surely prove itself as the critical success factor of the Web Service proliferation. In order to accomplish these interoperability various standardization bodies such as the W3C, UN or OASIS founded activities to create specifications and products implementing these building blocks.

As the sister event of the First International Conference on Web Services (ICWS 2003), which was held in Las Vegas, June 23 - 26, USA, has proven to be an excellent catalyst for research and collaboration, the 2003 International Conference on Web Services - Europe (ICWS-Europe 2003) is expected to continue this trend. The topics of papers collected in this proceedings volume ranges from issues like modeling, development, deployment, publishing, as well as discovery, composition and collaboration, plus monitoring and analytical control. Additional contributions summarize some research and development challenges of building Web Service solutions. Especially, some contributions present an emerging research direction, namely, Web Services collaboration. Moreover, some major research activities associated with facilitating extended business collaboration using Web services and semantic annotation are also covered.

Many people have worked very hard to make the Conference possible. We would like to thank all who have helped to make ICWS-Europe 2003 a success. The Program Committee members and referees each deserve credit for the excellent final program that resulted from the diligent review of the submissions.

July 2003   Mario Jeckle
Liang-Jie Zhang

Organization

General Co-chairs
Bogdan Franczyk, Leipzig University, Germany
Jen-Yao Chung, IBM T.J. Watson Research Center, USA

Program Co-chairs
Mario Jeckle, University of Applied Sciences Furtwangen, Germany
Liang-Jie Zhang, IBM T.J. Watson Research Center, USA

Industrial Chair
Zongwei Luo (University of Hong Kong)

Program Committee
Farhad Arbab (CWI Amsterdam)
Boualem Benatallah (University of New South Wales)
Christoph Bussler (Oracle Corp.)
Fabio Casati (Hewlett-Packard)
Schahram Dustdar (Vienna University of Technology)
Jean-Philippe Martin-Flatin (CERN)
Ulrich Frank (Koblenz University)
Garciela Gonzalez (Sam Houston State University)
Patrick C. K. Hung (Commonwealth Scientific & Industrial
    Research Organization)
Arne Koschel (Iona)
Zongwei Luo (University of Hong Kong)
Ingo Melzer (DaimlerChrysler Research and Technology)
Michael Stal (Siemens)
Son Cao Tran (New Mexico State University)
Rainer Unland (University of Essen)
Athanasios Vasilakos (University of Thessaly)

Table of Contents

Web Service Federations

Inter-organizational Business Processes

Confluence with Agent Technology and Semantic Web Enabled Web Services

Current and Future Issues

The Next Big Thing: Web Services Collaboration

Liang-Jie Zhang[1] and Mario Jeckle[2]

[1] IBM T.J. Watson Research Cente,
P.O. Box 218, Route 134
Yorktown Heights, NY, 10598
zhanglj@us.ibm.com
http://www.research.ibm.com/people/z/zhanglj8/
[2] Dept. Business Applications of Computer Science
University of Applied Sciences Furtwangen, Germany
mario@jeckle.de
http://www.jeckle.de

Abstract. In this paper, we introduce the lifecycle of a Web services solution that consists of Web services modeling, development, deployment, publishing, as well as discovery, composition and collaboration, plus monitoring and analytical control. Then some research and development challenges of building a Web services solution in the context of Web services solution lifecycle are described. Especially, we present an emerging Web services research direction, namely, Web services collaboration, followed by a few major research issues associated with facilitating extended business collaboration using Web services and semantic annotation.

1 Introduction

Web services are network enabled reusable components that conform to an interface with standard description format and access protocols. The basic enabling infrastructure of Web services consists of global registries like UDDI or local approaches like proposed by the Web Services Inspection Language (WSIL), SOAP-Protocol, Web Services Definition Language (WSDL), Process orchestration or choreography langauges like WSCI and BPEL4WS, and so forth.

For individual technology components, they have been extensively defined and explored in recent years. When building a solution using Web services, we can leverage the standard interface and communication protocols for information exchange and legacy application integration in most cases. For example, usually we use a Web service to represent an interface for a legacy application and then publish this Web service to Web services registries like UDDI registry or WSIL documents for public exposure and access. A more complicated case is to use BPEL4WS to capture the invocation sequences of a set of Web services and the related data exchange. No matter how simple the individual Web service case or how complicated Web services

M. Jeckle and L.-J. Zhang (Eds.): ICWS-Europe 2003, LNCS 2853, pp. 1–10, 2003.
© Springer-Verlag Berlin Heidelberg 2003

flow (a.k.a. composite Web service) are, they are just technology components in a solution.

Web service infrastructure itself can not fully understand the business context of an e-business solution. For example, basic syntactic information required to access the service is described in WSDL. However, an important part of the data about Web services is the relationships among business entities, business services, and operations, which are keys to composing and executing dynamic business processes. The fact is that the current Web services specifications and UDDI specification are lacking in the definitions and descriptions of such relationships. Therefore, in order to bridge the gap between the generic Web services infrastructure and the business solution context, we need to create a set of enabling technologies that can capture the semantic information about the business behaviors and IT system as well as provide an efficient bridging mechanism between the business requirements and IT infrastructure.

In this paper, we introduce the lifecycle of a Web services solution first. Then we summarize some research and development challenges of building a Web service solution. Especially, we present an emerging Web services research direction in the context of Web services solution lifecycle, namely, Web services collaboration, followed by some outstanding research issues associated with facilitating extended business collaboration using Web services and semantic annotation.

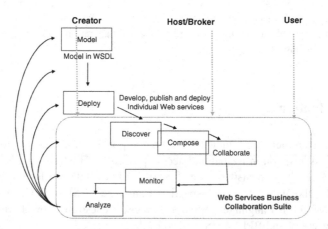

Fig. 1. Web Services Solution Lifecycle

2   Web Services Solution Lifecycle

Fig. 1 illustrates a Web services solution lifecycle which covers how Web services are created, composed and managed. A typical life cycle of a Web services solution consists of Web services modeling, development, deployment, publishing, as well as discovery, composition and collaboration, plus monitoring and analytical control. In this lifecycle, multiple parties may be involved.

As shown in Fig. 1, the Creator is responsible for modeling and deploying Web services. The Host/Broker and User will use Web services via discovery, composition and collaboration. Of course, the Creator himself can also consume the created Web services. The major steps involved in the life-cycle of a Web services solution and the corresponding research challenges are described in detail as follows.

Model: Web service is modeled in WSDL. This is a kind of top-down approach. Before implementing the execution code, one can define the service interface. This is similar to the Application Programming Interfaces (APIs) which have been used for years. Although, it should be noted that the usage for WSDL as a starting point is not necessarily the starting point of a Web Service development cycle it could make sense to start with the interface definition. The created service interface in the modeling phase should be platform independent. One of the research challenges on modeling is to find a way to carry more semantic information about method signature adaptation for dynamic Web services invocation. For example, MetaWSDL was proposed to represent the semantic information of WSDL for adaptive Web services invocation, such as the information for describing and quantifying the input and output parameters [13]. This kind of unit information is especially important when conversions between units are required. Additionally, UML based model driven architecture (MDA) proposed by OMG could be a good modeling approach to model the complexities of a business solution using Web services. Actually, since OMG introduced UML in 1997, it has been a dream to automatically bridge the gap between Business layer and IT layer in a solution.

Deploy: It includes developing, publishing, and deploying processes. We can develop Web services in different languages and deploy them on different application platforms as well as different operating systems. There are two types of Web services registries for one to publish Web services. One is the centralized UDDI (Universal Data Discovery and Interchange) registry. And the other one is Web Services Inspection Language (WSIL) documents, a kind of distributed Web services registry on the Web. Some example research challenges include the dynamic publishing Web services to multiple Web services registries and the tolerant invocation mechanism for communication with Web services registries. The concept of active UDDI proposed in [5] implements a proxy that is able to actively adapt to the changes to meet the requirements of fault tolerance by extending UDDI's invocation API for supporting dynamic service invocation.

In addition, how to find and compose Web services efficiently and effectively for adapting to the business context of an e-business solution is a real challenging research issue.

Discover: The problem is how to dynamically find a set of Web services from heterogeneous Web services registries for building a Web services-based solution. There are some research challenges in this space such as supporting multiple queries in one search request, providing a uniform Web services discovery interface without worrying about the complicated query invocation process, and aggregation search results in a controlled way. A federated Web services discovery framework, Business Explorer for Web Services (BE4WS) [11], can be used to automate the discovery process in a simplified programming model and more accurate search result aggregation mechanism. BE4WS is released in Emerging Technologies Toolkit [1].

Compose: After that, adaptively composing the available Web services to a business process flow that matches business requirements is another promising and challenging research topic as well. For instances, a flexible business requirement representation, a mechanism that automates search process based on business requirements, and a global optimization framework are needed to compose an optimal business process that matches business requirements. An example of dynamic composition framework for Web services flow, Web Services Outsourcing Manager (WSOM) [14], has been released on IBM alphaWorks [9], a public source for demonstrating the advanced technologies created by IBM.

Collaborate: In the current business-to-business application scenarios, a large amount of documents have to be transmitted to the receivers in different enterprises. Web services are the core facilitators to send, receive, and process messages or documents. SOAP attachment is one channel to exchange small-size documents between parties. Theoretically, the documents should be transmitted in an efficient and controlled way. That means the documents should be delivered to the right people with appropriate responses. Additionally, the status of the transmitted documents need be monitored in a distributed environment. In fact, for each document, it can be delivered to any receivers. After one of the receivers gets this document, he or she may modify this document and send back to the sender or distribute to other partners. From the original sender's point of view, he or she may not know who else will be the receivers. So the document delivery model across multiple enterprises or even within one organization forms a nonstructural and ad-hoc information exchange flow. Therefore, the most important thing is to find a flexible way to represent the control information and process them. In fact, along with the control information, created by the sender and re-created by the receivers for further distribution, the nonstructural and ad-hoc information exchange flow results in hierarchical linkages. We think this is a big space to explore service oriented collaboration using Web services.

Monitor: For example, there is a need to monitor and track collaborative development and design processes of a product involving multiple external parties within one's company. Moreover, there is the need to monitor and track the status of the exchanged documents in a peer-to-peer, distributed environment. This is a typical visibility control issue in an engineering design collaboration chain. For example, design center and design partners need to see different information which is exposed in terms of a set of visibility control policies. On the other hand, if there is a business exception, some control mechanisms are needed for handling that. One of the research challenges for monitoring the status of a design documents across multiple organization is to define a federated access control policy, which is used to coordinate the access control scope and access rights by leveraging existing trust and access control components provided in individual software components.

Control: After monitoring the real-time activities, data analysis and information analysis are needed for adjusting the current major steps for better modeling, deployment, discovery, composition, collaboration, and monitoring, if necessary.

This year's proceedings of the 2003 International Conference on Web Services covers a variety of papers, focusing on topics ranging from Web services framework, to Web services security, business process composition and management, QoS, performances and Web services applications. In this paper, we concentrate on the business scenarios and technical issues in the extended collaboration space which covers discovery, composition, collaboration, monitoring and analytical control.

3 Web Services Collaboration

As we know, different people see different models with different metrics at each level of a business. Lots of modeling means have been proposed to represent the behaviors of a business. There are corresponding to different number of layers models. However, no matter how many layers used in their models, they are basically include the higher business layer and the lower IT (Information Technology) layer. We should be familiar with traditional B2C (Business to Customer) model, ASP (Application Service Provider) model, A2A (Application to Application) model, and B2B (Business to Business) model. From these models' points of view, they are intentionally differentiated as intra-enterprise interactions and inter-enterprise interactions.

In this section, we introduce the natural home of the convergence of the existing e-business models. We believe the Extended Business Collaboration (eBC) is going to be a very important and emerging business model, which aims at reducing the boundary between enterprises in the inter-enterprise models and intra-enterprise models.

3.1 Extended Business Collaboration

As outsourcing and on-demand model are becoming more and more popular, the boundary between enterprises is becoming smaller and smaller. Yes, enterprises are not alone anymore. They have to collaborate with other enterprises at different levels. Here, we use a simple scenario to describe the collaboration between two companies.

For example, company A may want to do business with company B. Sometimes, the high level management teams will come up a strategy level agreement. The CEOs from company A and Company B plan to work together to create an alliance for providing adaptive enterprise solutions. This decision is made after conducting all the formal or informal communications at the strategy level.

Then both companies pass this strategic goal to the corresponding operation organizations to come up with some operation plans. One example operation plan is to launch a joint design of a new product in a few months. The communication and synchronization at this operation level should have some patterns which we can model. Then both companies put this operation plan into action. Lots of detailed execution plans such as budget allocation, development planning, press release, and so forth, should be coordinated between two companies.

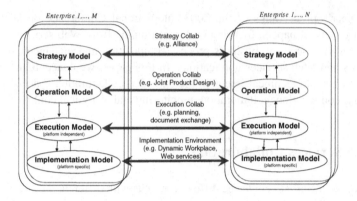

Fig. 2. Extended Business Collaboration Diagram

At the execution level, all the process flow, data format, data sources, which are platform independent, should be exchanged and synchronized between two parties. Last, they may use different implementation infrastructures, which are platform dependent, to run the collaborative product development process. The point here is that the interaction and collaboration are really conducted very often between levels within an enterprise as well as across multiple enterprises. In addition, human factor also plays a very important role in dealing with business exception handling and quick decision making required by a running business process or application. Human interactions with an application can be operated by his/her own enterprise or other enterprises. So we call this "Extended Business Collaboration (eBC)", which is a model for addressing industry value chain and people collaboration in the context of adaptive business solutions. Again, we think eBC is the natural home of the convergence of B2C model, A2A model, ASP model, and B2B model.

From this simple scenario, we can see the information formats exchanged maybe different at different levels. Meanwhile, the contents in the exchanged information containers such as documents may also be different. The dynamics of the virtual enterprise, extended business entity, are more active than before. In an engineering design collaboration scenario new design partners or trading partners could be invited to join a product design project. Additionally, a design center can also switch to another design partners dynamically in a product lifecycle management solution.

Although Web services infrastructure provides a good foundation to build such a flexible and extensive exchange protocol to support collaborative business information exchange, there are still lots of challenges. In our research agenda, we need to

- define a flexible information representation format;
- deliver the information in a standard way;
- process the information in a smart manner;
- control the information exchange flow dynamically;
- monitor the status of the process flow and documents exchanged;
- secure all the communication channels.

The following two sub-sections are used to address some ideas on the semantic representation and collaborative exchange protocols for enabling extended business collaboration.

3.2   Web Services Semantic Computing

In today's Web services infrastructure, shown in Fig.3, there is the lack of a uniform semantic representation about the individual solution components. For example, WSDL just describes the basic information about a Web service; Some information about WSDL are published in Web services registries, namely, UDDI registry or WSIL documents, which are two different type of Web services registries. But there is no place to describe capability information about a Web service, method signature mapping, and the like in current Web services related specifications. Moreover, there is still questionable on how the WS-Security mechanism interacts with the project context, business flow (e.g. BPEL4WS) context, and other solution components such as UDDI registry, SOAP invocation engine, and even WSDL documents. That's one of the reasons why WS-I Forum [8] is formed to address the interoperability issue among multiple standards specifications.

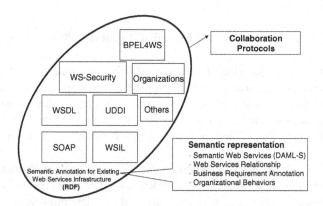

Fig. 3. Semantic Computing for Enabling Business Collaboration

Actually, most researchers in the field of Web services are realizing that the semantic information are needed for accurate Web services discovery, dynamic Web services composition as well as collaboration at run-time. Some semantic representation approaches have been proposed to address this issue. For example, (1) DAML-S is being proposed to describe more information about individual Web services for discovery and composition [9]; (2) Regular XML-based annotation languages have been defined to capture different types of semantic information. One example XML annotation, Web services relationship language (WSRL) [11], is proposed to capture the Web services relationships at different granularities, which we think will be an important facilitator in selecting and composing the right set of services that meets the customer's requirements. Additionally, a business requirement language, Business Process Outsourcing Language (BPOL), is proposed to capture the business requirements such as conceptual flow, preferences, business rules, relationship bindings, and event-action mappings for automating the Web services discovery and flow composition that matches customers' requirements [14]. (3) Organizational behaviors associated with an e-business solution refer to the semantic representations about the organizations, the on-going projects in an organization, tasks in a project, requirements and transactions in a task, additional annotation about any other related resources such as value-added services involved in an e-business solution.

For the first two, namely (1) and (2), as we mentioned earlier, we can find some example solutions to address the semantic representations for different aspects about individual Web services. The third is more systemic view of a semantic representation for building and managing a Web services based e-business solution. We think Resource Definition Framework (RDF) [6] could provide a uniform and efficient way to capture all the three types of semantic representations. So one of our research goals on Web services collaboration is to create an extended business collaboration ontology, which is built on top of RDF, DAML-S, and other XML-based semantic representations, to effectively create and manage the Web services based extended business collaboration solutions.

3.3   Collaboration Protocols for Extended Business Collaboration

After we described what kind of semantic information should be captured to support eBC solutions, we are now moving to protocols, which are used to transmit the semantic representation and control the information exchange flow as well as monitor the on-going activities in a dynamic way. As shown in Fig. 1, the Web Services Business Collaboration Suite is trying to address the issues above by leveraging the eBC ontology.

As an example B2B protocol, RosettaNet [7] only deals with transaction based scenarios like Purchase Order. Therefore, RosettaNet needs to be extended to support extended business collaboration in an ad-hoc and non-deterministic environment. The extensibility of the business document payload and configurable collaboration protocol are key challenging issues when realizing an eBC solution. It should cover an extensible message structure for carrying non-structural information. Let's take engineering design collaboration as an example, design center and design partners need to see different information which is exposed in terms of a set of visibility control policies. When there is a business exception or a quick decision is required in the running business process, people can be introduced for making quick decision or addressing problems. People collaboration tools such as dynamic workspace (e.g. Lotus Sametime, Quickplace) and pervasive devices can be used to perform more effective business collaboration.

4 Conclusions

We have introduced the lifecycle of a Web services solution which consists of Web services modeling, development, deployment, publishing, as well as discovery, composition and collaboration, plus monitoring and analytical control, followed by a summary of some research and development challenges of building a Web ser-vices solution. Especially, we present an emerging Web services research direction, namely, Web services collaboration in this paper. Additionally, we pointed out a few major research issues associated with facilitating extended business collaboration using Web services and semantic annotation. We would like to encourage people from industry and academia to join us to work on a flexible protocol creation and enabling platform for enabling extended business collaboration. This enabling infrastructure should allow ones to create an extensible message structure for carrying non-structural information as well as to dynamically configure business exchange protocols for on demand business process execution.

Note that the convergence of Web services, Grid computing [3], autonomic computing [4], and model driven business process integration and management methodology could pave a way to building extended business collaboration infrastructure. Among them, Web service is the integration technology and semantic computing is the glue to coordinate activities across multiple organizations.

References

1. ETTK, Emerging Technologies Toolkit, IBM alphaWorks,
   http://www.alphaworks.ibm.com/tech/ettk
2. DAML-S: DAML Services, http://www.daml.org/services/
3. Foster, I., Kesselman, C., Nick, J.M., Tuecke, S., Grid services for distributed system integration, Computer, Vol. 35, No. 6, pp.37–46, (2002)
4. Kephart, J.O., Chess, D.M., The vision of autonomic computing, Computer, Vol.36, No. 1, pp. 41–50, (2003)
5. M. Jeckle and B. Zengler, Active UDDI – An Extension to UDDI for Dynamic and Fault-Tolerant Service Invocation, in Web Databases and Web Services 2002, A. B. Chaudhri et al. (Eds.), LNCS 2593, pp. 91–99, (2003).
6. RDF: Resource Description Framework, http://www.w3.org/RDF/
7. RosettaNet, http://www.rosettanet.org
8. WS-I, Web Services Interoperability Organization, http://www.ws-i.org
9. WSOM, Web Services Outsourcing Manager, www.alphaworks.ibm.com/tech/wsom/, (2002)
10. Zhang, L.-J., Chang, H., Chao, T., Chung, J.-Y., Tian, Z., Xu, J., Zuo, Y., Yang, S., Ao, Q, Web Services Hub Framework for e-Sourcing, IEEE Conference on System, Man, and Cybernetics (SMC'02), Vol.6, pp. 163–168, (2002)
11. Zhang, L.-J., Chang, H., Chao, T., Web Services Relationships Binding for Dynamic e-Business Integration, International Conference on Internet Computing (IC'02), Las Vegas, pp. 561–567, (2002)

12. Zhang, L.-J., Chao, T., Chang, H., Chung J.-Y., XML-based Advanced UDDI Search Mechanism for B2B Integration, Electronic Commerce Research Journal, pp.25–42, (2003)
13. Zhang, L.-J., Chao, T., Chang, H., Chung J.-Y., Automatic Method Signature Adaptation Framework for Dynamic Web Service Invocation, 6th World Multi Conference on Systemics, Cybernetics and Informatics (SCI 2002), Orlando, Florida, (2002)
14. Zhang, L.-J., Li, B., Chao, T., Chang, H., On Demand Web Services-Based Business Process Composition, to appear in the proceedings of IEEE Conference on System, Man, and Cybernetics (SMC'03), (2003)

A Service Oriented Architecture for Managing Operational Strategies

Nektarios Gioldasis, Nektarios Moumoutzis, Fotis Kazasis, Nikos Pappas, and Stavros Christodoulakis

Laboratory of Distributed Multimedia Information Systems & Applications
Technical University of Crete – TUC/MUSIC
{nektarios,nektar,fotis,nikos,stavros}@ced.tuc.gr

Abstract. In this paper we present a case study where an e-business platform (OPERATIONS) has to be built in order to manage the operational strategies of a high volume coastal company. The platform is intended to support multiple operational scenarios that have to be executed when emergency situations or sudden changes of scheduled events unfold. In order to properly integrate all the involved parties that may take part in such a scenario, the system must support multiple interaction patterns according to the communication channel and the device that is used. Thus, its design must take into account multi-channel delivery of functionality and information. The design of the system follows a Service Oriented Architecture (SOA) in order to properly integrate back-office data sources and legacy systems with new required application extensions providing a complete e-business platform. The core business logic tier of the system is a Process Oriented Platform (POP) that is able to dynamically generate the appropriate workflows, to orchestrate the constituent services and to execute complex operational scenarios interacting with involved users and systems in a multi-channel fashion. Finally, appropriate knowledge bases have been defined to support the storage, evaluation, and evolution of the executed scenarios and to provide valuable Business Activity Monitoring information to the company's administration.

1 Introduction

The ultimate goal of the OPERATIONS platform is to provide a state-of-the art and reliable e-business environment supporting a regional coastal company. The company has a fleet of eleven modern and luxurious ships operating in the Aegean, Ionian and Adriatic Sea. In an attempt to improve its internal processes, to provide better services to its customers, and to capture and exploit its internal knowledge, the company asked for a requirements analysis and system architecture that satisfies its needs. The proposed e-business platform will be used to deploy and monitor in an extensible manner all the operational strategies and related processes of the company using multi-channel delivery of services and standard descriptions of operational scenarios. These scenarios represent procedures of major significance that today are either not considered at all or done in an empirical basis and it is consequently difficult to eva-

M. Jeckle and L.-J. Zhang (Eds.): ICWS-Europe 2003, LNCS 2853, pp. 11–23, 2003.
© Springer-Verlag Berlin Heidelberg 2003

luate their impact on the economic indicators of the company. Such scenarios that are going to be managed by the OPERATIONS system are:

- Management of emergency situations (e.g. mechanical breakdowns) that obstruct normal voyage.
- Management of urgent events that happen on-board (e.g. man on the sea, sudden death of a passenger, incidents that need special medical treatment).
- Management of changes on scheduled events (e.g. mass cancellations of reservations, cancellation of a scheduled trip).
- Management of passenger and/or vehicle overbooking due either to company policies or external events.
- Optimized cargo fitting dynamically, taking into account various constraints, and coordination of involved personnel.

It should be stressed that the above scenarios refer to polymorphic user roles that are impossible to manage at a strategic level without a system like OPERATIONS. Moreover they encapsulate numerous legal, spatial, temporal, economic and technical constraints arising from both the actual situations in which these scenarios unfold and the external environment (including e.g. legal framework for voyage safety) of the company. The dynamic nature of this setting calls for innovative technical solutions in order to reduce risks, increase flexibility, maintain low adaptation-times to changes in the external environment and increase the capability of the company to analyze and improve its performance by monitoring and reengineering its operational strategies.

One of the most important parts of this project is the software architecture, which is presented in this paper. The platform will be built on a multi-tier architecture that clearly distinguishes the application logic (presentation tier), the business logic (services or middleware tier), and the underlying IT infrastructure of the company (back-office tier). Knowledge bases are used to store scenarios' descriptions, user roles, as well as scenarios' instances. A well defined interface is used for the communication with the back-end systems of the company. The platform will be built following a Service Oriented Architecture. We strongly believe that this approach is the most suitable for such a system. According to the Gartner, by 2007 SOA will be the dominant strategy (more than 65%) of developing information systems. Moreover, the core business logic tier of the architecture will be a Process Oriented Platform (POP) in order to dynamically set the appropriate workflows of primitive services according to operational scenarios. Operational scenarios are well-defined manifests that drive the construction and execution of service oriented workflows.

The rest of this paper is organized as follows: In section 2 we mention the current state-of-the-art of the main technologies which will be utilized in the development of the OPERATIONS platform, while in section 3 we provide two typical scenarios that are to be supported by the proposed system. Section 4 illustrates the core platform architecture and section 5 concludes the paper.

2 State-of-the-Art

Service Oriented Architectures [1] has been proposed by W3C as reference architectures for building Web-based information systems. Service-Oriented Architecture

(SOA) refers to an application software topology according to which business logic of the applications is separated from its user interaction logic and encapsulated in one or multiple software components (services), exposed to programmatic access via well-defined formal interfaces. Each service provides its functionality to the rest of the system as a well-defined interface described in a formal markup language and the communication between services is platform and language independent. Thus, modularity and re-usability are ensured enabling several different configurations and achieving multiple business goals.

Web Services technology is currently the most promising methodology of developing web information systems. Web Services allow companies to reduce the cost of doing e-business, to deploy solutions faster and to open up new opportunities. The key to reach this new horizon is a common program-to-program communication model, built on existing and emerging standards such as HTTP, Extensible Markup Language (XML) [4], Simple Object Access Protocol (SOAP) [5], Web Services Description Language (WSDL) [2] and Universal Description, Discovery and Integration (UDDI) [6]. However, the real Business-to-Business interoperability between different organizations requires more than the aforementioned standards. It requires long-lived, secure, transactional conversations between Web Services of different organizations. To this end, a number of standards are under way. Some of these (emerging) standards are the Web Services Conversation Language (WSCL) [7], the Web Services Flow Language (WSFL) [8], the Business Process Execution Language for Web Services (BPEL4WS) [9], the Web Services Choreography Interface (WSCI) [10], the Web Services Coordination Specification (WS-Coordination) [11], the Web Services Transaction Specification (WS-Transaction) [12], and the Business Transaction Protocol (BTP) [13]. With respect to the description of service's supported and required characteristics the WS-Policy Framework [3] is under development by IBM, Microsoft, SAP, and other leading companies in the area.

On the other hand, other no "standard" languages and technologies have been proposed for composing services and modeling transactional behavior of complex service compositions. Such proposals include the Unified Transaction Modeling Language (UTML) [14], [17] and the SWORD toolkit [15]. UTML is a high level, UML-compatible language for analyzing, composing, designing, and documenting extended transaction models based on a rich transaction meta-model. Transaction nodes can be implemented by web services that exhibit specific transactional characteristics. The final design can be exported in XML format and thus it can be easily transformed to a web service description. SWORD is a toolkit that facilitates the process of service matchmaking in order to develop composite value – added services.

In the multi-channel delivery area, the main technologies referenced in this paper are the following:

- WAP (Wireless Application Protocol) [19] is a secure specification that allows users to access information instantly via handheld devices.
- Short Message Service (SMS) is the transmission of short text messages, usually to and from a mobile phone. Messages must be no longer than 160 alpha-numeric characters and contain no images or graphics.
- Multimedia Message Service (MMS), a store-and-forward method of transmitting graphics, video clips, sound files and short text messages over wireless networks using the WAP protocol. Carriers deploy special servers, dubbed MMS Centers (MMSCs) to implement the offerings on their systems.

- E-mail service is a simple and widely used service that is supported by the majority of the devices (including the hand-held) and could be used by a system that aims to implement multi-channel access. Technical specifications of SMS and MMS services can be found at [18].
- With the introduction of the Java 2 platform Micro Edition (J2ME) [20] the role of mobile wireless devices was enhanced from voice-oriented communication devices with limited functionality into extensible Internet-enabled devices. The use of Java Technology makes the application adequate for dynamic delivery of content, provides satisfactory user interactivity, ensures cross-platform compatibility and allows the offline access. Especially the offline access that allows the applications to be used without active network connection is of great importance since it reduces the transport costs and alleviates the impact of possible network failures.

3 Operational Scenarios

The OPERATIONS platform will be used in real operational scenarios such as management of emergency situations and urgent events that happen on-board, management of changes on scheduled events, overbooking situations, and dynamic optimized cargo fitting. These envisaged scenarios represent complex procedures that involve company's personnel, clients, and other external parties. The final decisions for the successful implementation of such scenarios including a detailed action plan will be supported by the OPERATIONS e-business platform in two complementary ways: First by coordinating all necessary flow of information and messages to the involved parties so that all actions are taken in correct order and by the most appropriate actor. Second, by retrieving, processing and presenting critical information from the company's extended IT Infrastructure so that alternatives could be efficiently evaluated and actions could be taken efficiently. Moreover, the execution history of the scenarios are finally filled in the OPERATIONS Knowledge Base for further off-line analysis and future use in similar situations, thus providing a formal way of expressing and reusing corporate knowledge that today more or less exists in a tacit manner.

To make things clear, consider the scenario of figure 1. An emergency or urgent event takes place on-board (step 1 of the scenario) and requires immediate treatment. A preliminary evaluation of the situation is done on-board by the authorized personnel (step 2) and immediately three complementary procedures are triggered:

- A detailed evaluation is initiated on-board (step 3) to investigate what are the details of the problem.
- The administration of the company is notified (step 5) about the event and starts working on possible solutions. The authorized people start to elaborate on a detailed assessment (step 7) on possible alternatives based on real cost estimations of each alternative (step 8) as well as hidden costs estimations (9) that refer to various factors including issues that could not be immediately quantified such as the credibility of the company. The alternatives considered at this time remain at a higher level, waiting for more detailed information about the

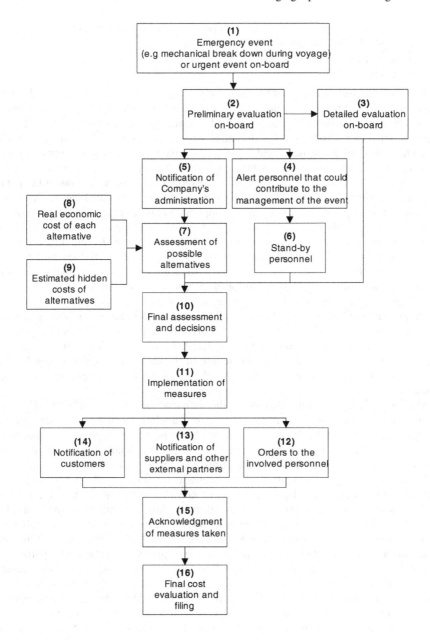

Fig. 1. A scenario concerning urgent of emergency situations happening on-board

exact problem and the readiness of the personnel that is necessary to handle the alternative solutions.

- Appropriate alerts are issued to the personnel considered as critical for the resolution of the problem and the implementation of the possible measures that could be taken (step 4). The involved persons may be on-board, on the land (at ports or in company's headquarters) or in other ships of the company that sail nearby. Some time later, the information about the readiness of the involved personnel starts coming and the personnel found to be ready to respond is brought into stand-by mode (step 6).

The information about possible alternatives, available personnel, and detailed evaluation of the problem is gathered to help find the optimal solution considering costs, company's policies and other critical constraints such as time, availability of supplies, customer satisfaction (or dissatisfaction), other related problems that could arise etc. This final assessment guides the final decision (step 10) that refers to a set of necessary measures along with a detailed schedule that takes into account all dependencies among the needed tasks. Then, all corresponding measures are taken (step 11) by issuing proper orders to the involved personnel (step 12), notification messages and corresponding acknowledgements to suppliers and other external parties involved (step 13) and possible notification messages to customers (step 14) that include both passengers on-board and customers that have made reservations for the next days that should be changed. The authorized personnel supervises the activities and finally, after the successful finish of the scenario, a final cost could be computed and the whole process could be filed (step 16) for future consideration and analysis.

This envisaged scenario is handled today in an empirical basis and in fact some of the steps illustrated in figure 1 are not at all taken or done in an ad-hoc way. For sure, there is no final evaluation and filing of the process (step 16) that leads to repetition of possible missteps in the future. Neither detailed cost estimations (steps 8 and 9), nor detailed monitoring of the implementation of the measures decided (steps 11, 12, 13, 14) is done due to high overheads and the great number of message exchanges induced.

This will change dramatically with the introduction of the OPERATIONS e-business environment which will be capable for handling the necessary message exchanges, exploiting multiple communication channels, processing the big amount of information necessary to evaluate alternatives, developing detailed action plans, coordinating the implementation of the measures and finally evaluating the actual costs endured, and storing the evolution of the scenario for future analysis and use. Note that this filing feature can be used for more knowledgeable future management of similar scenarios as it can provide information for cost estimations (steps 8 and 9), and action plans (steps 10 and 11), thus increasing responsiveness and overall efficiency of the company. It could also provide other valuable information such as concrete indicators of the efficiency and performance of personnel and external partners.

Figure 2 illustrates yet another class of possible scenarios that are distinguished from the previous one because they do not require immediate involvement of the company's administration. These scenarios refer to sudden changes on scheduled events and overbooking situations. As soon as such a situation is detected (step 1 of the scenario in figure 2), the authorized personnel elaborates a detailed plan of necessary measures (step 2). This plan takes into account similar situations that have happened in the past (step 3) and currently is handled empirically based on tacit knowledge and experience (the plan today usually exists in the mind of some of the most efficient employees of the company). Having decided on how to handle the problem, proper changes are made to reservations (step 4) triggering some notification messages to interested customers. At the same time, suppliers are communicated to handle necessary changes (step 6) after evaluating possible alternatives (step 7). The scenario finishes on reception of acknowledgements about the measures taken and leads to filing of the whole process (step 8).

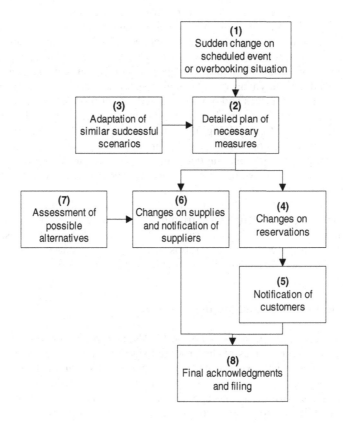

Fig. 2. A scenario concerning a sudden change of a scheduled plan or an overbooking situation

One could make similar comments as the ones made in the previous scenario with respect to the current management of such kind of situations: empirical management, high overheads, no final recording of the evolution of the scenario, dependence on experienced personnel to coordinate the activities.

Using the OPERATIONS e-business environment and corresponding multi-channel communication (affecting mainly steps 4, 5, 6, and 8) a detailed action plan on the optimal alternative could be elaborated and efficiently deployed, monitored and filed at the end. Successful scenarios could be re-used or properly adapted in the future (used as input to steps 4, 6 and 7) reducing processing times and possible risks. In addition, scenario analysis could provide concrete indicators of customer satisfaction as well as of the efficiency and performance of personnel and external partners.

4 System Architecture

The OPERATIONS platform adopts a multi-tier Service Oriented Architecture that clearly distinguishes the application logic (presentation tier), the business logic (services tier), and the underlying company's extended IT infrastructure (back-office tier). This approach ensures the company's investment in IT infrastructure and middleware tiers (through appropriate application integration using a service based approach) and supports modular deployment of both device specific user interfaces through multi-channel delivery of services and new or adapted operational processes and strategies. All connectivity interfaces are based on standard specifications. The architecture provides mechanisms for receiving, managing and coordinating information or service requests and corresponding messages, through the appropriate middleware components residing at the presentation tier at the one side and to the back-end systems of the company at the other. In addition the architecture incorporates sophisticated knowledge bases where scenarios and user roles are stored.

Figure 3 illustrates this architecture and clearly separates the presentation logic, the business logic, and back-office infrastructure. The service-based business logic components implement the various scenarios that reside in the Knowledge Bases using the information from the company's IT infrastructure and coordinating all flow of information and messages through multi-channel delivery mechanisms.

4.1 Application Logic and Multi-channel Delivery

A variety of devices (e.g. mobile phones, PDA's, laptops, PC's) and external partner servers are the client devices of the proposed system, exchanging formatted data via standard protocols. The external partner servers will have immediate access to the public business logic web services. The users will be using different devices that run device specific software (special applications, e-mail client, or web browsers). For example the cellular phone users could access the OPERATIONS system, using the SMS service or use mobile services (WAP, e-mail) or run special J2ME/MIDP applications, connecting to the server using a dialup or the more advanced GPRS connection (for a detailed description of these alternative see section 4.5 of this document). Special logic will be developed in the server-side presentation layer that dynamically discovers the device capabilities and redirects the information to the appropriate application logic adapters that, according to the capabilities of the device, will handle the interactions with the user, adapt the content and deliver it via the appropriate gateway. Thus, the presentation layer provides essentially a multi-channel information delivery that is a key feature of the system. It will be the front-end of the company's infrastructure, web servers, application servers and legacy systems, so that the same content could be efficiently delivered to different user devices.

4.2 Business Logic and Scenarios Support

The business logic is captured and implemented in the middleware through utilization of transactional services and complex orchestrated services guided by operational scenarios residing in the knowledge bases. This way, Process Oriented Architecture

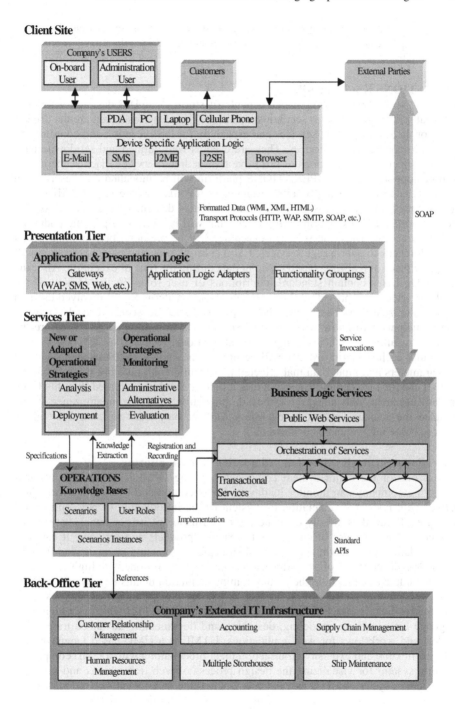

Fig. 3. The OPERATIONS Platform Architecture

(POP) is followed which distinguishes between primitive organizational activities, complex operational processes and operational scenario specifications, monitoring and evaluation.

OPERATIONS Knowledge-Bases

These are sophisticated components capable of storing standard descriptions of operational scenarios as well as scenarios instances. The scenarios stored are the driving force for the business logic services and especially for the execution and coordination of complex orchestrated services. They are used as well-defined and set down manifests for specific orchestrations of primitive transactional services. Each scenario that is to be supported by the OPERATIONS platform will be modelled and described in the knowledge bases using a suitable language for this purpose (e.g. UTML). This process includes also the association of the activities described in the scenario with the appropriate classes of primitive services that will be built on top of the underling IT infrastructure. Thus, the scenario execution will be pre-described in some extent with references to appropriate services. Extra configuration and parameterisation will be taking place at real-time based on input data during the time of execution. Also, the knowledge bases contain standard descriptions of user roles (in the context of the available scenarios), providing this way behavioural patterns for all involved users in a particular scenario. That is, in the scope of a specific scenario, each involved user/participant will know what are the expectations from him/her and what are the penalties resulting from not meeting these expectations.

Finally, each scenario instance will be filed in the knowledge bases along with all the parameters and input data that affected its execution and possibly some (administrative) conclusions about the success that it had. It should be stressed that this filing process has many advantages for the administration of the company since it can evaluate the scenario instances regardless whether they were successful or not in order to come into valuable conclusions.

Operational Strategies Creation, Adaptation, and Monitoring

This is one of the major system components. Using OPERATIONS' Knowledge-Bases, the company can monitor its day-to-day operation and evaluate various alternatives with respect to adaptation of existent or the introduction of new operational strategies. It can thus closely evaluate the performance of its personnel, its external partners or the response of customers to existing products and services. It can also deploy adapted or create new operational strategies by creating or modifying the corresponding descriptions of scenarios and user roles. This is done with high-level tools and methodologies that hide the complex implementation details encapsulated by the business logic components of the system. Scenarios will be modelled and described with the Unified Transaction Modeling Language (UTML) [17] which is a high level language for analyzing, modeling, designing and documenting advanced transaction models and workflows for web applications. UTML is a UML based language providing a flexible and extensible transaction meta-model along with a UML compatible notation system for visualizing the design process of web transactions and services. The notation system utilizes and extends UML finite state machines and state-chart technologies to describe the execution scenarios of the designed transactions. The UML compatibility of the language makes it a candidate for describing complex transactional scenarios. This holds due to the visual nature of UML and its multi-level (conceptual, specification, and implementation modelling) usage which greatly facilitates the description of complex business or software processes. A software tool is available that supports the design process with UTML and provides correctness checking based on built-in well-formedness and well behaving rules. It is an extension of the Rational Rose industrial UML design tool and provides description of the final UTML design into XML format. The description is based on an XML schema which has been developed to support transparent transaction description.

Transactional Services
The transactional services component integrates and provides the functionality and information of the back-office resources and applications in a platform and data independent manner. It does so, by providing primitive transactional services which directly interact with the underlying functionality and resources wrapping them accordingly, providing this way a transparent layer of interoperability. When called, this component retrieves the service descriptors, sets up the execution environment and issues appropriate execution requests to the resource providers.

Transactional services are used by the service orchestration component to compose new complex services. Transactional services are considered as the primitive services of the system that have access to the back-end systems. The purpose of these services is to perform standard transactional processing. These transactions are mapped to specific operations for the back-office systems, using the vendor specific programming interfaces. Thus, messages, sent through the multi channel access, are finally executed through transactions mapped to functions of the back-office systems.

Orchestration of Services
In this component, primitive transactional services are orchestrated accordingly to support involved business processes of the company. An embedded workflow engine is used to handle and execute compositions of existing services provided by the system and supports long-lived transaction processing. The orchestration done by this component is guided by the operational scenarios residing in the knowledge bases. In order to support the implementation and orchestration of complex operational scenarios, a mapping is required that transforms the scenario descriptions in the knowledge bases to appropriate service-based execution specifications (e.g. WSFL, BPEL4WS, BPML, etc.). Moreover, the notion of compensation is also supported, to allow the engine to reverse actions that have taken place if something goes wrong with the process.

Public Web Services
This component promotes orchestrated or primitive services as autonomous public web services to the outside world. These services will constitute the public interface of the company to the outside world and will be accessed by external users and partners. There are two important reasons for separating private from public business logic when building systems like OPERATIONS:

- The first is that businesses obviously do not want to reveal all their internal data management, decision making and processing logic to the outside world.
- The second is that, by separating public from private logic provides to businesses the freedom to change private aspects of the process implementation without affecting the public protocols and interaction patterns.

4.3   Company's IT Extended Infrastructure

The base layer of the architecture consists of the core IT Infrastructure of the company including the extensions and enhancements to be realised in the context of the project. It is essentially the back-office component of the system consisting of a number of different modules including:

- Human Resource Management
- Customer Relationships Management
- Supply Chain Management
- Ship maintenance
- Multiple Warehouses' Management
- Accounting

This is the major pool of information and functionality for transactional services that communicate through standard Application Programmatic Interfaces (APIs).

5   Summary

In this paper we presented the architecture for an e-business platform that will be used to support the operational strategies of a high volume coastal company. This work has been carried out in the scope of the OPERATIONS project in the e-Business application domain. The followed approach uses a Service Oriented Architecture in order to provide a reliable, integrated, configurable and extensible environment that will be able to serve multiple business goals and operational scenarios.

Additionally, multi-channel deliver of information and functionality has been taken into account and appropriate components have been defined that will ensure ubiquitous access of system's functionality through multiple communication channels and terminal devices.

The core business logic tier of the system is a Process Oriented Platform inspired by the SOA principles. It utilizes primitive services, dynamic workflow generation, and orchestration of services to serve multiple business goals in dynamic way.

The implementation of the OPERATIONS platform starts with the wrapping of the company's IT infrastructure and continues with the development of the primitive transactional services that will export this functionality, along with new extensions, to the rest of the system. The next step is the development of the Knowledge Bases and the scenario modeling and representation. Afterwards, the service orchestration will take place and the definition of the public web services. During these steps, prototype interfaces will be developed to facilitate the iterative system testing and evaluation. Then, the presentation tier will be finally developed to support all the multi-channel interaction models that are needed in the envisaged environment.

References

1. "Web Services Architecture", W3C, http://www.w3.org/TR/2002/WD-ws-arch-20021114/
2. Web Services Description Language (WSDL) Version 1.2, W3C, http://www.w3.org/TR/wsdl12/
3. Web Services Policy Framework, IBM, BEA, MICROSOFT, SAP, http://www.ibm.com/developerworks/library/ws-polfram/
4. eXtensible Markup Language (XML), W3C, http://www.w3.org/XML/
5. Simple Object Access Protocol (SOAP), W3C, http://www.w3.org/TR/SOAP/
6. Universal Description, Discovery and Integration, OASIS, http://www.oasis-open.org/committees/uddi-spec/doc/tcspecs.htm
7. Web Services Conversation Language (WSCL), W3C, http://www.w3.org/TR/wscl10/
8. Web Services Flow Language, IBM, http://www.ibm.com/developerworks/library/
9. Business Process Execution Language for Web Services (BPEL4WS), IBM, BEA, Microsoft, SAP, ftp://www6.software.ibm.com/software/developer/library/ws-bpel11.pdf
10. Web Services Choreography Interface, W3C, http://www.w3.org/2002/ws/chor/
11. Web Services Coordination (WS-Coordination), IBM, http://www.ibm.com/developerworks/library/ws-coor/
12. Web Services Transaction (WS-Transaction), IBM, http://www.ibm.com/developerworks/library/ws-transpec/
13. Business Transaction Protocol (BTP), OASIS, http://www.oasis-open.org/ committees/download.php/1184/2002-06-03.BTP_cttee_spec_1.0.pdf
14. UTML: Unified Transaction Modeling Language, Nektarios Gioldasis, Stavros Christodoulakis, in the proceedings of the 3rd International Conference on Web Information Systems Engineering (WISE 02), Singapore, December 2002
15. SWORD: A Developer Toolkit for Web Service Composition, Shankar R. Ponnekanti, Armando Fox, The 11th International WWW Conference 2002
16. Dynamic Composition of Workflows for Customized eGovernment Service Delivery, Soon Ae Chum, Vijayalakshimi Atluri, and Nabil R. Adam, 2nd Conf. on Digital Government, 2002
17. UTML: Unified Transaction Modeling Language, Nektarios Gioldasis, Doctoral Poster, VLDB 02, August 2002, Hong Kong, China
18. The European Telecommunications Standards Institute (ETSI). http://www.etsi.org
19. The WAP Forum http://www.wapforum.org
20. The Java 2 Platform Micro Edition. http://java.sun.com/j2me

Managing the Normative Context of Composite E-services

Olivera Marjanovic

School of Information Systems. Technology and Management
The University of New South Wales, Sydney, NSW 2052, Australia
o.marjanovic@unsw.edu.au

Abstract. As more and more companies provide their services over the Internet, the need to better understand and manage the normative context of composite services (including rights and responsibilities of all parties involved) becomes evident. Unfortunately the normative perspective of both individual and composite services seems to be left out from current e-service research and practice. Yet, this perspective of e-service provision is very important not only because of the possible legal consequences but also because of its implications on customer's trust. The main objective of this paper is to investigates the normative perspective of a composite e-service offered by independent as well as affiliated service providers. It proposes a formal model of the normative context investigates the problem of its management and defines the requirements for a value-added service that could be used both by customers and providers of composite e-services.

1 Introduction

"Let your customer do the work for you" is one of the new e-commerce strategies that is becoming increasingly popular in recent times. Consequently, more and more companies are entering the world of e-services, offering easy-to-use, Internet-based, applications that enable customers to perform a wide range of business transactions with the given company in their own time. When implemented properly, e-services not only create an added value for the customer, but also cut the cost of business interactions for the company by freeing its valuable resources.

As companies are gaining more and more experience in e-service provision their services are becoming increasingly complex. They have long moved from simple order and payment applications to provision of very sophisticated services such as for example integration of customer's value chain.

In addition to individual e-services offered by independent service providers, another very important trend has emerged in the form of composite e-services. Composite e-services enable flexible, on-demand, integration of individual e-services offered by different providers to meet the given business objective. This concept opens up new possibilities for cross-organisational integration through flexible business processes that consist of a number of coordinated e-services. Consequently, even the smallest providers can participate in composite e-services and cross-organisational business processes without sophisticated IT infrastructure.

M. Jeckle and L.-J. Zhang (Eds.): ICWS-Europe 2003, LNCS 2853, pp. 24–36, 2003.
© Springer-Verlag Berlin Heidelberg 2003

When it comes to the provision of composite e-services there are three business models that are currently in use. The first one sees a third-party service provider in charge of composition and provision of a composite e-service made of related but independent e-services. Thus the provider of the composite service is in charge of selection of individual services and their providers, as well as monitoring and coordination aspects. The second model involves self-regulatory and self-coordinated e-services where individual service providers take responsibility to coordinate their services with the others (see for example [1]).

This paper deals with the third model where customers (service users) are in charge of composition of complex-services. This model is likely to become more and more common especially with the companies using strategic alliance marketing to promote each others' products and services encouraging customers (through bonuses and discounts) to compose their related services. In many respects this is the most challenging concept among all three, as the typical customer does not usually have sophisticated tools or expertise to deal with complex services. At the same time, this customer has the ultimate choice not to proceed with a business transaction and will do just that in the case of any real or perceived problem.

Irrespectively of the chosen business model, the problem of e-service composition opens up a number of research and implementation challenges. Currently, there are many projects well under way to enable technical integration of independent e-services across different web-platforms. Equally important is the research problem of integration at the conceptual (modelling) level dealing with integration of business concepts.

There are several different aspects of service integration that require investigation at the conceptual level. For example [2] identifies four different perspectives: *the control-flow perspective* (that establishes the order individual services), *provider perspective, data exchange perspective* and *transactional perspective*. There is also a *temporal perspective* described in [3]. However, one of the important perspectives that is missing from current research and practical implementations is the *normative perspective*. This perspective includes modelling and management of normative context including rights and responsibilities of all parties involved in e-service provision. The normative perspective is crucial not only because of the legal implications but also because of its possible negative effects on customer trust that is so hard to establish and maintain in online world.

So how do e-services currently deal with this perspective? Simply by providing pages and pages of densely typed text including static terms and conditions for provision of a particular service usually followed by "I accept" or "Cancel" buttons. This is supposed to clearly communicate the normative context, yet in many cases customers have problems getting full information and more importantly understanding it, so they simply opt-out. On the other hand, if they decide to proceed with transaction, once they click on the "I accept" button they create a set of rights and obligations (normative context) for all parties involved. This may not be such a problem in the case of a simple e-service, however it could be very complex in the case of composite e-services offered by several affiliated service providers. Unfortunately, at this stage, there is no any support offered to customers to better manage their normative context. However, as composite services are getting more and more common, the problem of proper management of the normative context is likely to become even more important.

The main objective of this paper is to investigate the normative context of e-service provision including both individual and composite services with the following specific aims:

- to design a formal model of the normative context for both individual and composite e-services
- to investigate the problem of management of a normative context for both customers and service providers.
- to define the requirements for a value-added service (tool) for management of normative context and analyse if such a tool could be also offered as an e-service.

As a research framework, the paper proposes a simple model of an e-service lifecycle that consists of: *pre-service*, *service execution* and *post-service* phases and uses this model to analyse representation and management of the normative context for both individual and composite e-services.

The paper is organised as follows: Section 2 gives an overview of the related work. Section 3 introduces the e-service lifecycle that will be used as a framework for discussion of the normative perspective of e-services. Modelling of a normative context of single and composite e-services is described in Sections 4 and 5 respectively. Section 6 deals with the problem of management of the normative context and analyses the requirements for possible support that could be offered to customers and service-providers in a form of a value-added tool.

2 Related Work

In recent years, the area of e-service provision (and in particular e-service composition) has become increasingly relevant. As already mentioned, there are several research groups that deal with e-service integration both at technical and conceptual level (see for example [1], [2], [4], [5] etc.). At the modelling level, the emphasis seems to be mainly on the control flow and transactional perspectives of e-services. However, as already pointed out, the normative perspective of composite e-services is yet to be investigated.

Another related area of research is e-contracting in B2B. Lee [6] was one of the first researchers to propose the use of deontic logic to model electronic contracts. Later, the Reference Model of Open Distributed Processing (RM-ODP) [7] and in particular its component called the Enterprise View Point introduced a framework for modelling of contracts (including obligations, prohibitions and permissions) in an enterprise. Recent work in this area includes BCA (Business Contract Architecture) by [8], [9] and Agent –Based Electronic Contract Framework (ECF) by [10].

Although both B2B e-contracting systems and the normative perspective of e-services described in this paper, deal with formal modelling of deontic constraints there are several major differences. E-contracting systems deal with the B2B contracting process – including contract negotiation, drafting, verification, monitoring and enforcement. On the other hand, the process of generation of the normative context (rights and responsibilities) in e-services is different. Customers using composite e-services are presented with pre-defined set of explicit terms and conditions and they are not in a position to negotiate its content. However, terms and conditions are not yet a normative context. Only when customer performs certain type of actions (click on the "I accept" button"), the combination of actions and the offered terms and conditions will result in the creation of the normative context for both customer and service provider. This situation is especially complex in the case of composite e-services when a customer deals with the number of service providers at the same time and is expected to fully understand rights and obligations resulting from their intended actions. Thus, the main emphasis of this work is to primarily help customers in B2C to manage the normative context of both individual and composite e-services.

Finally, it is important to mention the emerging standards such as WSDL (Web Service Description Language) [11] that provides an abstract description of a particular service including all necessary information to invoke a particular service. Another relevant area is work on Service Level Agreement (SLA) as it also deals with obligations of service providers. SLA represents a contract between an Application Service Provider and end-user that is used to regulate mainly technical side of service provision including a guaranteed level of system performance, specified level of customer support etc. For more information on SLAs see [12]. So far, developments in both areas focus more on the technical side of service delivery rather than the business oriented service modelling at the conceptual level that is the main focus of this paper.

3   E-service Lifecycle and Its Normative Perspective

Irrespectively of whether an e-service is individual or composite it is possible to distinguish among three different phases of its lifecycle that are relevant for the analysis of the normative perspective. These are: *pre-service, service provision* and *post-service* phases. This section gives a brief overview of all three phases:

3.1   The Pre-service Phase

During the *pre-service phase,* service providers advertise their services along with their respective terms and conditions. Visitors browse the offered services and make their selection. (Note that the marketing of e-services and the actual selection of service providers are out of the scope of this paper).

There are several problems that can occur during this phase both on customer and providers' sides and that are related to the normative perspective of an e-service. First of all, on the customer's side, an important problem related to terms and conditions is obvious lack of choice (flexibility). "Under contract law, the terms and conditions that are applied to a transaction need to be offered and accepted. Usually at least some aspects are likely to be expressly offered and accepted, although the courts might impute conventional terms of trade in any particular industry sector and are very likely to regard some terms as being implied. ... An area of difficulty is the lack of consumer choice in such circumstances, because the only choice that exists is for consumer to accept the fixed terms and conditions or not do business" [13]. In addition to customer's lack of choice, another equally important problem is customer's lack of clear understanding of their rights and obligations even with regards to the *explicit* terms and conditions let alone the *implicit* ones (assumed to be known in a given business domain).

On the provider's side, they are required to clearly communicate customer's rights and responsibilities otherwise they may be held liable for provision of misleading information given by their terms and conditions. For example, in 1999, two computer manufacturing companies agreed to settle US Federal Trade Commission charges that they had disseminated misleading information to their consumers on their web site related to computer leasing plans and the total fees involved. The FTC investigators found out that both companies had included the required information on their Web pages, but "the important details, such as the number of payments and fees due at the signing of the lease, were placed in a small typeface at the bottom of a long Web page. A consumer who wanted to determine the full cost of leasing a computer would need to scroll through a number of densely filled screens to obtain enough information to make necessary calculations" [14].

From the normative perspective, it is important to observe that during pre-service phase, customers perform so called *informative* rather than *performative* actions. In other words, their actions do not generate any obligations for the customer to proceed with the service nor for the provider to offer the service. For example: customer clicks on the *Terms and condition* link and then on the "Cancel" button. The distinction between informative and performative actions, used in this paper, originates from the *Speech-act theory* (see [15]).

3.2   The Service Provision Phase

This phase is initiated by customer's very first performative action(s) (e.g. clicking on "I accept button"). Performative actions combined with terms and conditions given by service provider result in the creation of the *normative context* (specifying rights and responsibilities) for all parties involved. It is important to observe that service provision is a process rather than a single event. Therefore, even in the case of a very simple e-service, its provision may incorporate a number of both informative and performative actions.

In this paper, the normative context of an e-service is defined as a set of deontic constraints (obligations, permissions and prohibitions) that specify rights and responsibilities of all parties involved. Obviously, provision of a single service results in a number of deontic constraints as well as possible sanctions if actions are not performed as agreed. Deontic constraints are described in more details in the next section. The whole situation is even more complex in the case of composite services.

3.3   The Post-service Phase

The *post-service phase* deals with the analysis of the accumulated experience on service execution and is more relevant for service providers than customers. In the case of affiliated marketing strategies, data including deontic constraints and their fulfilment can be collected and analysed to evaluate the effectiveness of the partnership between affiliated service providers. This could be an integral part of the overall Customer Relationship Management (CRM) strategy for a given service provider.

4   Modelling of a Normative Context of a Single E-service

As already pointed out, the normative context of an e-service is defined as a set of deontic constraints. A formal model of obligations, permissions and prohibitions was first introduced by von Wright [16] in a form of formal logic called deontic logic. Later on it was widely used for modelling of organisational knowledge (see for example [5], [7], [9] etc). According to deontic logic, constrains include obligations, permissions and prohibitions, defined as follows. An *obligation* is a prescription that a particular behaviour is required. An obligation is fulfilled by the occurrence of the prescribed behaviour. A *permission* is a prescription that a particular behaviour is allowed to occur. A *prohibition* is a prescription that a particular behaviour must not occur. A prohibition is equivalent to there being an obligation for the behaviour not to occur. The original deontic logic didn't include the concept of time. It was later extended by [6] to include temporal constraints.

The formal model of the e-service normative context, proposed by this paper, is also founded in deontic logic. Here, deontic constraints are extended to include the following concepts: a set of *pre-conditions, period of validity*, and a set of *sanctions* for each deontic constraint.

Formally, a deontic constraint can be defined as:

$$Ci: \text{Deontic-Constraint-Type (Role, Action) valid (tb, te) -> Si}$$

where *Ci* represents a set of pre-conditions under which this deontic constraint becomes valid (effective). For unconditional constraints it is an empty set.

$$\textit{Deontic-Constraint-Type} \in \{P, O, F\}$$

indicates one of the three types of deontic constraints. Thus, it can be a permission (P), obligation (O) or prohibition (F).

Role represents a legal party involved in service provision i.e. a customer or service provider.

Action is the *performative* action that the given role is obliged/permitted or prohibited to perform during the period of validity of the given deontic constraint.

(tb, te) is a time interval that represents the period of validity for a given constraint. *tb* is the time when a given constraint becomes effective (valid). In the case of obligations *te* is the deadline by which this constraint has to be satisfied. In the case of permissions and prohibitions *te* is the end of validity period. The period of validity for a given constraint will be initiated at the beginning of the service provisioning phase.

Si is a set of sanctions that is applicable only to obligations and prohibitions in the case if they are not fulfilled by the given deadline.

For example:

$$\text{(Customer, Clicks-on-I-Accept, P1) :}$$

$$\text{O (Customer, buy-ticket-from-P1) valid (tb,tc) -> S1}$$

where tb= *Time*(Click-on-I-Accept) and

te=tb+14 days and

S1: Customer will be charged 10% of the ticket price

The above is a conditional obligation with the condition being expressed as: *(Customer, Clicks-on-I-Accept, P1)*. If and when this condition becomes satisfied, the corresponding obligation will take effect. Therefore, the above deontic constraint indicates that if *Customer* performs a performative action *Click-on-I-Accept* button on the web site of the provider *P1*, s/he is *obliged* to buy the ticket from this provider *within 14 days* otherwise *s/he* will be legally liable to pay a fee of 10% of the full ticket price.

It is important to observe that the above constraint is defined during the service pre-phase as a part of static terms and conditions for service provision. It is then instantiated (becomes effective) by the first performative action of the customer, during the service provisioning phase. The formal contract between the customer and the service provider will result in more even deontic constraints.

Formal modelling of terms and conditions for the provision of a single e-service may result in a large number of deontic constraints. *Deontic inconsistency* occurs when the same role is both *obliged* and *prohibited* or *obliged* and *forbidden* to perform the same action during the *same period of time*. Verification of deontic consistency is more complex (and relevant) for the service provider rather than for the customer (in a single e-service scenario) due to the large number of customers and their respective deontic constraints.

Obviously, deontic constraints have to be represented in a more user-friendly form, as customers cannot be expected to deal with formal models. A possible way to visualise deontic constraints could be a *deontic to-do* list that specifies not only constraints but also the associated performative actions. Deontic to-do list is an extension of a concept of a role widow that was originally introduced in [17] in the area of electronic contracting. Figure 1 depicts an example of deontic to-do list that is divided into 3 different areas that correspond to obligations (O), permissions (P) and prohibitions (F) assigned to a particular role for a given service *Si*. Within each area, each timeline has a corresponding time interval that indicates the period of validity of a gi-

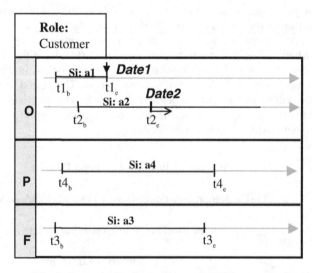

Fig. 1. An example of a deontic-to-do list for service Si

ven constraint. Deontic to-do list can be used to visualise both hard deadlines (e.g. action a1 *must* be completed by Date1) as well as soft deadlines (action a2 *should* be completed by Date2). It can be also used for verification of deontic inconsistency.

Simply, if time intervals associated with an obligation or permission for the given role and perfomative action, overlap with a prohibition defined for the same role and action there is a deontic inconsistency.

Deontic to-do list can be used on both customer's and provider's sides. On the customer side it could be used for visualisation, deontic verification and monitoring of the normative context. Thus it can help customer to better understand and manage the normative context of a given service. On the provider's side, it could be used active tracking of their rights and responsibilities including monitoring and query composition and execution. For example it could be used to determine for a given time interval all pending obligations and associated sanctions. This could be used not only in B2C but also in B2B commerce.

5   Normative Context of a Composite E-service

The normative context of a composite service is a combination of normative contexts of individual services. Its complexity is determined not only by the number of individual e-services, but also by the type of service providers and nature of their business relationship. Thus, we distinguish between composite services offered by independent or affiliated service providers.

5.1   Independent Composite E-services

If a customer combines individual independent e-service into a composite service the resulting normative context is a union of all deontic constraints from individual normative contexts. For example, a customer planning a trip purchases an airline ticket via one service provider, books a rental car through a car-rental agency and books a guided tour through a local tourist agency. All service providers in this example are independent and under no obligation to coordinate their activities in any way. In fact, they are not even aware that their services are a part of a composite e-service.

Thus, it is up to the customer to coordinate services and negotiate service delivery dates in accordance with the given (static) terms and conditions for each individual service. Obviously, deontic to-do list on the customer's site will include actions and corresponding deontic constraints for all different service providers. As they are independent the likelihood of deontic inconsistency between individual constraints is very low (and can be easily detected). However, the main problem on the customer's site is possible temporal inconsistency that can occur as the result of a coordination problem. For example, a customer is obliged to be at two different places at the same time or is obliged to pay the car rental without securing the air ticket. Therefore, it would be useful to have a coordination tool on the customer's side to help them schedule individual actions and obligations and even negotiate service delivery dates.

A coordination tool that could be used in this case is the *time map* [3]. The nodes of the time map correspond to the beginning/end time of individual e-services (i.e. customer's and providers' performative actions). Arcs are relative time values that correspond to a distance between the corresponding two time points (e.g. duration of an e-service or time between two e-services). All arcs are labelled by temporal operators (e.g. "<") and some by relative time values indicating time limits (e.g. "<*d1*" means that the distance between two time points should be less than *d1*). An absolute time value attached to a node correspond to a deadline or estimated occurrence. To indicate repetitive time, a set of absolute time values is attached to a node. To distinguish temporal constraints (when services have to be completed by) from estimates (when services could be completed by), a darker font/colour is used. For example, Figure 2 indicates that the estimated duration of Si is less than d1 time. Service *Sj* must start before *Si*. Service *Sj* is expected to occur on *Date2, Date3* or *Date4*. Service *Sk* is expected to start after or at the same time (no earlier) when service *Si* ends. Service *Sk* must take no more than *d2* time to complete. Services *Sk* and *Sl* must start at the same time (i.e. *Date1*).

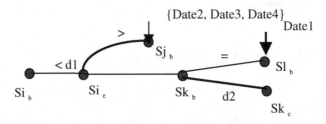

Fig. 2. An example of a time map

The time map can be used for scheduling of individual services (including negotiation of service delivery dates and times), verification of their temporal consistency and monitoring of service execution. It could be used as a complement to the deontic to-do list. For more details on modelling and verification of temporal constraints in e-services see [3]

5.2 Affiliated (Dependent) E-services

Under the affiliated marketing strategy, one service provider advertises related services of another service provider. They may offer discounts or other special deals to customers who combine their services in a certain way. It is important to note that there is a third party service provider that combines individual services. Various marketing strategies are used to encourage customers to combine individual services, however services can still be used independently. For example, suppose that a local airline is affiliated with a car rental agency and a hotel chain and on its web site offers a promotional package "City Getaway" until the end of April 2003. Suppose they offer the following deal to their customers. All customers who purchase a local adult airfare to one of the capital cities in Australia by the end of April 2003, if they book a car through the affiliated rental agency within 48h after purchasing the ticket, will receive 15% discount on the standard rental fee. They will also receive a 10% discount coupon to be used in any of the restaurants of the affiliated hotel chain valid till the end of April 2003. This type of affiliation is quite common, especially in event management (organisation of conferences and major sporting events).

The normative context on the customer's side includes deontic constraints that combine performative actions of more than one service provider. On the other hand, service providers deal with conditional obligations and permissions where the actions of one service provider become conditions for deontic constraints of another provider. Therefore, in addition to temporal interdependency between individual performative actions, there is deontic interdependency between deontic constraints of affiliated service providers. For example, service provider B is obliged to perform an action aj (e.g. give a discount for car-rental), only if the customer performed a set of performative actions (book a car within 48h after purchasing the ticket on provider A's web site).

A possible formal representation of this conditional constraint is given as follows:

(Customer, buy-ticket (Airline-A)) before 30-04-03 and

(Customer, book-car(car-rental-C1) and

Time (book-car (Car-rental-C) < Time (buy-ticket(Airline-A) + 48 h:

O (Car-rental-C1, give-discount(%15)) valid (tb, te)

where: $tb = Time$(book-car (Car-rental)) and

te <= 30-04-03 is the agreed car pickup date/time.

Obviously, this conditional obligation will becomes active if customer's performative actions satisfy its conditions. Variables tb and te that specify validity of this obligation will be instantiated at the time action *book-car* is completed.

Therefore, service providers are expected to deal with both temporal interdependency (to track and coordinate relative performative actions both on the customer's web site and the sites of all affiliated service providers) as well as deontic interdependency (including mutual verification of deontic constraints). To be able to do it, all affiliated service providers will need to "share" the normative context created by the provision of the composite service (i.e. to be aware of customer's performative actions on the affiliated web site). That means they need to have access to a shared deontic to-do list or at least to exchange messages or use any other coordination awareness mechanism to detect events on the affiliated web site that will trigger their own obligations.

Formal representation of the normative context is only the first step towards efficient management of the normative context on both customer's and provider's web site. The following section deals with the problem of normative context management in more details.

6 Managing the Normative Context of a Composite E-service

As already pointed out in Section 3, it is possible to distinguish three different phases of an e-service lifecycle: pre-service, provision and post-service phases. Recall that the normative context gets created at the beginning of the second phase by customer's first performative action. Therefore, management of the normative context is relevant only during service provision and post-service phases. In this section we concentrate on the *service-provision phase*. Table 1 summarises the most important requirements for normative context management support during provision of both individual and composite e-services.

Table 1. The Main Support Requirements for Management of the normative context

Role / Service Type		Customer	Service Provider(s)
I N D I V I D U L		• user-friendly visual represen-tation of deontic constraints (e.g. deontic to-do list) • detection of possible temporal and deontic inconsistency of a set of deontic constraints (by using the time map and deontic to-do list) • event management including: automatic generation of remin-ders and alerts	• user-friendly visual represen-tation of deontic constraints (e.g. deontic to-do list) for number of customers • detection of possible temporal and deontic inconsistency • event management including: automatic generation of remin-ders and alerts for all custom-ers • exception handling including "what if" analysis tool
C O M P O S I T E	I N D E P E N D E N T	• as in the case of individual ser-vices plus - integraton of normative con-texts (i.e. integrated to-do list) - coordination tool (e.g. time map)	As in the case of individual service providers
	A F F I L I A T E D	• as in the case of individual services extended to manage the increased number of roles and their performative actions	• as in the case of independent composite e-service plus: – awareness management – management of conditional deontic constraints

This table also illustrates new opportunities to create added value on top of an e-service being provided. This could be even taken one step further. Thus, provision of support for management of normative context could be even offered as another value-added service provided to the customers. However, provision of such a service would open up a number of interesting research challenges that need to be solved before such a service could be implemented. First of all, it is necessary to consider which party could offer such a service. For example, in the case of individual services, it could be offered by the same e-service provider. In the case of composite e-services (both independent and affiliated), provision of such a value-added service is much more challenging due to the number of reasons. For example, it would require the "integration" of normative contexts offered by different (dependent or independent) providers. However, the first step towards integration is standardisation of the representation of the normative context for all providers. A possible solution for standardisation of the representation of the normative context, or at least the first step, could be through an extension of the existing Web Services Description Language (W3C, 2001) that is becoming widely recognised both by researchers and industry.

7 Conclusions

As more and more companies provide their services over the Internet, the need for better understanding and ultimately better management of the normative context of composite services (including rights and responsibilities of all parties involved) becomes evident. Unfortunately the normative perspective of both individual and composite services seems to be left out from current e-service research and practice.

Yet, the normative perspective of e-service provision is very important not only because of the possible legal consequences but also because of its implications on customer's trust.

This paper investigates the normative aspect of individual and composite e-services offered by independent and affiliated service providers. It also defines requirements for management of the normative context on both customer and provider(s) sides during the service execution phase.

However, there are many interesting research problems that should be further explored. First of all, user-friendly representation of the normative context is very important. The proposed model of deontic constrains and deontic to-do list is only a starting point in this direction. Another problem is related to data interoperability and possible standardisation of the deontic context. This would require dealing with the problem of ambiguities in terms and conditions and generalised expression of purpose such as "other services" or "for the performance of agency's functions' (as pointed out in [13]) as they cannot be easily translated into deontic constraints.

Finally, from the business perspective, it is necessary to investigate if full disclosure and standardised description of all terms and conditions (without "small prints" and "conditions apply " statements) is likely to affect provider's marketing strategy and ultimately its competitive position.

Research presented in this paper hopes to provide a starting point for further investigation of the management of the normative context of composite e-services.

Future work includes further analysis of terms and conditions from the perspective of a possible standardisation, analysis of the accumulated experience (in particular normative contexts) and creation of "deontic profiles" on the provider side.

References

1   Sheng, Q.S., Benatallah, B., Dumas, M. and Mak E.O. (2002) "SELF-SERV: A Platform for Rapid Composition of Web Services in a Peer-to-Peer Environment", Proc. Of the 28th VLDB Conference, Hong Kong, China, 2002

2   Fauvet, MC et al. (2001), "Peer-to-Peer Traced Execution of Composite Services", Proc. Of the Second International Workshop on Technologies for E-Services, Springer, Heidelberg, Germany, pp 103–117

3.   Marjanovic, O. (2002), "Supporting Coordination in Dynamic Virtual Enterprises", Proc. Of the 15th Bled Electronic Commerce Conference: eReality: Constructing the eEconomy, Bled, Slovenia, June 17–19, 2002

4   Durante, A. et al. (2000), "A Model for the E-Service Marketplace", *Hewlett-Packard Company*

5   Kuno, H. (2000), "Surveying the E-Services Technical Landscape", *Hewlett-Packard CompanY*

6   Lee, R.M. (1998), "A logic model of electronic contracting", Decision Support Systems, 4, 27–44

7   ISO/IEC WD 15414. (1998) Open Distributed Processing – Reference Model – Enterprise Viewpoint, January 1998

8   Herring, C. and Milosevic, Z. (2001), "Implementing B2B Contracts Using BizTalk", Proc. of *HICSS-34 Conference,* Hawaii, Honolulu.

9   Cole, J. et al. (2001), "Author Obliged to Submit Paper before 4 July: Policies in an Enterprise Specification", Policy2001 workshop, Bristol, UK, January

10   Salle (2002) "An Agent-based Framework for the Automation of Contractual Relationships" AAAI-2002 Workshop on Agent-Based Technologies for B2B Electronic Commerce, 28. July 2002, Edmonton, Alberta Canada

11   W3C (2001) Web Services Description Language (WSDL) available from http://www.w3.org/TR/wsdl

12   Ludwig, H, Keller, A. Dan, A and King R. (2002) "A Service Level Agreement Language for Dynamic Electronic Services", Proceedings of WECWIS 2002, IEEE Computer Society, Los Alamitos, pp. 25–32

13   Clarke, R. (2002), "eConsent: A Critical Element of Trust in eBusiness", Proc. Of the 15th Bled Electronic Commerce Conference: eReality: Constructing the eEconomy, Bled, Slovenia, June 17–19, 2002

14   Schneider, G.P. and Perry, J.T. (2001), *Electronic Commerce*, Thomson Learning, Boston, MA

15   Searle, J.R. (1969) *Speech Acts – An Essay in the Philosphy of Language*, The Universiy Printing House, Cambridge

16   Von Wriht, C.G. (1968), "An essay in Deontic Logic and the General Theory of Action", Acta Philosophica Fennica, 21, North-Holland

17   Marjanovic, O. and Milosevic, Z (2001), "Towards Formal Modelling of e-Contracts", Proceeding of the 5th IEEE International Enterprise Distributed Object Computing Conference EDOC'01, September 4–7, Seattle, Washington, USA

Constructing Web Services out of Generic Component Compositions

Johann Oberleitner and Schahram Dustdar

Distributed Systems Group
Information Systems Institute
Vienna University of Technology
Argentinierstrasse 8/E1841
A-1040 Wien, Austria
{joe,sd}@infosys.tuwien.ac.at

Abstract. Todays information systems are built using various component models such as Enterprise Java Beans, JavaBeans, Microsoft COM+, and CORBA distributed objects. In this paper we argue that it is crucial for designers of information systems to interactively build and test systems constructed from (a) components (enabling interoperability across component models) and (b) Web services at the same time. The contribution of this paper is threefold: Firstly, we introduce a visual tool the Component Workbench - for designing information systems out of components from different component models (e.g. EJB, COM+, CORBA) and combine them with Web services. Secondly, we show how component compositions can be turned into Web services using SOAP as a communications protocol. Thirdly, we show how to interactively test compositions before creating the actual Web services out of components.

Keywords: composition, components, component models, interactive testing.

1 Introduction

Increasingly Web services [1] are gaining momentum for intra- and interorganizational integration of information systems. Current systems are built using various component models such as Enterprise Java Beans [2], JavaBeans [3], Microsoft COM+ [4], and CORBA distributed objects [5]. Furthermore, we may safely expect that required application logic will continue to be developed using those component models in the foreseeable future. Most of todays Web service development systems are based on the idea that components (and legacy systems) used in organizations should be first developed using component models and as a next step be equipped with Web services interfaces and communications means (i.e. SOAP [6]). The argument of this paper is that it is crucial for designers of information systems to interactively build and test systems constructed from (a) components (enabling interoperability across component models) and

M. Jeckle and L.-J. Zhang (Eds.): ICWS-Europe 2003, LNCS 2853, pp. 37–48, 2003.
© Springer-Verlag Berlin Heidelberg 2003

(b) Web services at the same time. In order to provide a proof-of-concept, we introduce a prototype system - the Component Workbench based on our Vienna Component Framework.

The contribution of this paper is threefold: firstly, we introduce a visual tool the Component Workbench - for designing information systems out of components from different component models (e.g. EJB, COM+, CORBA) and combine them with Web services. Secondly, we show how component compositions can be turned into Web services using SOAP as a communications protocol. Thirdly, we show how to interactively test compositions before creating the actual Web services out of components.

The remainder of the paper is structured as follows. In section 2 we explain background information about the Vienna Component Framework (VCF) we have built to access different component models in a uniform way. How component compositions can be built with VCF are illustrated in section 3. The Component Workbench, our graphical tool, is illustrated in section 4. How such compositions are turned into Web services is explained in section 5. Section 6 discusses related work. Section 7 concludes the paper and provides an brief overview for our future research directions.

2   The Vienna Component Framework

We have built the Vienna Component Framework (VCF) [7] to support the interoperability and composability of components from different component models such as Enterprise JavaBeans (EJB) [2] or Microsoft COM+ components [4].

VCF provides a Java API to reuse components that adhere to different component models within one single application. VCF abstracts the internals of the different component models, therefore simplifies the use of different component models and reduces the difficulties inherent in these models.

VCF uses plugins to simplify the extension with new component models. Currently, we have implemented plugins that provide uniform access for components that adhere to either JavaBeans, Enterprise JavaBeans, Microsoft COM+, CORBA distributed objects, and Web services that use SOAP as communication medium.

Each plugin provides the functionality to access a component model's metadata facility to find out about the *operations*, *properties*, and *event callbacks* a component supports. For each of those features VCF defines an interface that contains operations for accessing them. For instance, the interface for a components method has operations invoking this method and query methods to find out about the method parameters and its return values. The interface for callback events allows registration and unregistration of notification listeners for the events. The plugin provides implementations of each of the interfaces to provide uniform access for the corresponding component model.

Clients do not use plugin classes directly, but use a façade class to access the features of components. This allows the integration of new functionality in the façade class for all component models and all components, without changing the syntactic or semantic structure of a plugin. Furthermore, this supports per-instance modification of components on the external component interface.

A client creates an instance of a component by using a factory method that is aware of all plugin classes. This factory method takes as parameters data to identify a component's model and the corresponding plugin class and plugin-specific information for instantiating the component. The factory method returns an instance of the façade class that contains an instance of the appropriate plugin and a component-model dependent reference to the instance of the component. During this instantiation step the plugin creates instances of the implementation classes for each feature found with the metadata facility. For each operation found, an instance of the implementation class that implements the interface IMethod will be created and stored in a feature container (see figure 1). The same happens for properties and event-sets.

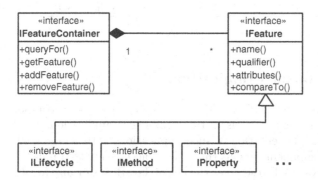

Fig. 1. Features and Feature Containers

The façade class provides a flexible mechanism to make queries for features, such as a component's operations. The queries return the feature interfaces that provide mechanisms to access a component instance's functionality.

The set of feature interfaces allows to use different components in a reflective programming style, similar to Java reflection or CORBA Dynamic Interface Invocation. This programming style is well supported by graphical composition environments such as the Component Workbench (section 4) or when components are added at runtime but is tedious to use by programmers, since even the simplest calls get complicated. Hence, we allow the generation of wrappers around the feature interfaces. This is more convenient for programmers, allows a programming style similar to use regular Java classes, and is statically typed.

Table 1 shows the component models supported by VCF, the metadata facilities used for each model, and how dynamic calls are built. Although the existing plugins all rely on such built-in metadata facilities other plugins could use data provided by component clients. This can be used to build plugins for legacy systems that do not adhere to a particular component model.

```
public interface IConnectorControl {

    public void connect () throws Exception;
    public void disconnect () throws Exception;
}
```

Fig. 2. Interface Declaration for IConnectorControl

Table 1. VCF plugins

Component Model	Metadata	Dynamic Calls
COM+	Type Library	IDispatch interface
CORBA	Interface Repository	Dynamic Invocation Interface (DII)
EJB	Java Reflection	Java Reflection
JavaBeans	Java Reflection	Java Reflection
Web services (SOAP)	WSDL	Dynamic SOAP calls (WSIF)

3   Component Composition

One of the primary goals of VCF was to allow the use of components built for different component models in the same client application. VCF supports the design and implementation of such applications with one unified programming model for component models that can be accessed with a plugin.

Using Java, VCF resembles the use of JavaBeans or any regular Java classes. Furthermore, VCF supports component composition with connectors that link components with predefined communication semantics. This allowed us to support different communication primitives in different connector types such as building a connector for component method calls or component callbacks.

Similar to building component model plugins, connectors use a similar plugin architecture. Each connector plugin has to provide an implementation for the IConnectorControl interface. As shown in figure 2 this interface defines a method for making a connecting, and another one for canceling a connection.

In addition each connector supports a number of roles. These roles represent the end-points of a connector (see figure 3).

We do not restrict ourselves to binary connectors, but allow an arbitrary number of roles, allowing virtually any kind of connection among an arbitrary

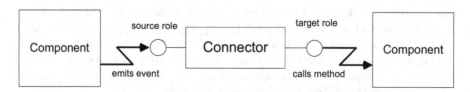

Fig. 3. Connector, Roles, and Bindings

```
public interface IRole{

    public void linksTo (IBinding binding) throws Exception;
}
```

Fig. 4. Interface Declaration for IRole

number of components. The connector plugin has to provide implementation classes for roles. Figure 4 shows the interface that has to be implemented for one particular role. It has only one method that links a connector's role, i.e. a connector's end-point, to a component binding.

A binding is an encapsulation of a concrete component plus an executable part of a component. A typical example of connectors are event connectors that model component callbacks. Such callbacks are realized by VCF's event set feature. This feature allows clients to register notification listeners that implement a particular Java interface.

The source role of this connector will be linked to a particular component's event set feature while the target role will be linked to one or more method feature. The corresponding bindings contain also all arguments necessary to call the bound feature. For instance, in case of the event connector the target binding will bind a method and all argument values for calling this method. These argument values in turn can be retrieved by bindings to other components, hence allowing for recursively resolved structures.

Bindings are evaluated either at connect time of the connector, or at run-time when a certain communication between roles happens. In case of the event connector the source role binding calls the register listener method of the event set feature. This happens when the connector is made concrete, with the `IConnector Control` interface. On the target role side, a particular method is called, and arguments are forwarded. This is done only when an event occurs.

Since VCF can be enhanced with new connector types and bindings many different compositions among components are possible.

Two other VCF characteristics ease the construction of compositions. First, since no client addresses components directly but always uses a façade class for accessing a component's feature, it is easily possible to instrument this façade class for modifying the behavior of one particular component's feature. For instance, it is possible to inform other components or other clients when a particular method has been called by clients. This facility exists, even when a different component model will be used later.

Second, VCF allows the arrangement of components, connectors, or both in composite components. This allows the construction of hierarchical composition structures. Nevertheless, it is possible to expose a subset of those composition elements to clients that reside on other levels, also allowing conversational composition.

4   The Component Workbench

This section briefly introduces the CWB [8] which is a graphical composition environment developed in [9]. It allows developers to construct compositions out of existing components in a graphical and interactive way. Figure 5 shows the architecture of the CWB. It uses VCF to allow the use of arbitrary component models and it also supports the connector mechanism described in section 3. Component instances can be arranged within other components, so-called composite components, hence building a hierarchical structure of components. Internally a composite component consists of instances of child components that are linked by connectors. A composite component is represented either by an entire window to allow modification of its child components or it can be represented by a graphical icon in its parent component. This allows to link together composite components to other components.

Once, a component instance has been put onto a CWB window they are fully functional. This means it is possible to change a component instances' state or call an instances' operation directly within the CWB.

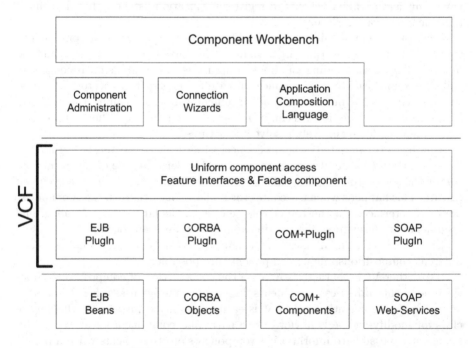

Fig. 5. Architecture of the Component Workbench

A wizard allows the user to define the roles and its bindings within the CWB by drawing connections. A connection can be visualized by a class provided by the connector plugin. For binary connections, by far the most common, this means that an arrow will be drawn from the source-role to the target-role. However, the visualization is not limited to this kind of representation.

A composition built with the CWB can be stored to an XML file that describes the arrangement of components and connectors [10]. Later this file can be reloaded to work on a composition again. The set of available components is stored in a different type of XML file that describes the necessary parameters to instantiate a component and the component model to which it adheres. Another type of XML file is available that describes connector types, its roles, the classes that implement the connector and the required wizard dialogs. New components or connectors can be added to the CWB by adding a new file that describes a component or a connector to the appropriate directory.

5   Web Service Construction

A primary contribution of this paper is to show how a component composition built with VCF can be turned into a Web service that uses SOAP as communication protocol. This section explains how a composition that has been built with the Component Workbench can be converted into a Web service.

We propose a tool-supported approach that relies on several steps. Each of these steps corresponds to a Component Workbench wizard. Initially the developer invokes the Web-Service Designer (section 5.1) to create a new Web service. This allows for defining static properties of a service, such as its service name. The Message Designer (section 5.2) enables the definition of messages used within services. These messages can be linked to components as described

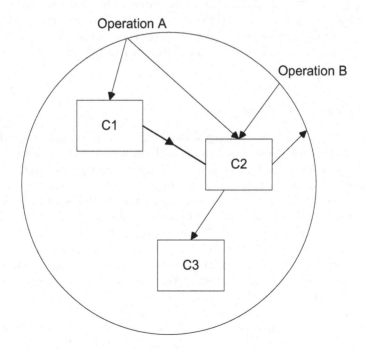

Fig. 6. Web service boundaries

in section 5.3. Figure 6 shows a composition of the components C1, C2, C3. The tasks of the Message Designer and the Component Link wizard are to let ingoing operations map to invocations of appropriate components. A service modeled with CWB can be used to create Java source code (section 5.5) and the corresponding description information. The CWB also allows interactive testing of Web services built out of components (section 5.4).

5.1   Web Service Designer

The developer has to select one of CWB's composite components to be converted to a Web service or a fresh composite component can be created if the developer wants to design a new composition. The developer also can propose a name and a namespace for the service.

5.2   Message Designer

The message designer allows users to define new messages for operations used in Web services. In the CWB this message designer is implemented as a dialog that allows the user to compose messages out of existing data types.

Since SOAP messages rely on XML Schema declarations the result of this designer is an XML Schema declaration. Furthermore, the user can provide data to fill the types declared in the wizard for both, documentation and testing purposes. Since VCF uses Java as implementation language, Java classes will be created automatically that match the newly created Schema types.

To support users in defining new messages the designer allows browsing of existing components, and Web service definitions to take SOAP *message part types* and *part names* from.

5.3   Message-Component Links

Links from components to messages and links from messages to components are defined with the Message-Component Link wizard. This wizard provides mappings from messages to methods. An ingoing message can lead to the invocation of one or more methods. Different parts of an ingoing message can be distributed to the parameters of the components' methods being called. The methods can be called synchronously or asynchronously. If one of the methods is called synchronously, the whole Web service supports synchronous communication semantics. Otherwise the Web service supports asynchronous interaction semantics. Return messages are mapped similar to the ingoing messages.

When the user has designed messages that use *part types* and *part names* that identically map to types and names of components then the message-component link wizard automatically proposes standard mappings.

Furthermore, it is possible to add filters on ingoing and outgoing messages for parameter conversion. The actions that are invoked when a message occurs are shown visually.

Figure 7 shows a simplified representation of the wizard. On the left an input message for a student grading Web service is displayed. Each row shows the parts of this message with its part type and part name. On the right part component invocation boxes are shown. These invocations are initiated when the input message arrives. The figure shows that the parts of the message have a different natural order than the arguments of the gradeDB's storeGrade method. Hence, the wizard shows this reordering with arrows that start in the parts and end in the arguments. Furthermore, the input message's instructor part does not match the type of the instructor argument of the storeGrade method. Hence, an additional call that makes a lookup for an id of the instructor in an instructor database has been added. This call is shown as another invocation box. The box has an arrow on its right side that leads to the instruction parameter of the storeGrade method.

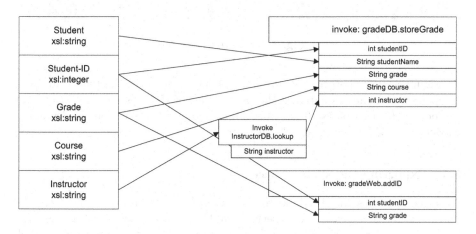

Fig. 7. Message Component Link Wizard

5.4 Interactive Testing

When a Web service has been declared, and its messages and the links to components completed this composition can already be tested within the CWB. It is possible to open another window, instantiate the designed Web service, connect CWB provided components that allow entering of ingoing message parts, and displaying return value parts. Although the Web service is not created at this time, it is possible to test the composition as if it were a Web service. In addition, later when the Web service has been created it is possible to use the same test case. Instead of the designed Web service, the concrete Web service is used.

The CWB provides components to enter and display message arguments, directly on the screen. These components use VCF to find out about the method parameters, and provides an input mask for entering and displaying message parts.

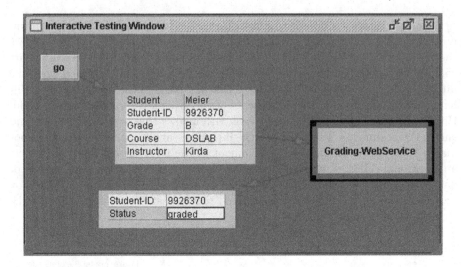

Fig. 8. Interactive testing

Figure 8 shows how a *student grading Web service* is connected to an input component that allows entering the part values of the message and an output component that displays the acknowledgment message. The communication is started when the user presses the *ok* button.

5.5   Exporting the Web Service

Once the messages, and the links to the corresponding components has been defined, the source code for a Web service can be generated. We currently support the generation of source code that uses the Apache SOAP engine. For each Web service operation, a method is generated that uses VCF to call the corresponding components. The Component Workbench uses an XML format for storing component compositions [10]. We apply an XSLT style sheet to convert such a composition into the source code for the Java Web service. We plan to support different target environments in the future.

In addition to the generation of the source code the Web service description is created. The information gained from the user in the Web service designer, and the message designer is used to create this file.

6   Related Work

Recently, initiatives have been started to provide transparent SOAP access for Enterprise JavaBeans [11] and CORBA objects [12]. Similarly, Microsoft supports the access of COM+ objects via SOAP in a recent release of the Internet Information Server (IIS). However, most of these initiatives are currently only specifications and implementations are rare.

Graphical composition environments have gained some attention by the research community in the last years [13]. The CWB is specific with respect to the support of arbitrary component models. VCF supports interoperability across component models. Microsoft's .NET framework supports transparent kind of functionality for COM+ components, .NET classes, and SOAP Web services [14]. However, support for applications that rely on Sun's JDK cannot transparently integrated into .NET easily. IBM's Web service invocation framework (WSIF) [15] has similarities to VCF. Like VCF it is primarily used on the client, and provides transparent access to different providers such as SOAP Web services. A recent addition was a provider that supports Enterprise JavaBeans.

Some commercial application servers that support Web services provide tools to define workflow applications. These tools can be compared to our extensions of the Component Workbench for exporting component compositions. Usually these tools are restricted to Web services itself and don't support the use of multiple component models.

7 Conclusions and Future Work

This paper presented a graphical composition environment for integrating arbitrary component models as well as Web services and enabling interoperability across them. Today, most tools in the Web services domain are focused (and restricted) solely to composition of Web services. In our paper we demonstrated a prototype system allowing the use of a combination of multiple component models and Web services within one system. We think that such an open and integrated approach will foster the Service-oriented computing approach and demonstrate its viability. Our future work includes increased attention towards interactive testing of Web services, which becomes more and more challenging, while Web services providers are distributed on the Internet and Quality-of-Service issues become more relevant [16].

References

1. Benatallah, B., Casati, F., Toumani, F., Hamadi, R.: Conceptual modeling of web service conversations. In: Proceedings of 15th International Conference on Advanced Information Systems Engineering (CAiSE'03), Springer (2003)
2. DeMichiel, L.G., Yalcinalp, L.Ü., Krishnan, S.: Enterprise JavaBeans Specification, Version 2.0. Sun Microsystems. (2001)
3. Hamilton, G., ed.: JavaBeans. Sun Microsystems, http://java.sun.com/beans/ (1997)
4. Kirtland, M.: Designing Component-Based Applications. Microsoft Press (1999)
5. Siegel, J.: CORBA 3: Fundamentals and Programming. Second edn. John Wiley & Sons, Inc. (2000)
6. W3C: SOAP – Simple Object Access Protocol. (2001)
7. Oberleitner, J., Gschwind, T., Jazayeri, M.: The Vienna Component Framework: Enabling composition across component models. In: Proceedings of the 25th International Conference on Software Engineering (ICSE), IEEE Press (2003)

8. Oberleitner, J., Gschwind, T.: Component distributed components with the component workbench. In: Proceedings of the 3rd International Workshop on Software Engineering in Middleware 2002 (SEM), LNCS 2596, Springer (2002)

9. Oberleitner, J.: The Component Workbench: A Flexible Component Composition Environment. Master's thesis, Technische Universität Wien (2001)

10. Oberleitner, J., Gschwind, T.: Transforming application compositions with xslts. In Assmann, U., Pulvermueller, E., Borne, I., Bouraqadi, N., Cointe, P., eds.: Electronic Notes in Theoretical Computer Science. Volume 82., Elsevier Science Publishers (2003)

11. Sun Microsystems: Enterprise JavaBeans Specification, Version 2.1 – proposed final draft. (2002)

12. OMG: CORBA-WSDL/SOAP Interworking. (2003)

13. Lüer, C., van der Hoek, A.: Composition environments for deployable software components. Technical Report UCI-ICS-02-18, Department of Information and Computer Science, University of California, Irvine (2002)

14. Richter, J.: Applied Microsoft .NET Framework Programming. Microsoft Press (2002)

15. Duftler, M.J., Mukhi, N.K., Slominski, A., Weerawarana, S.: Web Services Invocation Framework (WSIF), http://ws.apache.org/wsif/references.html. (2001)

16. Zeng, L., Benatallah, B., Dumas, M., Kalagnanam, J., Sheng, Q.Z.: Quality driven web services composition. In: Proceedings of the 12th International World Wide Web Conference 2003 (WWW), ACM (2003)

Adaptation Space: A Design Framework for Adaptive Web Services

Henrique Paques, Ling Liu, and Calton Pu

Georgia Institute of Technology
College of Computing
Atlanta, GA 30332-0280 USA
{paques,lingliu,calton}@cc.gatech.edu

Abstract. Web service adaptation is an important feature for mission critical Web services. It is widely recognized that thrashing and crashes occur in system saturation for many statically adaptive resource management algorithms, including CPU, memory, and network congestion. Service adaptation supports alternative responses to saturation control, maintaining service and server system stability and progress, instead of thrashing. In this paper, we present a design framework for developing adaptive web services. The core of this framework is the adaptation space model, which is based on the concepts of adaptation space and adaptation case. An adaptation space is defined by a use context and a partial order of adaptation cases. Each adaptation case describes a specific adaptation of a program or component of a web service. There are three main thrusts of the adaptation space approach. First, it defines a multi-dimensional adaptation context for capturing and coordinating different kinds of adaptation at different levels of a web service. Second, it provides a uniform way for representing and viewing a collection of alternative adaptations for a given web service component. Third, it promotes a declarative and incremental approach to adaptation specification, allowing the incorporation of new adaptation behavior of a web service in terms of existing adaptation cases. We evaluate the adaptation space approach using Ginga, an adaptive query processing service for handling queries over multiple data sources with diverse capabilities across the Internet. Our experimental results show that Ginga query adaptation can achieve significant performance improvements (up to 40% of response time gain) for processing distributed queries over the Internet in the presence of end-to-end delays.

Keywords: program adaptation, adaptation space.

1 Introduction

Most of the current efforts on developing web services concentrate mainly on how to guarantee that these services can interoperate. Well-known examples of these

M. Jeckle and L.-J. Zhang (Eds.): ICWS-Europe 2003, LNCS 2853, pp. 49–63, 2003.
© Springer-Verlag Berlin Heidelberg 2003

efforts are the WSDL[1], SOAP[2], and UDDI[3] standards. However, an important problem that still needs to be solved is related to the design of web services. Assuming that these services are executed in a distributed open environment that dynamically changes over time, how can we guarantee the maintenance of the performance optimality of these services at runtime. To illustrate this problem, take a web service S that needs to contact other remotely located services in order to complete its task. Considering that the implementations of web services are independent from each other, and that the bandwidth of the network connections between these services can fluctuate quite unpredictably, it is difficult to anticipate the performance behavior of each service. Consequently, it is very likely that S will have unpredictable performance. The problem becomes aggravated when S is responsible to execute a task that is part of a mission critical application, where each task has a specific deadline to be completed.

In order to overcome unpredictable changes to the runtime environment, such as network bandwidth fluctuations, the web service needs to be able to *adapt* its program (or component) execution accordingly. If we take service S, one possible way to adapt its execution when a remote web service W is taking too long to respond to a S's request, is to contact an alternative service that can provide similar response to the same request. Another possible adaptation of S for coping with the same delay problem is to modify S's program (if possible) to perform other parts of its task while waiting on W's response. A third adaptation is to close and re-open the connection with W and submit the request again. It is possible that the previous route established between S and W was too crowed, resulting in network congestion. Observe that we can have more than one alternative for adapting a given web service. The challenge is then how to coordinate and integrate these alternative adaptations.

In this paper we propose an adaptation space based approach to web service adaptation. The core of this adaptation model is the notion of adaptation space and the mechanisms for coordinating and integrating different kinds of adaptations. An adaptation space is defined by a use context and a partial order of adaptation cases. Each adaptation case describes a specific adaptation of a program or component of a web service. Given a program or component, say T, the adaptation process typically consists of three steps:

- **Step 1: What to Adapt.** Construct an adaptation space for T where preferred adaptation alternatives are specified by a use context and a partial order of adaptation cases (see Sect. 3 for concrete syntax);
- **Step 2: When to Adapt.** Monitor the use conditions of each specified adaptation alternative in the adaptation space of T, and notify the adaptation engine whenever a use condition becomes true;
- **Step 3: How to Adapt.** Turn on the appropriate adaptation case to prevent the running program or component from unnecessary lost of performance, thrashing, abnormal exit, or crash. The selected adaptation case fulfills this

---

[1] http://www.w3.org/TR/wsdl
[2] http://www.w3.org/TR/SOAP
[3] http://www.uddi.org

job by redirecting the ongoing program to run using specialized code that can accomplish the intended task through partial evaluation, such as using specialized code with either fewer resources or requiring fewer capabilities.

There are three main thrusts of adaptation space based approach: First, program adaptation presents a unified framework for representing and viewing of multi-dimensional adaptation context and adaptation opportunities for a given program or component of a web service. Second, program adaptation provides a uniformed way of capturing and coordinating different kinds of adaptation at different levels of a web service. Third, program adaptation promotes a declarative and incremental approach to define the multi-dimensional adaptation context and adaptation alternatives, allowing the seamless incorporation of new adaptation behavior of a web service into the existing adaptation framework.

The rest of this paper proceeds as follows: Sect. 2 motivates the adaptation space based approach using a real world example. Sect. 3 provides an informal introduction to the concept, the syntax, and the semantics of adaptation cases and adaptation spaces. Sect. 4 presents the formal semantics of the adaptation space model. We illustrate the adaptation space concept and semantics by walking through the application scenario introduced in Sect. 2. Sect. 5 examines the issues that should be addressed by the adaptation space model. Sect. 6 describes a concrete application for the proposed adaptation space model. We discuss related work in Sect. 7 and conclude the paper in Sect. 8.

2 Motivating Application Scenario

Let us briefly motivate the adaptation space based approach using an application scenario drawn from the Bioinformatic domain: One of the common applications of the growing number of Bioinformatic data sources[4] is the discovery of new drugs that may efficiently treat serious diseases caused by virus such as Human Immunodeficiency Virus (HIV). As we describe next, such applications will involve contacting different web services that have unpredictable response times. The main challenge in this scenario is to execute a user request over these unstable remote services with expected responsiveness.

Example 1 (Application Scenario). Consider Next Generation Drugs (NGD), a company specialized in developing state-of-the-art drugs. For each new drug that NGD starts to develop, the first step is to gather all the needed information about the virus that the new drug will attack. In general, this information describes the nucleotides, proteins, and protein structures associated with the virus. Once the necessary information has been collected, the pharmacologist can then start the process of finding the new drug.

Let us assume that NGD has an internal web service NGD-WS responsible for gathering the needed data for starting the development of a new drug. The pharmacologist enters the virus name, and NGD-WS executes query Q expressed

---

[4] There are more than 500 Bioinformatic data sources available on the Internet.

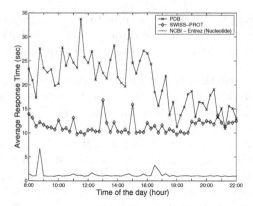

Fig. 1. Average response time measured every 15 min. for 32 days (from 4/11/02 to 5/13/02) between 8:00 and 22:00 EST. Keyword search on "HIV" using PDB, SWISS-PROT, and NCBI Entrez.

in a SQL statement[5] shown in Fig. 2(a), and returns the result back to the pharmacologist. The information on nucleotides, protein, and protein structures is typically provided by remote web services such as NCBI Entrez[6](nucleotides), SWISS-PROT[7](proteins), and PDB[8] (protein structures). However, the response time from these web services can be very unpredictable as shown in Fig. 1. Even though NCBI Entrez has fast response time (in the order of a few seconds), waiting for PDB results can take up to 34 seconds depending on what time of the day the query request was posted to the site. Considering that NGD-WS has to combine this data collected before delivering them to the pharmacologist, such difference in response time could become costly. The situation may become aggravated when NGD needs to execute this type of queries repeatedly (practically, one for each new chemical compound that can potentially affect the virus). The accumulative effect of these delays can significantly affect the company's productivity.

One possible solution for NGD-WS is to adapt the execution of query Q by modifying the data collection and integration process so that the fluctuation on end-to-end delays can be masked. We illustrate next how to implement this solution using adaptation space.

Example 2 (Adapting to End-to-End Delays). Let us assume that NGD-WS generates the optimized query plan P_0 (see Fig. 2(b)) for executing Q, and that the expected transfer rate for the network connection[9] L_i is $Rate(L_i) = 1Mbps$, for $1 \leq i \leq 3$. Now, suppose that as NGD-WS starts the execution of P_0

---

[5] Any other query language, such as XQuery, could very well be used instead.

[6] http://www.ncbi.nlm.nih.gov/Entrez

[7] http://ca.expasy.org/sprot

[8] http://www.rcsb.org/pdb

[9] We use the term *end-to-end delay* to refer to the delays experienced by the clients due to both bandwidth fluctuation in networks and contention at the servers. In this paper, we concentrate our study on end-to-end delays caused by bandwidth

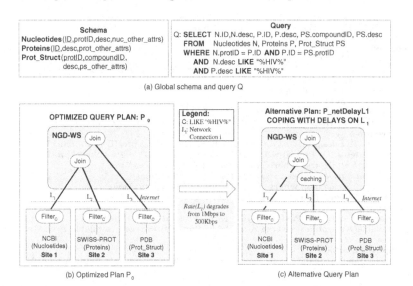

(a) Global schema and query Q

(b) Optimized Plan P_0 (c) Alternative Query Plan

Fig. 2. (a) Query Q and associated global schema; (b) Optimized query plan P_0; (c) Alternative query plan $P_{netDelayL1}$ for coping with delays on network connection L_1.

the transfer rate of connection L_1 degrades from 1Mbps to 500Kbps causing the data from *NCBI* to be slowly delivered. Assuming that P_0 is executed according to the iterator-based model [3], i.e., query operators are scheduled in a left-deep recursive way, without adaptation, the execution of P_0 will be delayed. One way to solve this problem is to start collecting the data from *SWISS-PROT* and caching it locally *while* slowly receiving data from *NCBI*. Fig. 3 presents a sketch of such an adaptation case, declaring an adaptation opportunity: mask the slow delivery of data from *NCBI* while executing other parts of the query. If *NCBI* is completed downloaded by the time the data from *SWISS-PROT* is fully cached, the query execution can then proceed without affecting considerably the final response time.

Based on this adaptation specification, the adaptation engine can infer that this adaptation can be done at compile time if the connection to remote source *NCBI* is known to be slow. Otherwise, the adaptation must be done at runtime, and query plan P_0 will be replaced by $P_{netDelayL1}$ shown in Fig. 2(c).

3 Adaptation Space Model: An Overview

3.1 Adaptation Cases

Adaptation cases define the adaptation behavior of a web service program in anticipation of resource shortage or in the need for performance optimization. More concretely, an adaptation case defines a context for adaptation through program

---

fluctuation, which results in slow delivery, i.e., the data from the remote server arrives at a rate slower than expected.

ADAPTATION CASE ac_caseNetDelayL1 **adapts execution of query** Q.
  goal: query adaptation when $Rate(L_1)$ degrades.
  context
    resource objects
      Nucleotides = {NCBI}; *Proteins* = {SWISS-PROT}; *Prot_Struct* = {PDB};
      NetworkLinks = $\{L_1, L_2, L_3\}$
    resource object parameters
      must-provide
        ID, desc **from** *Nucleotides*; ID, desc **from** *Proteins*;
        compoundID, desc **from** *Prot_Struct*; bandwidth **from** *NetworkLinks*
      require
        Nucleotides.protID, *Proteins*.ID **where** *Nucleotides*.protID = *Proteins*.ID
        Proteins.ID, *Prot_Struct*.protID **where** *Proteins*.ID = *Prot_Struct*.protID
        Nucleotides.desc **where** *Nucleotides*.desc LIKE *virusName*
        Proteins.desc **where** *Proteins*.desc LIKE *virusName*
        Prot_Struct.desc **where** *Prot_Struct*.desc LIKE *virusName*
    adapted query plan: $P_{netDelayL1}$ (see Fig. 2(c))
  use-condition
    $(Rate(L_1) < 1Mbps) \wedge (Rate(L_2) \geq 1Mbps) \wedge (Rate(L_3) \geq 1Mbps) \wedge$
    available(*Nucleotides*) = **true** $\wedge$ available(*Proteins*) = **true** $\wedge$ available(*Prot_Struct*) =
    true
  adaptation action
    "collect and cache data from *Protein* while slowly receiving data from *Nucleotide*."
end ac_caseNetDelayL1

Fig. 3. Adaptation case that adapts the execution of Q when $Rate(L_1) < 1Mbps$.

ADAPTATION CASE ac_initialP **adapts execution of query** Q.
  goal: fast response time with survivability to network delays.
  context
    resource objects
      // Same as **resource objects** described in ac_caseNetDelayL1 (Fig. 3).
    resource object parameters
      // Same as **resource object parameters** described in ac_caseNetDelayL1 (Fig. 3).
    adapted query plan: P_0 (Fig. 2(b))
  use-condition
    available(*Nucleotides*) = **true** $\wedge$ available(*Proteins*) = **true** $\wedge$ available(*Prot_Struct*) =
    true $\wedge$
    $\{\forall \ell \in NetworkLinks, Rate(\ell) \geq 1Mbps\}$
  adaptation action
    none.
end ac_initialP

Fig. 4. Initial adaptation case definition.

specialization or generalization. For instance, it identifies what components of a web service should be specialized for adaptation to resource availability or for performance optimization in the presence of certain quasi-invariants [2,13,11].

Generally, adaptation cases are concerned with data and control flow exchanges between a collection of program components, modules, and systems. Resources[10] are the currency of exchange among these system components. In object-oriented systems, all resources are ultimately provided by *classes*. However, it is not always the case in most of the legacy systems. Therefore, in the proposed adaptation space model, both classes and modules are units that provide a set of resources and require another set of resources.

---

[10] A resource is any entity that can be named in a programming language (e.g., variables, type definitions, etc.) and which can be made available for reference by other program components within a large software system.

ADAPTATION CASE ac_netDelayL2 **adapts case** ac_initialP.
  goal: query adaptation when $Rate(L_2)$ degrades.
  context
    resource objects
      // Same as **resource objects** described in ac_caseNetDelayL1 (Fig. 3).
    resource object parameters
      // Same as **resource object parameters** described in ac_caseNetDelayL1 (Fig. 3).
    adapted query plan: P_{12} (see Fig. 8)
  use-condition
    $(Rate(L_2) < 1Mbps) \wedge (Rate(L_1) \geq 1Mbps) \wedge (Rate(L_3) \geq 1Mbps) \wedge$
    available($Nucleotides$) = **true** $\wedge$ available($Proteins$) = **true** $\wedge$ available($Prot\_Struct$) =
    true
  adaptation action
    "collect and cache data from $Prot\_Struct$ while slowly receiving data from $Protein$."
end ac_netDelayL2

Fig. 5. Adaptation case that adapts the execution of Q when $Rate(L_2) < 1Mbps$.

ADAPTATION CASE ac_netDelayL12 **adapts case** ac_netDelayL1.
  goal: query adaptation when $Rate(L_1)$ and $Rate(L_2)$ degrade.
  context
    resource objects
      // Same as **resource objects** described in ac_caseNetDelayL1 (Fig. 3).
    resource object parameters
      // Same as **resource object parameters** described in ac_caseNetDelayL1 (Fig. 3).
    adapted query plan: P_{21} (see Fig. 8)
  use-condition
    $(Rate(L_1) < 1Mbps) \wedge (Rate(L_2) < 1Mbps) \wedge (Rate(L_3) \geq 1Mbps) \wedge$
    available($Nucleotides$) = **true** $\wedge$ available($Proteins$) = **true** $\wedge$ available($Prot\_Struct$) =
    true
  adaptation action
    "collect and cache data from $Prot\_Struct$ while slowly receiving data from $Nucleotides$
    and $Proteins$."
end ac_netDelayL12

Fig. 6. Adaptation case that adapts the execution of Q when $Rate(L_2) < 1Mbps$ and $Rate(L_2) < 1Mbps$.

Specifically, given a target web service and a reference program unit, an adaptation case description includes

- *Case Name*, described by a character string;
- *Goal Description* (optional), specified by the synopsis of the goal;
- *Context* of the case, defined by (1) a list of resource parameters internal to the reference program unit and critical to the specification of adaptation behavior of the reference program; and (2) a pointer to the adapted code for the reference program;
- *Use Condition*, expressed by a Boolean expression that indicates when it is appropriate to use this adaptation case. Variables in use conditions are defined in the adaptation case context;
- *Adaptation Action*, described by an action to be fired when the use condition is satisfied.

To enable on-demand generation of adaptation action, we need to capture type, state, and alternation of each resource parameter specified in the adaptation case context. The **type** of a resource parameter can be either primitive types such as *integer, char, float, Boolean,* or structured types as those defined in object-oriented systems. The **state** of a resource parameter includes *provide, must-provide, require, must-require*. Such state information distinguishes (1) the *required* resources from the *provided* resources, and (2) the *mandatory* provide-parameters or require-parameters from *optional* ones. The attribute **alternation** indicates the possible alternatives of the given resource and a list of degradation attributes such as extra-cost, freshness, extra-overhead, to name a few.

Example 3. The initial adaptation case for the execution of query Q is depicted in Fig. 4. It describes the target program (in this case the query Q) in terms of the adaptation model syntax and the particular adaptation context defined in its adaptation space (see Sect. 3.2). For instance, from the SQL statement given in Fig. 2(a), Q provides two output data items from each input source (i.e., *Nucleotides*, *Proteins*, and *Prot_Struct*), and requires the input condition that the data collected is relevant to HIV. We list these resources along with the network links in the initial case ac_initialP as critical parameters for defining the adaptation behavior of Q.

We can define as many as needed adaptation cases for a given query execution plan. For instance, in addition to degradation of $Rate(L_1)$ (Fig. 3), we can also define one adaptation case for Q that deals with degradation of only $Rate(L_2)$ (Fig. 5) and another that deals with degradation of both $Rate(L_1)$ and $Rate(L_2)$ (Fig. 6).

The automatic generation of program adaptation code from the original code may not always be feasible, especially when the target software is a legacy system with sophisticated procedures and state transitions. The development of mechanisms for semi-automatic or automatic generation of specialized adaptation code for given adaptation cases are part of our ongoing research work.

3.2   Adaptation Space

An adaptation space consists of a reference context, which sets up the scope of adaptation behavior and a partial order of adaptation cases, each case representing a specific way of adapting the same program unit. In addition to the set of adaptation cases, an adaptation space description includes the following header information:

- *Name* of the adaptation space, served as a unique identifier;
- *Goal Description*, consisting of a list of objectives and a set of quasi-invariants for this adaptation space;
- *Reference Context*, describing the common resources that all adaptation cases may share, and the nominal functionality and behavior of the program component that this adaptation space deals with. A reference context can be an initial adaptation case, which describes the original, unspecialized program component. The reference context has three main components: (1) the initial case (also called the root case); (2) the set of common resource parameters that all adaptation cases may share; and (3) the set of local parameters used in the goal description and use condition specification.
- *Use Condition*, specifying the general condition to turn on this adapt. space.

Example 4. The initial adaptation case ac_initialP (Fig. 4) and the specialized adaptation cases for coping with network delays (Fig. 3, Fig. 5, and Fig. 6) together form an adaptation space named as_spaceQ as shown in Fig. 7. The reference context of as_spaceQ includes the resource objects and their descriptive attributes that are involved in Q, in addition to the initial adaptation case ac_initiaP. This adaptation space is equipped with a single goal: to cope with network delays with the price of increasing memory contention once concurrent caching processes are fired.

```
ADAPTATION SPACE  as_spaceQ adapts the execution of query Q.
   goal: g₁: fast response time with survivability in the presence of network delays.
   reference context
      initial-case: ac_initialP;
      resource-object: Nucleotides
         parameters
            ID, protID, desc, nuc_other_attrs; instance:  NCBI
      resource-object: Proteins
         parameters
            ID, desc, prot_other_attrs; instance:  SWISS-PROT
      resource-object: Prot_Struct
         parameters
            prot_ID, compound_ID, desc, ps_other_attrs; instance:  PDB
      resource-object: NetworkLinks
         parameters
            bandwidth; instances:  L₁, L₂, L₃
      use-condition
         ∃x ∈ NetworkLinks, Rate(x) < 1Mbps
end  as_spaceQ
```

Fig. 7. Example of an adaptation space description for the execution of query Q.

4   Adaptation Space Model: Formal Semantics

In this section we formally describe the concept of adaptation case, adaptation space, and related notions (such as adaptation-of relationship) using graph-based notation. The formal definitions introduced in this section will be served as THE basis for defining adaptive coordination mechanisms that guarantee the correct use of adaptation cases and adaptation spaces. Due to space limitation, in this section we only formalize the key concepts of the adaptation space model. A more detailed discussion on this model can be found in [10].

Given a program component T in a target web service, we can define the adaptation behavior of T through introduction of multiple adaptation cases. Each adaptation case is applicable when its use-conditions become true.

Definition 1 (Use Condition). Let T denote a program component in a target web service. Let $Param(T)$ denote the list of adaptation context parameters of T, and $dom(P_i)$ denote the domain of possible values of an adaptation parameter P_i $(P_i \in Param(T))$. A use-condition, denoted by F, can be defined recursively as follows:

(a) $F = \emptyset$ is a use-condition (empty condition);
(b) $F = P_i \Theta P_k$, $P_i \Theta v_{ij}$, or $v_{ij} \Theta P_i$ are use-conditions, where
  (i) P_i and P_k are comparable functions returning atomic values, $P_i, P_k \in Param(T)$, $v_{ij} \in dom(P_i)$, and $\Theta \in \{==, =, \neq, <, \leq, >, \geq\}$;
  (ii) P_i and P_k are comparable functions returning set values, $v_{ij} \subseteq dom(P_i)$, and $\Theta \in \{==, =, \neq, \subset, \subseteq\}$;
(c) If F, F_1, and F_2 are use-conditions, then the conjunction $F_1 \wedge F_2$, the disjunction $F_1 \vee F_2$, and the negation $\neg F$ are use-conditions;
(d) If F is a use-condition, and x is a free variable in F, then $(\exists x)F(x)$ and $(\forall x)F(x)$ are use-conditions;
(e) Nothing else is a use-condition. □

Definition 2 (Adaptation Case). Let T denote a program component in a target web service. An adaptation case of T is described by a tuple $(N, TARG, GOAL, CTX, UC, AACTION)$ where

- N is the name of the adaptation case.
- $TARG$ is the identifier of the target adaptation unit. It can be a regular class, a module, a program, a procedure, or an existing adaptation case.
- $GOAL$ describes the goal description of the adaptation case.
- CTX is the context description of the case, defined by three components: a pointer to the adapted code, the *list of resource objects* used in the reference program, and the *list of resource object parameters*, where each parameter is further described by a quadruple $(Pr, State, Type, Rdom)$, where Pr is a name for the resource parameter; $State(Pr)$ specifies one of the following use states of the resource parameter Pr: *provide, must-provide, require, must-require*; $Type(Pr)$ defines the type of the resource parameter Pr and optionally the domain constraint of the parameter Pr; and $Rdom(Pr)$ defines the set of permissible values of the resource parameter Pr.
- UC is a set of use-condition, expressed by a Boolean expression, indicating when it is appropriate to use this adaptation case. Variables in use conditions are defined in the adaptation case context.
- $AACTION$ is the adaptation action to be fired when UC is satisfied. □

Example 5. Recall adaptation case ac_netDelay2 (Fig. 5). According to Definition 2, we can describe this adaptation case as follows:

$N(\text{ac\_netDelayL2}) = \text{ac\_netDelayL2}$.
$TARG(\text{ac\_netDelayL2}) = \text{ac\_initialP}$.
$GOAL(\text{ac_netDelayL2}) = $ "query adaptation when Rate(L_2) degrades".
$CTX(\text{ac\_netDelayL2}) = \{ (P_{12}), (NetworkLinks, \{(bandwidth, \text{must-provide})\}),$
         $(Proteins, \{ (ID, desc, \text{must-provide})\}), (Nucleotides, \{(ID, desc, \text{must-provide})\})$
         $(Prot\_Struct, \{ (compoundID, desc, \text{must-provide})\})\}$
$UC(\text{ac\_netDelayL2}) = \{(Rate(L_2) < 1Mbps) \wedge (Rate(L_1) \geq 1Mbps) \wedge (Rate(L_3) \geq 1Mbps) \wedge$
    $available(Nucleotides) = \textbf{true} \wedge available(Proteins) = \textbf{true} \wedge available(Prot\_Struct) = \textbf{true} \}$
$AACTION(\text{ac_netDelayL2}) = $ "collect and cache data from $Prot\_Struct$ while slowly receiving
                    data from $Protein$."

Definition 3 (Adaptation-of Relationship). Let T denote a program component in a target web service. Let α and β denote two adaptation cases of T, where each case is described by a tuple $(N, TARG, GOAL, CTX, UC, AACTION)$. The case β is said to have an *adaptation-of* relationship with the case α, denoted by $\alpha \implies \beta$, if and only if the following conditions are verified:

1. $TARG(\beta) = $ case α.
2. $\forall x \in CTX(\beta) \exists y \in CTX(\alpha)$ s.t. $identical(x, y) \vee$
   $(specialized\_version\_of(x, y) \wedge N(x) = N(y))$.
3. $\forall p \in UC(\alpha) \exists q \in UC(\beta)$ s.t. $degradation\_of(q, p)$.
4. $\forall p \in UC(\alpha) \forall q \in UC(\beta), (q = p) \vee degradation\_of(q, p)$.
5. $AACTION(\beta) = AACTION(\alpha) + new\_action$ □

This definition states that new adaptation cases can be defined incrementally in terms of existing adaptation cases, rather than being defined from scratch. However, the intuition between supercase and subcase is quite different from the superclass and subclass relationship in object-oriented systems. For example, a subcase in the adaptation model may have more restricted use conditions but may consume fewer resources than its supercase. More concretely,

- Condition (1) specifies that each subcase takes its immediate supercase as the target unit of adaptation.
- Condition (2) amounts to saying two points: (i) not every resource of a supercase will be used in its subcases, and (ii) for any resource of a subcase, its implementation may be more specialized than the corresponding one in its supercase (e.g., an alternative remote data source, which has better response time, can be accessed instead).
- Condition (3) states that there must exist at least one condition in $UC(\beta)$ that represents a *degradation of* some resource parameter used by T.
- Condition (4) asserts that the state of all resource parameters listed in case α are either degraded or remain unchanged in case β.
- Condition (5) specifies that the adaptation action of a subcase consists of all the actions considered by its supercase plus a new one.

In general, given an adaptation case, each of its immediate subcases describes an adaptation alternative. The subcases that are siblings with one another may have use-conditions that are either mutually exclusive or overlapping. Thus, it is possible that more than one sibling cases are eligible for adaptation at the same time. Selection policies [5] are therefore required to reconcile the situation and guarantee that there is only one adaptation case being activated at any specific point in time. We call such case the *active case* of the adaptation space.

Definition 4 (Adaptation Space). Let T denote a program component in a target web service. An adaptation space of T is defined as a labeled directed graph $G = (V, L, E)$ where V is a finite set of adaptation vertices of G; L is an ordered set of labels, each described by a set of use-conditions; E is a ternary relation on $V \times L \times V$, representing adaptation edges. For any α, $\beta \in V$ and $\ell \in L$, if $\alpha \Longrightarrow \beta$, then $(\alpha, \ell, \beta) \in E$.   □

Given an adaptation space graph $G = (V, L, E)$, each vertex in V represents an adaptation case and each label in $(u, \ell, v) \in V \times L \times V$ represents a use condition describing when to switch off case u and turn on case v.

Example 6. Recall the four examples of adaptation cases for Q presented previously. The four cases are related with one another through the adaptation-of

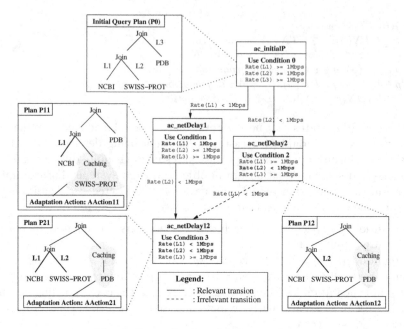

Fig. 8. Example of an Adaptation Space.

relationship, and together they form an adaptation space for Q, as shown in
Fig. 8. Formally, this adaptation is described as a graph $G = (V, L, E)$, where

$V = \{ac\_initialP, ac\_netDelayL1, ac\_netDelayL2, ac\_netDelayL12\}$

$L = \{(L_1 < 1Mbps), (L_2 < 1Mbps)\}$

$E = \{(ac\_initialP, L_1 < 1Mbps, ac\_netDelayL1), (ac\_netDelayL1, L_2 <$
$1Mbps, ac\_netDelayL12),$

$(ac\_initialP, L_2 < 1Mbps, ac\_netDelayL2), (ac\_netDelayL2, L_1 < 1Mbps, ac\_netDelayL12)\}$

5   Issues of Using Adaptation Space Model

In this section, we summarize our discussion on the adaptation space model by
classifying the concepts introduced into the following three categories: (1) what
to adapt, (2) how to adapt, and (3) when to adapt.

What to Adapt. The first task we need to deal with in adaptation specification
is how to identify the program components of a web service that should be
adapted. We have addressed this issue by identifying what should be included
in an adaptation context and what are the target units that we consider in our
adaptation model.

When to Adapt. We have defined the use condition and the incremental
approach for adaptation case specification in Sect. 3 and Sect. 4. A use condition
is a set of predicates over some parts of the program state or adaptation space
state, which hold over a period of time. It identifies when the corresponding
adaptation case should be activated. Usually, a set of use conditions may not

become true all at once. Some use conditions may even be in conflict with each other. Therefore it is useful to be able to describe a partial order of adaptation contexts for a given program so that it can be adapted further as more use conditions become satisfied.

How to Adapt. The question of how a program component should be adapted involves the operational aspects of adaptation, which include issues such as how to monitor the use conditions, when to produce the adaptation code, how to apply (trigger) an adaptation, and how to integrate the adaptation code into the program.

In general, given an adaptation case, if its use condition can be evaluated at compilation stage, then we refer to the use condition as compile-time use condition and the adaptation case as compile-time adaptation. Otherwise, it is called runtime adaptation and its use condition is called runtime use condition.

In the runtime adaptation case, we need some runtime support, which detects when all the predicates in the use condition become valid, and when the adaptation is triggered to replace the target component. There are a number of ways to conduct situation monitoring. For example, we can use periodic monitoring with regular or irregular time interval [4].

Once the use condition becomes true, an immediate question to ask is when to apply adaptation. Both eager approach and lazy approach can be used here. When the use condition is evaluated to be true, the eager approach applies adaptation and replaces the component immediately, whereas the lazy approach only replaces the component at the time when the component is used.

For a runtime adaptation case, the runtime support must preserve the validity of the adaptation. This implies two basic tasks: (1) detecting when the predicates in the use condition are invalidated, and (2) replacing the adaptation component by an appropriate adaptation case whose use condition is satisfied.

6   Adaptation Space Model Application

We are currently developing, at Georgia Institute of Technology, a web service called Ginga [7,8], a self-adaptive query processing system, which has in its core the adaptation space model described in this paper. Ginga has two main phases: Proactive Engagement and Reactive Control. At Proactive Engagement, prior to runtime, Ginga generates an initial adaptation space for the input query. At runtime, Ginga Reactive Control phase monitors the use conditions. Whenever one or more use conditions become true, Ginga then navigates the adaptation space, selects the most appropriate adaptation case, and fires the associated adaptation action which replaces the current query plan with an alternative one optimized for the changes to the runtime environment configuration.

We have evaluated the benefits and trade-offs of adapting distributed queries using Ginga. Fig. 9 shows the comparative benefits of using Ginga versus no query adaptation when slow delivery is detected while downloading the remote data from the left-most operand (base relation called A) of a 7-way join query plan. All other base relations were also considered remote. The x-axis repre-

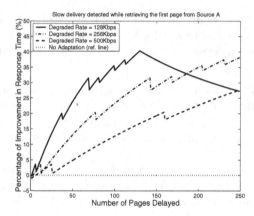

Fig. 9. Ginga adaptation engine performance: benefits of adaptation over no adaptation.

sents the number of pages from A that were delayed, and the y-axis represents percentage of improvement in response time obtained by using Ginga. Three degraded transfer rates were considered: $128Kbps$, $256Kbps$, and $500Kbps$. Normal transfer rate was $5Mbps$. As we can see from the graph, Ginga can provide up to 40% of improvement on the query response time when compared with the no adaptation case.

7   Related Work

The adaptation space based approach for program adaptation described in this paper can be seen as a seamless generalization and evolution of program specialization concept [1,12,13,11,6]. Program adaptation is a generalization of program specialization in both the objectives of adaptation and the methods of adaptation. Similar to program specialization, program adaptation presents an approach for adapting a generic program component to a given use context. However, *program specialization* is commonly viewed as a means for performance optimization. *Program adaptation* aims at a wider spectrum of enhancement of system capabilities, including performance, quality of service, and survivability. Program adaptation provides a uniformed framework for adapting programs to different levels of code specialization or capability relaxation (degradation) according to the various quality of service requirements and resource availability.

8   Conclusion

We have described the notation and the formal semantics of the adaptation space model used for designing adaptive web services. There are three main thrusts of the adaptation space approach. First, it defines a multi-dimensional adaptation context for capturing and coordinating different kinds of adaptation at different levels of a web service. Second, it provides a uniformed way for representing and viewing a collection of alternative adaptations for a given query program or component of a web service. Third, it promotes a declarative and incremental approach to adaptation specification, allowing the incorporation of new adaptation behavior of a web service in terms of existing adaptation cases.

We have also described a web service called Ginga [7,8], which has in its core the adaptation space model described in this paper. Our experimental results show that Ginga query adaptation can achieve significant performance improvements (up to 40% of response time gain) for processing distributed queries over the Internet in the presence of end-to-end delays. We are currently extending the Ginga work to study other kinds of changes to system resource availability (e.g., CPU and memory constraints [9]) and their interactions with end-to-end delays and sudden unavailability of remote servers.

Acknowledgements. The first author was partially supported by CAPES - Brasilia, Brazil - and DoE SciDAC grant. The other two authors were partially supported by DARPA, DoE, and NSF grants.

References

1. C. Consel, L. Hornof, F. Noel, J. Noye, and E. Volanschi. A uniform approach for compile-time and run-time specialization. In *Partial Evaluation, International Seminar*, 1996.
2. C. Cowan, A. Black, C. Krasic, C. Pu, and J. Walpole. Specialization classes: an object framework for specialization. In *International workshop on object-oriented in Operating Systems*, 1996.
3. G. Graefe. Query Evaluation Techniques for Large Databases. *ACM Computing Surveys*, 25(2), 1993.
4. L. Liu, C. Pu, W. Tang, J. Biggs, D. Buttler, W. Han, P. Benninghoff, and Fenghua. CQ: A Personalized Update Monitoring Toolkit. *ACM-SIGMOD'98*.
5. D. Maier. Adaptation spaces: Concepts and realization. Technical report, OGI CSE Technical Report, 1997.
6. D. McNamee, J. Walpole, C. Pu, C. Cowan, C. Krasic, A. Goel, P. Wagle, C. Consel, G. Muller, and R. Marlet. Specialization tools and techniques for systematic optimization of system software. *ACM TCS*, 19(2), 2001.
7. H. Paques, L. Liu, and C. Pu. Ginga: A self-adaptive query processing system. In *CIKM*, 2002.
8. H. Paques, L. Liu, and C. Pu. Distributed Query Adaptation and Its Trade-offs. In *ACM-SAC'03*.
9. H. Paques, C. Pu, and L. Liu. Query adaptation to changes in memory constraints. Technical report, Georgia Institute of Technology, 2003.
10. H. Paques, L. Liu, and C. Pu. The Adaptation Space Model. Technical report, Georgia Institute of Technology, 2003.
11. C. Pu, T. Autrey, A. Black, C. Consel, C. Cowan, J. Inouye, L. Kethana, J. Walpole, and K. Zhang. Optimistic incremental specialization: Streamlining a commercial operating system. In *SOSP*, 1995.
12. F. Tip and P. Sweeney. Class hierarchy specialization. *OOPSLA'97*.
13. E. N. Volanschi, C. Consel, and C. Cowan. Declarative specialization of object-oriented programs. *OOPSLA'96*.

Design and Implementation of an Asynchronous Invocation Framework for Web Services

Uwe Zdun[1], Markus Voelter[2], and Michael Kircher[3]

[1] Department of Information Systems
Vienna University ofEconomics, Austria
`zdun@acm.org`
[2] voelter – Ingenieurbro für Softwaretechnologie, Germany
`voelter@acm.org`
[3] Siemems AG, Corporate Technology
Software and System Architectures, Germany
`michael.kircher@siemens.com`

Abstract. Asynchronous invocations are an important functionality in the context of distributed object frameworks, because in many situations clients should not block during remote invocations. There should be a loose coupling between clients and remote services. Popular web service frameworks, such as Apache Axis, offer only synchronous invocations (over HTTP). An alternative are messaging protocols but these implement a different communication paradigm. When client asynchrony is not supported, client developers have to build asynchronous invocations on top of the synchronous invocation facility. But this is tedious, error-prone, and might result in different remote invocation styles used within the same application. In this paper we build a framework using patterns for asynchronous invocation of web services. The framework design is based on the asynchrony patterns and other patterns from the same pattern language.

1   Introduction

In this paper we discuss the problem of asynchronous invocation of web services. Although there are many kinds of distributed object frameworks that are called web services, a web service can be described by a set of technical characteristics, including:

- The HTTP protocol [7] is used as the basic transport protocol. That means, remotely offered services are invoked with a stateless request/response scheme.
- Data, invocations, and results are transfered in XML encoded formats, such as SOAP [4] and WSDL [6].
- Many web service frameworks are extensible with other transport protocols than HTTP.
- The services are often implemented with different back-end providers (for instance, a Java class, an EJB component, a legacy system, etc.).

Advantages of this approach to invoke REMOTE OBJECTS [16] are that web services provide a means for interoperability in a heterogeneous environment. They are also

M. Jeckle and L.-J. Zhang (Eds.): ICWS-Europe 2003, LNCS 2853, pp. 64–78, 2003.
© Springer-Verlag Berlin Heidelberg 2003

relatively easy to use and understand due to simple APIs, and XML content is human-readable. Further, firewalls can be tunneled by using the HTTP protocol. In the spirit of the original design ideas of XML [5] (and XML-RPC [18] as the predecessor of today's standard web service message format SOAP) XML encoding should also enable simplicity and understandability as a central advantage. However, today's XML-based formats used in web service frameworks, such as XML Namespaces, XML Schema, SOAP, and WSDL, are quite complex and thus not very easy to comprehend.

Liabilities of the approach are that the functionality of current web service frameworks is relatively limited compared to other standard middleware. The string-based, human-readable transport formats are bloated compared to more condensed (binary) transport formats. This results in larger messages and a more extensive use of network bandwidth. Also more processing power is consumed because XML consists of (human-readable) strings for identifiers, attributes, and data elements. String parsing is more expensive in terms of processing power than parsing binary data. The HTTP protocol may also cause some overheads because it is not as optimized for distributed object communication as protocols specifically designed for this task.

Many web service frameworks, such as Apache Axis [3], only allow for synchronous invocations (for synchronous transport protocols such as HTTP). That means the client process (or thread) blocks until the response arrives. For client applications that have higher performance or scalability requirements the sole use of blocking communication is usually a problem because latency and jitter makes invocations unpredictable. In such cases we require the client to handle the invocation asynchronously. That means, the client process should resume its work while the invocation is handled. Also the intended loose coupling of web services is something that suggests asynchronous invocations, that is, the client should not depend on the processing times of the web service. Note that various messaging protocols are integrated with web services, such as the use of Java Messaging Service (JMS) in Axis and WSIF [2], JAXM, or Reliable HTTP (HTTPR) [10]. These protocols provide asynchrony at the transport protocol level. They are more sophisticated than simple asynchronous invocations (e.g. they support reliability of message transfers as well) and use a different communication paradigm than synchronous transport protocols. Under high volume conditions, messaging might incur problems such as a bursty and unpredictable message flow. Messages can be produced far faster than they can be consumed, causing congestion. This condition requires the messages to be throttled with flow control. In this paper, we do not directly deal with messaging protocols, even tough it is possible to use a messaging protocol in the lower layers of our framework design.

Hard-coding different styles of asynchronous invocation into a client application by hand for each use is tedious, error-prone, and results in different styles of invocation. Instead one invocation model should be offered to the developer that supports all invocation variants with a simple and intuitive interface. In this paper, we present an asynchronous invocation framework for Apache Axis. Its design is based on a set of asynchrony patterns [17] to fulfill the specific client-side requirements for integrated asynchronous invocation in the web service context (on top of HTTP). The framework is designed to be easily adapted to other web service frameworks and/or other synchronous (or asynchronous) transport protocols.

The paper is structured as follows: First we give an overview of the goals of an asynchronous invocation framework in the context of web services. Next we present the asynchrony patterns from [17] briefly. Then we discuss the design of an asynchronous invocation framework for Apache Axis and compare its performance with synchronous invocations. Finally, we present some related work and conclude.

2   Goals of an Asynchronous Invocation Framework in the Context of Web Services

There are a number of issues about web services because of the limitation to synchronous invocations only. To avoid hard coding asynchronous invocations in the client code, we provide an object-oriented framework [11] to offer a flexible and reusable software implementation. In particular our framework aims at the following issues:

- *Better Performance of Client Applications*: Asynchronous invocations can lead to better performance of the client application, as we can avoid idle times waiting for a blocking invocation to return. This is specifically important because handling of XML encoding and HTTP is not the fastest variant of remote invocation.
- *Simple and Flexible Invocation Model*: A simple invocation model should be offered to client developers. Asynchronous invocation should not be more complicated to use than synchronous invocation. That is, the developer should not have to deal with issues such as multi-threading, synchronization, or thread pooling.
- *Support for Multiple Web Services Implementations and Protocols*: The strength of web services is heterogeneity, thus an asynchronous invocation framework should (potentially) work with different protocols (such as JMS or Secure HTTP) and implementations. If the invocation framework can be built on top of an existing web service framework (that already integrates different protocols), then they are automatically integrated in the invocation framework as well.
- *Avoiding the Use of Messaging Protocols*: Messaging protocols such as JMS or HTTPR can provide asynchrony on the protocol level. To provide for heterogeneity, web services should not depend on a special protocol such as JMS, but all required functionality should be provided for all supported protocols. For instance, if asynchrony is required and HTTP should be used for firewall tunneling, then asynchrony should be provided for HTTP natively.
- *Client as a Reactive Application*: Some clients are reactive applications, such as GUI applications or servers that are clients to other servers. In such reactive clients a blocking invocation is not possible because that would mean to block the reactive event handling as well. A blocking server or GUI is usually not acceptable.

3   Client Asynchrony Patterns

In this section, we present a set of client asynchrony patterns [17] that are part of a larger pattern language for distributed object communication[1] (see also [16]).

---
[1] The complete pattern language will be published in a book entitled "Remoting Patterns" in Wiley's pattern series in 2004.

A pattern[2] is a proved solution to a problem in a context, resolving a set of forces. Each pattern is a three-part rule, which expresses a relation between a certain context, a problem, and a solution [1]. A pattern language is a collection of patterns that solve the prevalent problems in a particular domain and context, and, as a language of patterns, it specifically focuses on the pattern relationships in this domain and context. As an element of language, a pattern is an instruction, which can be used, over and over again, to resolve the given system of forces, wherever the context makes it relevant [1].

The client asynchrony patterns are in particular:

- FIRE AND FORGET: In many situations, a client application needs to invoke an operation on a REMOTE OBJECT simply to notify the REMOTE OBJECT of an event. The client does not expect any return value. Reliability of the invocation is not critical, as it is just a notification that both client and server do not rely on. When invoked, the CLIENT PROXY sends the invocation across the network, returning control to the caller immediately. The client does not get any acknowledgment from the REMOTE OBJECT receiving the invocation.

- SYNC WITH SERVER: FIRE AND FORGET is a useful but extreme solution in the sense that it can only be used if the client can really afford to take the risk of not noticing when a remote invocation does not reach the targeted REMOTE OBJECT. The other extreme is a synchronous call where a client is blocked until the remote method has executed successfully and the response arrives back. Sometimes the middle of both extremes is needed. The client sends the invocation, as in FIRE AND FORGET, but waits for a reply from the server application informing it about the successful reception, and only the reception, of the invocation. After the reply is received by the CLIENT PROXY, it returns control to the client and execution continues. The server application independently executes the invocation.

- POLL OBJECT: There are situations, when an application needs to invoke an operation asynchronously, but still requires to know the results of the invocation. The client does not necessarily need the results immediately to continue its execution, and it can decide for itself when to use the returned results. As a solution POLL OBJECTS receive the result of remote invocations on behalf of the client. The client subsequently uses the POLL OBJECT to query the result. It can either just query (poll), whether the result is available, or it can block on the POLL OBJECT until the result becomes available. As long as the result is not available on the POLL OBJECT, the client can continue asynchronously with other tasks.

- RESULT CALLBACK: The client needs to be actively informed about results of asynchronously invoked operations on a REMOTE OBJECT. That is, if the result becomes available to the CLIENT PROXY, the client wants to be informed immediatly to react on it. In the meantime the client executes concurrently. A callback-based interface for remote invocations is provided on the client. Upon an invocation, the client passes a RESULT CALLBACK object to the CLIENT PROXY. The invocation returns immediately after sending the invocation to the server. Once the result is available, the CLIENT PROXY calls a predefined operation on the callback object, passing it the result of the invocation.

---

[2] We present pattern names in SMALLCAPS font.

Table 1. Alternatives for applying the patterns

Client Asynchrony Pattern	Result to client	Acknowledgment to client	Responsiblity for result
FIRE AND FORGET	no	no	-
SYNC WITH SERVER	no	yes	-
POLL OBJECT	yes	yes	Client is responsible for getting the result
RESULT CALLBACK	yes	yes	Client is informed via a callback

Table 1 illustrates the alternatives for applying the patterns. It distinguishes whether there is a result sent to the client or not, whether the client gets an acknowledgment or not, and, if there is a result sent to the client, it may be the clients burden to obtain the result or it is informed via a callback.

4   Design and Implementation of an Asynchronous Invocation Framework for Apache Axis

In this section, we explain a framework design to implement the client-side asynchrony patterns, explained in the previous section, in a generic and efficient way for a given web service implementations. We use the popular Apache Axis framework for our implementation in Java, though the general framework design can also be used with other web service implementations.

4.1   Client Proxies

Our general design relies on the CLIENT PROXY pattern [16]. A CLIENT PROXY is provided as a local object within the client process that offers the REMOTE OBJECT'S interface and hides networking details. Client proxies can dynamically construct an invocation, or alternatively they can use an INTERFACE DESCRIPTION [16] (such as WSDL). In our description, we first concentrate on CLIENT PROXIES that build up a remote invocation at runtime. We also discuss how to use the stubs that are automatically generated from WSDL in an asynchronous CLIENT PROXY in Section 4.6.

In our framework, we provide two kinds of CLIENT PROXIES, one for synchronous invocations and one for asynchronous invocations. Both use the same invocation scheme. The synchronous CLIENT PROXY blocks the invocation until the response returns. Thus it is just a wrapper to the ordinary CLIENT PROXY of the Axis framework for convenience. A client can invoke a synchronous CLIENT PROXY by instantiating it and waiting for the result:

```
SyncClientProxy scp = new SyncClientProxy();
String result =
  (String) scp.invoke(endpointURL, operationName, null, rt);
```

This CLIENT PROXY simply instantiate a handler for dealing with the invocation, and after it has returned, it returns to the client.

The asynchronous CLIENT PROXY is used in a similar way. It offers invocation methods that implement the four client asynchrony patterns discussed in the previous section.

For this goal a client invocation handlers, corresponding to the kind of invocation, is instantiated in its own thread of control. The general structure of asynchronous invocation is quite similar to synchronous invocation. The only difference is that we pass an `AsyncHandler` and `clientACT` as arguments and do not wait for a result (`AsyncHandler` and client invocation handlers are described in the next sections in detail):

```
AsyncHandler ah = ...;
Object clientACT = ...;
AsyncClientProxy ascp = new asyncClientProxy();
ascp.invoke(ah, clientACT, endpointURL, operationName, null, rt);
```

Note that the `clientACT` field is used here as a pure client-side implementation of an ASYNCHRONOUS COMPLETION TOKEN (ACT) [15]. The ACT pattern is used to let clients identify different results of asynchronous invocations. In contrast to the `clientACT` field, the ACT (in the description in [15]) is passed across the network to the server, and the server returns it to the client together with the result. We do not need to send the `clientACT` across the network here because in each thread of control we use synchronous invocations and use multi-threading to provide asynchronous behavior. We thus can identify results by the invocation handler that has received it (or, more precisely, on basis of its socket connection). This handler stores the associated `clientACT` field.

4.2   Client Invocation Handlers

In the case of a synchronous invocation, invocation dispatching and subsequent invocation handling do not need to be decoupled. This is because the invoking process (or thread) blocks until the invocation is completely handled. In contrast, asynchrony means that multiple invocations are handled in parallel, and the invoking thread can continue with its work while an invocation is handled. Therefore, invocation dispatching and invocation handling should be decoupled.

Synchronous and asynchronous invocation handling is performed by different kinds of invocation handlers. These, however, require the same information about the invocation, such as endpoint URL and operation name as web service IDs, an argument list, and a return type. Also constructing a `Call` from these information is common for all different kinds of invocation handlers (see Figure 1).

The synchronous invocation handler mainly provides a method `invoke` that synchronously invokes the service constructed with `constructCall`. The invocation returns when the response arrives.

The asynchronous invocation handler (`AsyncInvocationHandler`) implements the `Runnable` interface. This interface indicates that the handler implements a variant of the COMMAND pattern [8] that can be invoked in the handler's thread of control using a method `run`. The class `AsyncInvocationHandler` associates a handler object to hand the result back to the client thread. It also contains a `clientACT` field that stores the ASYNCHRONOUS INVOCATION TOKEN supplied by the client. Usually, the field is used identify the invocation later in time, when the response has arrived.

The `AsyncInvocationHandler` decides on basis of the kind of handler object which asynchrony pattern should be used, RESULT CALLBACK, POLL OBJECT, or SYNC WITH SERVER (see Section 4.4). The decision is done using Java's `instanceof` primitive.

Finally, FIRE AND FORGET is implemented in its own invocation handler class (see next Section).

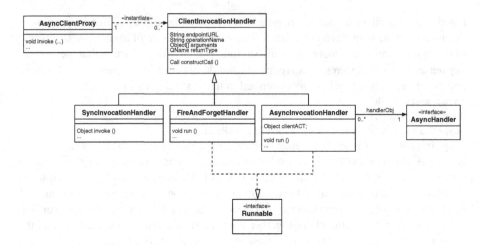

Fig. 1. Invocation Handlers

4.3   Fire and Forget Invocations

The FIRE AND FORGET pattern is not implemented in the class
`AsyncInvocationHandler` (or as a subclass of it) due to a specialty of web services: the WSDL standard [6] that is used for interface description of web services
supports so-called one-way operations. These are thus implemented by most web
service frameworks that support WSDL. Therefore, we do not implement FIRE
AND FORGET with the `AsyncInvocationHandler` class, but use the one-way invocations to support FIRE AND FORGET operations. All invocations dispatched by the
`AsyncInvocationHandler` class are request-response invocations.

A FIRE AND FORGET invocation executes in its own thread of control. The FIRE
AND FORGET invocation simply constructs the `Call`, performs the invocation, and then
the thread terminates.

A FIRE AND FORGET invocation is invoked by a special `invokeFireAndForget`
method of the `AsyncClientProxy` class:

```
AsyncClientProxy clientProxy = new AsyncClientProxy();
clientProxy.invokeFireAndForget(endpointURL, operationName,
                                null, rt);
```

Figure 2 shows the dynamic invocation behavior of a FIRE AND FORGET invocation.

4.4   Asynchrony Pattern Handlers

To deal with the asynchrony patterns RESULT CALLBACK, POLL OBJECT, or SYNC
WITH SERVER the client asynchrony handler types `ResultCallback`, `PollObject`, and
`SyncWithServer` are provided. These are instantiated by the client and handed over to
the CLIENT PROXY (for instance, in the `invoke` method).

The asynchronous CLIENT PROXY handles the invocation with an
`AsyncInvocationHandler`. Each invocation handler runs in its own thread of

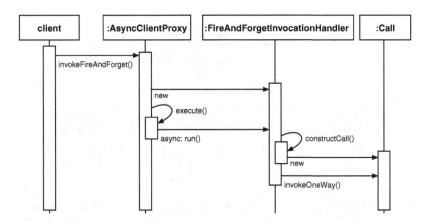

Fig. 2. Fire And Forget Dynamics

control and deals with one invocation. A thread pool is used to improve performance and reduce resource consumption (see Section 5.1). The client asynchrony handlers are sinks that are responsible for holding or handling the result for clients.

For an asynchronous invocation, the client simply has to instantiate the required client asynchrony handler (a class implementing one of the following interfaces: ResultCallback, PollObject, or SyncWithServer) and provide it to the CLIENT PROXY'S operation invoke. This operation is defined as follows:

```
public void invoke(AsyncHandler handler, Object clientACT,
                   String endpointURL, String operationName,
                   Object[] arguments, QName returnType)
   throws InterruptedException {...}
```

The parameter handler determines the responsible handler object and type. It can be of any subtype of AsyncHandler. clientACT is a user-defined identifier for the invocation. The client can use the clientACT to correlate a specific result to an invocation. The four last arguments specify the service ID, operation name, and invocation data.

For instance, the client might invoke a POLL OBJECT by first instantiating a corresponding handler and then providing this handler to invoke. Subsequently, it polls the POLL OBJECT for the result and works on some other tasks until the result arrives:

```
AsyncClientProxy clientProxy = new AsyncClientProxy();
SimplePollObject p = new SimplePollObject();
clientProxy.invoke(p, null, endpointURL, operationName,
                   null, rt);

while (!p.resultArrived()) {
  // do some other task ...
}
System.out.println("Poll Object Result Arrived = " +
                   p.getResult());
```

Note that the clientACT parameter is set to null in this example because we can use the object reference in p to obtain the correct POLL OBJECT.

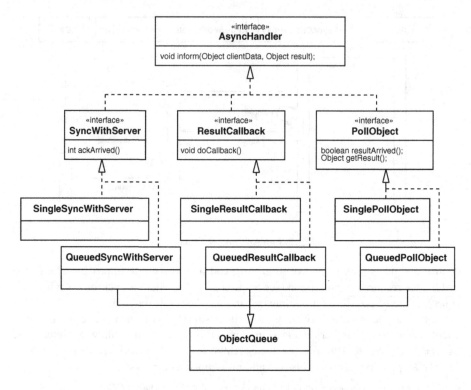

Fig. 3. Handlers for Obtaining Asynchronous Results

The pre-defined client asynchrony handlers and interfaces are depicted in Figure 3.

The client asynchrony handlers that are informed of the results run in the invoking thread. To enable synchronization of the access from different threads (and clients) we apply the MONITOR OBJECT pattern [15], which is supported by Java's synchronized language construct. The operations of each client asynchrony handler are synchronized and the access is scheduled.

Figure 4 shows the dynamic invocation behavior of a POLL OBJECT invocation. The dynamics of handling a RESULT CALLBACK are identical, with the exception that a RESULT CALLBACK asynchrony handler is passed to the CLIENT PROXY, and the client does not poll it. A SYNC WITH SERVER uses the SYNC WITH SERVER asynchrony handler and does not obtain the result, but only an acknowledgment.

4.5   Queued Asynchrony Handlers

Sometimes we want to use one instance to handle multiple responses. A simple implementation of such behavior is an asynchrony handler that queues the arriving responses. Such queuing handlers with FIFO (first-in,first-out) behavior are pre-defined in our framework for RESULT CALLBACK, POLL OBJECT, and SYNC WITH SERVER (as depicted in Figure 3).

In the queuing variant the client cannot use the handler object reference to identify the invocation that belongs to the result. Thus generally the clientACT field should be

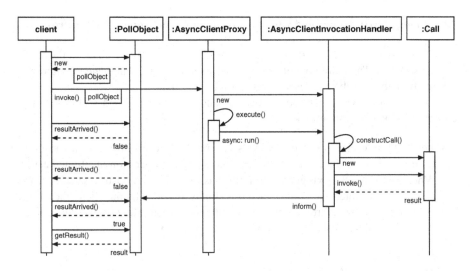

Fig. 4. Poll Object Dynamics

used to identify the invocation that belongs to an asynchrony handler. The `clientACT` field is also important for clients, if they need to customize the handler objects. For instance, if a RESULT CALLBACK should forward the callback to an operation of the client object, a reference to the client object is needed. This reference can be passed as part of a client ACT structure, which is then used by the custom asynchrony handler to dispatch the callback to the client.

Consider a RESULT CALLBACK as a second example. A developer might define a RESULT CALLBACK class as an extension of the existing RESULT CALLBACK type `ResultCallbackQueue`:

```
class DateClientQueue extends ResultCallbackQueue {...};
```

Then the client can use this custom type to handle invocations. When we use a queue handler type, we usually want to handle more than one result with the same handler; thus we instantiate a number of invocations in different threads of control:

```
AsyncClientProxy clientProxy = new AsyncClientProxy();
DateClientQueue results = new DateClientQueue(10);
for (int i = 0; i < 10; i++) {
  String id = "callback" + i;
  clientProxy.invoke(results, id, endpointURL, operationName,
                     null, rt);
}
```

In this example the ten invocations are all reported to one queuing RESULT CALLBACK object. This object can either handle the result on its own (e.g. if the client is just a `main` method) or forward the callback to the client object that has invoked it. Of course, if the client is an object that implements the `ResultCallback` interface it can also be itself handed over as a RESULT CALLBACK object.

4.6   Using WSDL Generated Client Stubs in an Asynchronous Client Proxy

WSDL [6] is used as a standard INTERFACE DESCRIPTION [16] language in the context of web services. The main goal of using WSDL is to provide a language to interchange information about web services and transfer these to clients.

Axis provides two models of invocation and both can be used within our asynchronous invocation framework:

– The Call interface provided by Axis can be used to construct an invocation at runtime. This interface is used by the constructCall operation mentioned earlier.
– When using WSDL, Axis generates a stub class that already constructs the invocation using the Call interface. Thus, when this stub is provided by the client, the CLIENT PROXY in our asynchronous invocation framework can directly use the stub and does not need to invoke the constructCall operation.

5   Performance Considerations

Providing an asynchronous invocation framework provides a better performance regarding the invocation times because the client can resume its work after dispatching an invocation. Yet, compared to synchronous invocation dispatching, multi-threaded invocations also incur an invocation overhead due to instantiating the threads. This overhead can be minimized with thread pooling discussed in Section 5.1. Next, we compare the performance of asynchronous invocations to synchronous invocations in our framework.

5.1   Thread Pooling

To optimize resource allocation for threading, the threads can be shared in a pool using the POOLING pattern [12]. Clients can acquire the resources from the pool, and release them back into the pool, when they are no longer needed. To increase efficiency, the pool eagerly acquires a pre-defined number of resources after creation. If the demand exceeds the available resources in the pool, it lazily acquires more resources. POOLING thus reduces the overhead of instantiating and destroying threads.

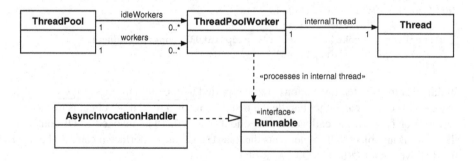

Fig. 5. Thread Pooling

We use a generic thread pool with thread pool workers that require the client to provide COMMANDS [8] of the type `Runnable` (see Figure 5). The thread pool acquires a pre-defined number of thread pool workers in its idle workers list. Whenever a thread pool worker is required, it is obtained from the pre-instantiated worker pool, if possible. If there is no worker idle, the thread pool lazily instantiates more workers. After the work is done, the (pre-defined) workers are put back into the pool.

The asynchronous invocation handlers implement the `Runnable` interface and can thus be used with the thread pool. Thus each invocation handler runs in its own thread of control and is automatically pooled.

5.2 Performance Comparison

As a performance comparison we have used a simple web service that just returns the current date as a string.

For each variant we have tested 1, 3, 10, and 20 invocation in a row. The thread pool had a size of 10 pre-initialized workers. All results are measured in milliseconds. We have used the Sun JDK 1.4, Jakarta Tomcat 4.1.18, Xerces 2.3.0, and Axis 1.0. All measurements were performed on an Intel P4, 2.53 GHz, 1 GB RAM running Red Hat Linux. We have measured all performance tests 10 times and used the best results (the average results were quite close to the best results and therefore we omit them here).

The results are summarized in Table 2.

For synchronous invocations we have simply measured the time that all invocations took. We can see that the invocation times increase as the number of invocations increases.

Table 2. Performance Comparison

Performance Test	Synchronous Invocation	FIRE AND FORGET	SYNC WITH SERVER	POLL OBJECT	RESULT CALLBACK
1 invocation	30ms	1ms	1ms	1ms/39ms	1ms/42ms
3 invocation	68ms	2ms	2ms	2ms/89ms	2ms/69ms
10 invocation	204ms	2ms	2ms	2ms/265ms	2ms/189ms
20 invocation	378ms	5ms	4ms	5ms/409ms	4ms/368ms

For FIRE AND FORGET and SYNC WITH SERVER we have measured the time until the requests were sent. We can see that the times are much shorter than the synchronous invocations, as expected. Only the 20 invocations case is 2-3ms slower than it could be expected when a linear progression would be assumed. This overhead is approximately the time needed to instantiate 10 thread pool workers.

For POLL OBJECT and RESULT CALLBACK we have measured the times until the invocations are dispatched and the invoking thread can resume its work. These numbers are more or less equal to the times of FIRE AND FORGET and SYNC WITH SERVER. Also we have measured the times until the last response has arrived. We can see that these numbers are similar to the synchronous invocation times yet there is a slight overhead.

6   Related Work: Other Known Uses of the Patterns

In this section we summarize some known uses of the asynchrony patterns as related work.

There are various messaging protocols that are used to provide asynchrony for web services on the protocol level, including JAXM, JMS, and Reliable HTTP (HTTPR) [10]. In contrast to our approach these messaging protocols do not provide a protocol-independent interface to client-side asynchrony and require developers to use the messaging communication paradigm. Yet these protocol provide a reliable transfer of messages, something that our approach does not deal with. Messaging protocols can be used in the lower layers of our framework.

The Web Services Invocation Framework (WSIF) [2] is a simple Java API for invoking Web services with different protocols and frameworks (similar to the internal invocation API of Axis). It provides an abstraction to circumvent the differences in protocols used for communications, similar to our invocation framework. However, it deals with asynchrony using messaging protocols (HTTPR, JMS, IBM MQSeries Messaging, MS Messaging) only. The approach presented in this paper can also be used on top of with WSIF.

For a long time CORBA [9] supported only synchronous communication and unreliable one-ways operations, which were not really an alternative due to the lack of reliability and potential blocking behavior. Since the CORBA Messaging specification appeared, CORBA supports reliable one-ways. With various policies the one-ways can be made more reliable so that the patterns FIRE AND FORGET as well as SYNC WITH SERVER, offering more reliability, are supported. The RESULT CALLBACK and POLL OBJECT patterns are supported by the Asynchronous Method Invocations (AMI) with their callback and polling model, also defined in the CORBA Messaging specification.

.NET [13] provides an API for asynchronous remote communication. Similar to our approach, client asynchrony does not affect the server side. All the asynchrony is handled by executing code in a separate thread on the client side. POLL OBJECTS are supported by the IAsyncResult interface. One can either ask whether the result is already available or block on the POLL OBJECT. RESULT CALLBACKS are also implemented with this interface. An invocation has to provide a reference to a callback operation. .NET uses one-way operations to implement FIRE AND FORGET. SYNC WITH SERVER is not provided out-of-box, but it can be implemented with a similar approach as used in this paper.

Actiweb [14] is a web object system implemented in Tcl. It provides sink objects for all kinds of blocking and non-blocking communication. A client can register a callback for the sink (to implement RESULT CALLBACKS), block on the sink, or use the sink as a POLL OBJECT. FIRE AND FORGET can be implemented by using sink with an empty RESULT CALLBACK. Similarly, SYNC WITH SERVER can be implemented by a RESULT CALLBACK that raises an error if a timeout exceeds and does nothing if the server responds correctly.

7 Conclusion

In this paper we have provided a practical approach to provide asynchronous invocations for web services without using asynchronous messaging protocols. The framework was designed with a set of patterns from a larger pattern language for distributed object frameworks. The functionalities as well as the performance measurements indicate that the goals of the framework (as introduced in Section 2) were reached; in particular:

- A client can significantly faster resume with its work so that the performance penalty of web services can be avoided to a certain degree.
- The invocation API provided by the framework is very simple and can flexibly be extended with custom handlers.
- As the framework is built on top of Axis we automatically can use its heterogeneity regarding transport protocols and back-ends of web services (so-called "service providers").
- If the client is a reactive server applications, a remote invocation does not block it.

As a drawback, an asynchrony framework on top of a synchronous invocation framework always incurs some overhead in terms of the overall performance of the client application. Further functionalities of messaging protocols, for instance, are not supported. But as messaging protocols can be used internally this is not a severe drawback. Our framework does not introduce any security functionalities (yet) at the invocation layer, and can thus only use security functionalities implemented at lower layers, say, at the transport protocol layer.

References

1. C. Alexander. *The Timeless Way of Building*. Oxford Univ. Press, 1979.
2. Apache Software Foundation. Web services invocation framework (WSIF). http://ws.apache.org/wsif/, 2002.
3. Apache Software Foundation. Apache axis. http://ws.apache.org/axis/, 2003.
4. D. Box, D. Ehnebuske, G. Kakivaya, A. Layman, N. Mendelsohn, H. F. Nielsen, S. Thatte, and D. Winer. Simple object access protocol (SOAP) 1.1. http://www.w3.org/TR/SOAP/, 2000.
5. T. Bray, J. Paoli, and C. Sperberg-McQueen. Extensible markup language (XML) 1.0. http://www.w3.org/TR/1998/REC-xml-19980210, 1998.
6. E. Christensen, F. Curbera, G. Meredith, and S. Weerawarana. Web services description language (WSDL) 1.1. http://www.w3.org/TR/wsdl, 2001.
7. R. Fielding, J. Gettys, J. Mogul, H. Frysyk, L. Masinter, P. Leach, and T. Berners-Lee. Hypertext transfer protocol – HTTP/1.1. RFC 2616, 1999.
8. E. Gamma, R. Helm, R. Johnson, and J. Vlissides. *Design Patterns: Elements of Reusable Object-Oriented Software*. Addison-Wesley, 1994.
9. O. M. Group. Common request broker architecture (corba). http://www.omg.org/corba, 2000.
10. IBM developerWorks. Httpr specification. http://www-106.ibm.com/developerworks/webservices/library/ws-httprspec/, 2002.
11. R. E. Johnson and B. Foote. Designing reusable classes. *Journal of Object-Oriented Programming*, 1(2): 22–35, June/July 1988.

12. M. Kircher and P. Jain. Pooling pattern. In *Proceedings of EuroPlop 2002*, Irsee, Germany, July 2002.
13. Mircrosoft. .NET framework. http://msdn.microsoft.com/netframework, 2003.
14. G. Neumann and U. Zdun. Distributed web application development with active web objects. In *Proceedings of The 2nd International Conference on Internet Computing (IC'2001)*, Las Vegas, Nevada, USA, June 2001.
15. D. C. Schmidt, M. Stal, H. Rohnert, and F. Buschmann. *Patterns for Concurrent and Distributed Objects*. Pattern-Oriented Software Architecture. J. Wiley and Sons Ltd., 2000.
16. M. Voelter, M. Kircher, and U. Zdun. Object-oriented remoting: A pattern language. In *Proceeding of The First Nordic Conference on Pattern Languages of Programs (VikingPLoP 2002)*, Denmark, Sep 2002. http://wi.wu-wien.ac.at/~uzdun/publications/vikingPlop02.pdf.
17. M. Voelter, M. Kircher, and U. Zdun. Patterns for asynchronous invocations in distributed object frameworks. submitted, a draft can be found at http://wi.wu-wien.ac.at/~uzdun/publications/AsynchronyDraft.pdf, 2003.
18. D. Winer. XML-RPC specification. http://www.xmlrpc.com/spec, 1999.

Using Corporate Firewalls for Web Services Trust

Ingo Melzer and Mario Jeckle

DaimlerChrysler AG
P. O. Box 2360, D-89013 Ulm, Germany
paper@ingo-melzer.de, mario@jeckle.de
http://www.ingo-melzer.de, http://www.jeckle.de

Abstract. Web Services allow collaboration of different systems independent of their operating system or the programming languages being deployed. They enable also the integration of legacy systems and grant access to external partners to those systems. Therefore, it is necessary to implement protection against misuse. Such an addition should be achieved transparently for users and developers. This paper illustrates how to integrate important security features into corporate firewalls or proxies.

1 Introduction

The variety of today's computer systems is a real burden when collaboration is desired or even required. An encouraging approach are Web Services which offer a great possibility for companies and institutions to allow others to access important information to enable a better cooperation.

However, at the same time, the introduction of Web Services for accessing possibly critical business systems may offer other users of the Internet the possibility to gain access to those legacy systems. Most of the time, Web Service deployment is based on the well known HTTP protocol as transport media. Content of this type is normally not inspected or filtered by most firewalls at all. The efficiency of a firewall is therefore significantly reduced. Also, SOAP, the lightweight XML-based protocol of Web Services, does not come with any security features. Though, a firewall or proxy is a commonly used security facility.

However, this does not constitute SOAP based Web Services as a general security hole. SOAP is not secure or insecure — security is simply not its job! According to SOAP's underlying philosophy the application has to take care of this topic. Taken XML's co-standard for digitally signing into account, arbitrary SOAP calls could be secured with respect to authentication, non-reputation, and integrity of the transmitted data. Based on this, the receiver is able to grant authorization to system's access. Since the creation of a digitally signed message requires modifications to the message itself by adding security information, the application creating the SOAP payload is required to be modified as well.

M. Jeckle and L.-J. Zhang (Eds.): ICWS-Europe 2003, LNCS 2853, pp. 79–87, 2003.
© Springer-Verlag Berlin Heidelberg 2003

An alternative to changing numerous business systems to introduce SOAP security is presented here. For secured and closed environments like today's intranets behind corporate firewalls, it could be an option to concentrate the handling of digital signatures at a single point within the network's structure. The machine devoted to this task could sign all outbound Web Service calls and vice versa check the signatures of all signed inbound calls as part of corporate's security infrastructure. Therefore, the inclusion of such a facility will disburden applications and even leverage the usage of digital signatures. As an option, such a facility could reside on a firewall or proxy machine.

Such an add-on to the proxies can be a service which signs all outgoing SOAP calls with a signature owned by the company. On the other side, the firewall of the other partner will block all SOAP calls which do not have an appropriate signature. The key issue of authorization based on authentication can therefore be eased significantly whenever a call passes an enterprise's boundary.

This paper first illustrates a typical infrastructure for most Web Services. It also provides the necessary basics of web services security and digital XML signatures. Based on this, the most important steps for implementing such a proxy for web services, which will be called *Signing Proxy*, to achieve a federated or corporate trust are shown.

2   Web Services Infrastructure

The technical basis of the Web Service philosophy is grounded on the idea of enabling various systems to exchange structured information in a decentralized, distributed environment. In essence this lead to the definition of lightweight protocols for synchronous remote procedure calls as well as asynchronous document exchange using XML encoding via well-known Internet protocols such as HTTP.

After some introductory approaches which were popularized under the name XML-RPC [4] the seminal SOAP[1] protocol which has recently been standardized by the World Wide Web Consortium [5,6] establishes a transport-protocol agnostic framework for Web Services that could be extended by the user on the basis of XML techniques.

The SOAP protocol consists of two integral parts: A messaging framework defining how to encode and send messages. And an extensibility model for extending this framework by its user.

First a brief introduction of the messaging framework is given before showing value of the extensibility mechanisms to accomplish the goals defined above.

Technically speaking SOAP resides in the protocol stack above a physical wire protocol such as HTTP, FTP, or TCP. Although, the specification does not limit SOAP to HTTP-based transfers this protocol binding is currently the most prominent one and is widely used for Web Service access. But it should be noted that the approach introduced by this paper is designed to operate completely independent of the chosen transport protocol and resides solely on the SOAP layer.

---

[1] At the time of it's definition the acronym stood for *Simple Object Access Protocol*. In the standardized version SOAP is no longer an acronym.

All application data intended to be sent over a network using the SOAP protocol must be transferred into an XML representation. To accomplish this SOAP defined two message encoding styles. Therefore the specification introduces rules for encoding arbitrary graphs into XML. Most prominent specialization of this approach is the *RPC style* introduced by the specification itself which allows the exchange of messages that map conveniently to definitions and invocations of method and procedure calls in commonly used programming languages. As introduced before SOAP is by nature protocol agnostic and can be deployed for message exchange using a variety of underlying protocols. Therefore a formal set of rules for carrying a SOAP message within or on top of another protocol needs to be defined for every respective transport protocol. This is done by the official SOAP specification for HTTP as well as SMTP.

Inside the SOAP protocol the classical pattern of a message body carrying the payload and an encapsulating envelope containing some descriptive data and metainformation is retained. Additionally SOAP allows the extension of the header content by the use of XML elements not defined by the SOAP specification itself. For distinguishing these elements from those predefined by the specification the user has to take care that they are located in a different XML namespace.

The example below shows a SOAP message (the body's content is omitted for brevity) together with the transport protocol specific data necessary when using the HTTP binding. Additionally a user defined header residing in a non-W3C and thus non normative namespace is shown as part of the SOAP `Header` element.

```
POST /axis/theService/ HTTP/1.1 Content-Type: text/xml;
charset=utf-8 Accept: application/soap+xml
Host: 10.0.0.1:8080
Content-Length: nnn
<?xml version="1.0" ?>
<env:Envelope
 xmlns:env="http://www.w3.org/2002/06/soap-envelope">
 <env:Header
    env:mustUnderstand="true"
    env:role="http://10.0.0.99/FWProxy">
  <sp:SigningRequest
      xmlns:sp="urn:xmlns:daimlerchrysler.com:research:sp">
    <sp:Path>env:Body</sp:Path>
    <sp:Username>JohnDoe</sp:Username>
    <sp:Token>SGVsbG8gd29ybGQh</sp:Token>
  </sp:SigningRequest>
 </env:Header>
 <env:Body>
    //some XML encoded payload here
 </env:Body>
</env:Envelope>
```

In contrast to the payload which is intended to be sent to the receiver of the SOAP message clearly identified by HTTP's `Host` header, SOAP headers may or may not be created for processing by the ultimate receiver. Specifically they are only processed by machines identified by the predefined `role` attribute. By doing so the extension framework offers the possibility of partly processing a message along its path from the sender to the ultimate receiver. These intermediate processing steps could fulfill arbitrary task ranging from problem oriented ones like reformatting, preprocessing, or even fulfilling parts of the requests to more infrastructural services such as filtering, caching, or transaction handling. In all cases the presence of a node capable of (specification compliant) processing of a SOAP message is prescribed. This is especially true since an intermediary addressed by the `role` attribute is required to remove the processed header after executing the requested task. Additionally the specification distinguishes between headers optionally to be processed (e.g. caching) and those which are interspersed to trigger necessary message behavior. The latter ones must additionally be equipped with the attribute `mustUnderstand`. If a header addressed to an intermediary flagged by this attribute cannot be processed, the SOAP node is forced to raise an exception and resubmit the message to the sender. Thus it is ensured that all headers mandatory to be processed are consumed by the respective addressees and removed afterwards.

3   Security for Web Services

Three of the most important issues when dealing with security are message integrity, authorization, and authentication. The Signing Proxy presented in Section 4 on page 84 addresses these requirements. Another important security issue is privacy. It is ignored in this paper, because methods to obtain privacy cannot be applied transparently for the users and do not keep valid XML/SOAP documents, which causes some more problems to be solved. Instead of integrating privacy functionality into the Signing Proxy, the use of appropriate transport layer methods is assumed in this paper.

SOAP does not address security issues; it has not been designed to do this. The job has been left to other (mostly XML based) standards. This section briefly introduces the most important standards necessary for building the Signing Proxy which provide more secure SOAP calls.

3.1   XML Signature

RFC3275 defines in [1] how a digital document can be signed and how the result can be represented in XML. Whereas this specification is not limited to XML documents, it is still especially useful for XML documents like SOAP messages, because the result is also an XML document. Using XPath, it is possible to sign only certain parts of an XML file.

A typical Web Service example using XML Signature is shown is Figure 1 on page 83. For simplicity reasons, the firewalls are simplified on both sides.

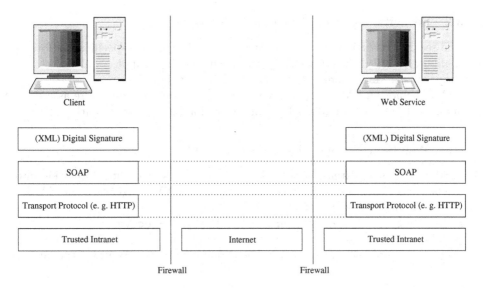

Fig. 1. Web Service Infrastructure

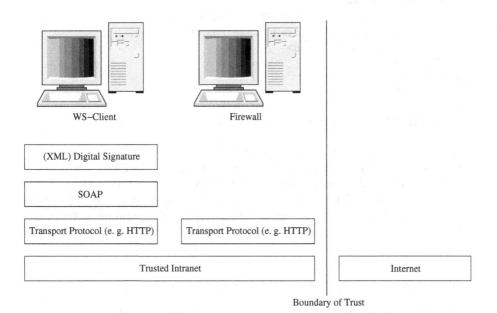

Fig. 2. Web Service Infrastructure including Firewall

Firewalls which parse HTTP are more and more frequently used. This changes both, the Web Service and client side. The according change is shown for one side in Figure 2 on page 83.

3.2   Security Assertion Markup Language

The security assertion markup language, short SAML, is a specification for exchanging security credentials. A specification can be found at
http://www.oasis-open.org/committees/security/.
SAML defines an XML vocabulary which allows to specify and share assertions about security relevant topics like authentication and authorization.

3.3   Web Services Security (WS-Security)

WS-Security is an extension of SOAP to add security relevant information into the header of each message. It is a combination of XML Signature and SAML. A specification can be found at
http://www.ibm.com/developerworks/library/ws-secure/
     The following listing shows a possible extension of a SOAP header which contains a username and a password as defined in the WS-Security standard:

```
<soap:Header>
   <wsse:Security>
      <wsse:UsernameToken>
         <wsse:Username>Ingo</wsse:Username>
         <wsse:Password>oiraM</wsse:Password>
      </wsse:UsernameToken>
   </wsse:Security>
</soap:Header>
```

4   Security Proxy for Web Services

Due to the fact that SOAP does not care about security, it is necessary to develop solutions which add required security features. An ideal solution hides the additional effort such that users and even developers of Web Services do not even notice the additions. This also means that an integration into existing systems in possible without changing a single Web Service. The solution described in this section reaches these goals by means of a SOAP security proxy and a SOAP firewall.

4.1   Intercepting Outgoing SOAP Messages

Proxies are commonly used in an HTTP environment. They reduce network traffic by caching techniques and allow to control Web usage by blocking specific sites or pages with explicit content. Given richer and thus stricter settings a firewall may intercept also content which is operated on a higher level than plain transport protocols like SOAP messages are.
     Such a SOAP proxy acts as an intermediary receiving the SOAP request before it is sent over the Internet to the requesting receiver. The header of the SOAP message can be expanded by security credentials. It is advisorable

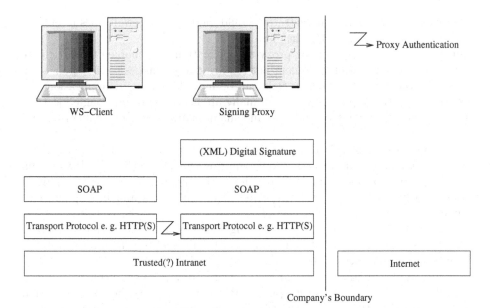

Fig. 3. Signing Proxy inserted into Web Service Infrastructure

to use an existing standard like WS-Security for this step to gain an easier interoperability. The message is thereafter sent to the next destination within the message path.

It is important to keep in mind that the outgoing call is still a valid SOAP message. The receiver can use the additional information, but it is also valid to simply ignore it.

The installation of such a signing proxy into the architecture shown in Figure 2 on page 83 moves the responsibility of creating signatures to the proxy service as shown in Figure 3 on page 85.

4.2   Processing Incoming SOAP Messages

The firewall of the receiver intercepts the incoming SOAP message. In addition to the usual steps which are always executed, it authenticates the message using the information which has been added to the header by the proxy of the sender. Thereafter, a check if the sender has permission to use the requested Web Service is performed. The security credentials could be removed to make the whole process completely transparent for both sides, but this is not necessary since they do not bother the receiver and might still be useful.

4.3   Integration into Existing Infrastructure

One of the main advantages of the presented approach is the small number of changes which have to be made by users and administrators. The users only have to change their proxy settings to contact the signing proxy which contacts the regular proxy. The administrator should modify the firewall rules to enforce valid signatures in the SOAP header.

But by introducing the singing proxy all applications are enabled to participate instantly in a secured environment not requiring any changes to the application code. On the contrary, security code can be moved from many application layers (i.e. from the application layer of many applications) to one single location. Hence also the amount of auditing and maintenance could be centralized and thus lowered.

As a consequence of this the proposed approach could be transparently integrated into existing processes without requiring changes to the workflow or even the supporting business applications. Hence the Signing Proxy forms a plug-in solution which could easily be deployed at existing sites and be expanded to further partners.

Since the inner nature of the Signing Proxy is hidden by the usage of a standard communication infrastructure (i.e. HTTP and SOAP) interoperability problems are conceptually impossible.

Since currently most practical Web Service applications are concentrated to closed and trusted communities (e.g. B2B communication) the communication path connecting the application with the Signing Proxy is always part of a trusted intranet and can thus be regarded as secured a priori.

Due to the fact that most calls can be regarded to be symmetric, a SOAP message is sent to the Web Service and thereafter a SOAP message is sent back to the caller, those changes have to be made on both sides.

In a bigger environment, it can be useful to install a policy server to get a single point of administration for each intranet.

5   Summary

Securing web services is an important and not impossible task. Due to the fact that this issue has been left out of the SOAP specification, it is important to apply security steps which are appropriate to the given environment.

This paper demonstrates how to develop a proxy service to automatically add security features to web services without saddling the users with this burden.

In addition, the given approach only uses open standards like WS-Security or SAML. This allows an easy integration into existing systems or infrastructures. Also, since these formats are, like SOAP, XML based, it is possible to allow this add-on and still keeping valid XML/SOAP documents.

Advantages.
- Platform-independent (high interoperability)
- transparent integration – even into existing systems
- smooth integration into existing processes
- uses only open standards
- plug-in security
- central administration of security policies
- ideal for B2B (trust)

References

1. D. Eastlake, J. Reagle, D. Solo: XML-Signature Syntax and Processing, RFC3275, March 2002 `http://www.ietf.org/rfc/rfc3275.txt`
2. Roy Fielding, et al.: Hypertext Transfer Protocol – HTTP/1.1, RFC2616, June 1999 `http://www.ietf.org/rfc/rfc2616.txt`
3. IBM, Microsoft, Verisign: Web Services Security (WS-Security) Version 1.0, April 2002
   `http://www-106.ibm.com/developerworks/webservices/library/ws-secure/`
4. Winer, D.: XML-RPC Specification, available electronically (1999)
   `http://www.xmlrpc.com/spec`
5. Gudgin, M., Hadley, M., Mendelson, N., Moreau, J.-J., Nielsen H. F. (eds.): SOAP Version 1.2 Part 1: Messaging Framework, W3C Proposed Recommendation (2003)
6. Gudgin, M., Hadley, M., Mendelson, N., Moreau, J.-J., Nielsen H. F. (eds.): SOAP Version 1.2 Part 2: Adjuncts, W3C Proposed Recommendation (2003)

Specification and Enforcement of Access Control in Heterogeneous Distributed Applications

Torsten Fink, Manuel Koch, and Cristian Oancea

Institut für Informatik
Freie Universität Berlin, 14195 Berlin, Germany
{tnfink,mkoch,oancea}@inf.fu-berlin.de

Abstract. Security is a crucial aspect in any modern software system. We consider in this article the specification and the management of access control in in-house business applications which are coupled over the Internet using Web services. In-house business applications are usually built on a middleware in which security is an established aspect and security management tools are available. The integration of security in SOAP, however, is still an ongoing activity.

Therefore, we propose an access control model for Web services which originates from CORBA-based applications. This integration has the advantage of a unique access control policy for both the CORBA-based in-house application and the Web services. We implemented an infrastructure to enforce the access control policy and a comprehensive set of powerful XML based management tools.

Keywords: SOAP-based web services, access control, RBAC, CORBA, security management, interoperability.

1 Introduction

Security is an integral part of most modern software systems that are not used in completely trusted environments. We consider in this article in-house business applications that are integrated over the Internet by SOAP-based Web services. There is an established support for security in the middleware, e.g. CORBA [15] or Java RMI, used in in-house business applications, but there is still an ongoing effort in establishing standards for Web service security.

Nowadays, due to the lack of a Web security standard and corresponding implementations, Web security is mostly delegated to the security mechanisms of the Web server which acts as application server. For example, the Tomcat Web server [2] provides a security manager for the administration of users, groups, roles, and permissions to access Java-Web applications. The authorization in Tomcat, however, is coarse-grained, in the sense, that it is not possible to restrict the access on single operations of Web services. Moreover, delegation of access decision is as well a problem as the reuse of access control policies in different frameworks, e.g. .Net [11].

There are emerging XML-based security standards from W3C and OASIS for Web security. The Web Services Security (WSS) specification [13] from OASIS

M. Jeckle and L.-J. Zhang (Eds.): ICWS-Europe 2003, LNCS 2853, pp. 88–100, 2003.
© Springer-Verlag Berlin Heidelberg 2003

describes a mechanism for securely exchanging SOAP messages. It provides the following three main security features: the ability to send security tokens (e.g., user name, certificates) as part of a SOAP message to authenticate users, to provide message integrity, and message confidentiality.

The Security Assertion Markup Language (SAML) [12] from OASIS is an XML framework for exchanging authentication and authorization information, whereas the eXtensible Access Control Markup Language (XACML) [14] presented by OASIS lets you express authorization and access control policies in XML. XACML defines a vocabulary to specify subjects, rights, objects, and conditions. Implementations of the XACML standard already exist, for example Sun's XACML implementation [19] written in Java or the access control engine *jiffyXACML* by Jiffy Software [10]. To our knowledge, however, there is no implementation which enforces a given XACML policy in an application.

Unlike all approaches mentioned above which concentrate on developing new approaches for security in Web services, we propose to integrate a well-established security model from a different domain into Web service applications. This security model is called *View-based Access Control* (VBAC) [6] which originates from CORBA-based applications. VBAC is a variant of role-based access control [16] and provides a specification language, *View Policy Language* (VPL), in which access control policies can be specified. Authorizations can be specified fine-grained on the level of single Web service operations and authorization rights can change dynamically, triggered by operation calls. The VBAC model is implemented in the CORBA-based infrastructure Raccoon [5] accompanied with a comprehensive set of powerful XML based management tools. Raccoon enforces a VPL policy for CORBA-based systems.

We identified the features needed to describe access control for Web services, extended the VPL accordingly and applied the VPL to the specification of access control requirements in Web services. We use the Raccoon infrastructure to enforce a Web service security policy. Therefore we developed a proxy which intercepts SOAP messages. This proxy extracts the authentication and service information and delegates access decision to the Raccoon infrastructure. The Raccoon infrastructure decides if the request is rejected or if the Web service is executed.

The advantages of an integration of a well-established security model into Web services are:

- A unique access control model and access control language for both in-house applications and Web services. This reduces the expert security knowledge required by system designers and administrators.
- A powerful access control language in which dynamic right changes can be expressed and authorization can be explicitly granted or denied on the level of Web service operations. For example, XACML does not provide a possibility for dynamic right changes, Tomcat specifies access control on the level of entire Web applications only.
- The VPL was especially designed for readability and an easy use by developers and system administrators. XACML is mainly designed to describe access

control policies in a format that allows for an efficient machine evaluation of access requests against access requirements. So, the VPL is more suitable for system designers and administrators and reduces design and administration errors.

- VPL supports automatic type and consistency checks. For example, contradicting authorization assignments can be statically detected.
- VBAC and VPL are accompanied by an infrastructure which enforces access control policies written in VPL. There are XML based graphical management tools for policy deployment and policy administration. These tools can be used without any new implementation.

The VPL access control specification and the XACML specification, however, do not mutually exclude, since the VPL specification can be transformed in a XACML specification by an XSL stylesheet. Therefore, the proposed specification language VPL can be also used as a manageable front-end for a XACML specification. Moreover, the VPL is independent of Raccoon and can be used also with other access control enforcement engines.

The remainder of this paper is organized as follows: Section 2 introduces a video rental example which is used throughout the paper. In section 3 we identify the access control requirements of the video rental example and introduce the VPL and the VBAC model. Section 4 presents a brief overview of the Raccoon infrastructure and shows how it can be used to enforce a VPL access control policy for Web services. Section 5 concerns related work and section 6 concludes the paper and points to future work.

2 Example – Video Central

Video Central is a Web service sample application provided by IBM [9]. The Video Central contains a central data repository that can be accessed by registered Web-based applications (see fig. 1).

There is one business-related Web service, the *business registration*, that allows a business (a video store) to register with the Video Central. Once a video store registered with Video Central, it is able to use the following customer-related Web services:

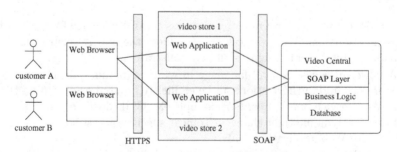

Fig. 1. Video Central architecture.

- *Customer Registration*: Enables the registered video store to register their own customers with Video Central.
- *Customer Infraction*: Enables the registered video store to add and query infraction information to and from the central repository.
- *Customer Rented List*: Enables the registered video store to add and query rented videos for each customer.
- *Customer Wish List*: Enables the registered video store to add and query the titles of videos the customer has expressed an interest in watching.
- *Movie Search*: Enables the registered video store to search for movie titles. This Web Service can be used by the staff or customers of the store.

The UML design of Video Central is given in [9]. Figure 2 shows the part of the class diagram needed for the paper.

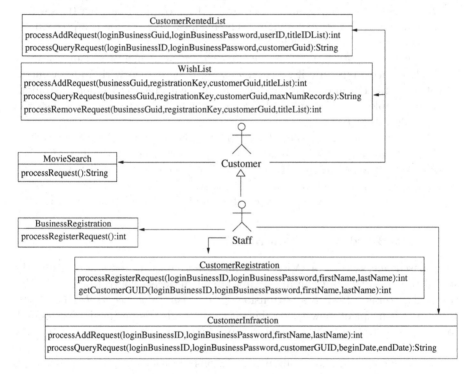

Fig. 2. Video Central class diagram.

It shows the classes for the six Web services and their operations. The operation parameters for the operations of the classes BusinessRegistration and MovieSearch are not shown, since we will not need them later in the paper. The operation parameters of the remaining classes are relevant and are depicted in the class diagram. The arrows between actors and Web services show in which Web services the actors participate.

3   Access Control

We identify in this section the access control requirements in the Video Central application and introduce afterwards the View Policy Language and the View-based Access Control model in which we express the Video Central access control requirements.

3.1   Access Control in Video Central

In the Video Central application, the accesses on the services are performed by video store staff members and video store customers. We get the following access control requirements for the above Web services:

- *Business Registration*: Can be used by a video store staff member (this will be in general a video store manager). The business registration is a prerequisite for all remaining Web services.
- *Customer Registration, Customer Infraction*: Staff members can use these Web services, but only if their video store is registered with Video Central. Staff members can use the Web services only with respect to their customers. For example, a staff member of video store A is denied to register a customer for video store B.
- *Customer Rented List, Wish List*: Staff members can use these Web services (again only for their customers). Customers can check the list of videos rented by themselves, but they cannot add requests to the list. Customers can add, remove, and query their wish list.
- *Movie Search*: This Web service can be used by staff members and customers.

3.2   View-Based Access Control

View-based access control (VBAC) is an access control model specifically designed to support the design and management of access control policies in distributed systems. VBAC is an extension of *role-based access control* (RBAC) [16, 17] by the concept of views and schemas. A *view* groups permissions or denials to access objects (e.g., a file, a method, printer) and views are assigned to roles. A subject (e.g., a user, a process) can access an object if the subject has a role to which a view with the required permissions is assigned. If such a view does not exist for the role, the subject cannot access the object. A *schema* specifies dynamic assignments or removals of views to and from roles. These assignments are performed automatically whenever a given operation is executed.

The View Policy Language (VPL) is a declarative language to specify VBAC policies [6,4]. The VPL is used to specify roles, views, and schemas. Roles are defined in a role declaration (after the keyword **roles**), the views in several view definitions (introduced by the keyword **view**) and the schemas in several schema definitions (introduced by the keyword **schema**).

The role clause defines the available roles in the policy together with their initial views. Figure 3 depicts the role definition for the Video Central application in which we have two roles, namely `customer` and `staff`. The role `staff` has initially the view `BusinessRegistration` (keyword **holds**), the role `customer` does not have an initial view.

A VPL view defines the authorization for a subset of operations of a single Web service, which is referenced in the **controls** clause. For example, the view `BusinessRegistration` gives the permission to call the operation *processRegisterRequest* of Web service BusinessRegistration. A VPL view can be statically restricted to certain roles listed after a **restricted to** clause, so that it can only be assigned to these roles. For example, the view `BusinessRegistration` can be assigned only to the role `staff`, but not to `customer`.

The view `CustomerRegistration` gives the permission for the operations *getCustomerGUID* and *processRegisterRequest*. Since a video store can only register its own customers (see requirements in Sec 3.1), the operation can be called only with a subset of the possible operation parameters. In our example, *getCustomerGUID* can be called only with the *loginBusinessID* of the calling video store (a video store gets its *loginBusinessID* after registering with Video Central by the Web service BusinessRegistration). Analog, the operation *processRegisterRequest* can only be called with the *loginBusinessID* of the calling video store.

This restriction of parameters is not necessary in the VPL originating from CORBA-based applications. An operation can be granted so that it can be called with all possible operation parameters or it is denied. This is due to the fact that in CORBA-based applications a common design pattern is used that creates an object on the server side for each client. The client communicates with this object and thus no identification is necessary. For example, in a Video rental CORBA application each client would get its own *CustomerRegistration* object on the

```
role customer
     staff holds BusinessRegistration

view BusinessRegistration controls BusinessRegistration restricted to staff {
     processRegisterRequest }

view CustomerRegistration controls CustomerRegistration restricted to staff
{
     getCustomerGUID(loginBusinessID,_,_,_) if caller = loginBusinessID

     processRegisterRequest(loginBusinessID,_,_,_) if caller = loginBusinessID
}

view CustomerInfraction controls CustomerInfraction restricted to staff {
     processAddRequest( loginBusinessID,_,_) if caller = loginBusinessID

     processQueryRequest( loginBusinessID,_,_,_,_) if caller = loginBusinessID
}
```

Fig. 3. The VPL role and view declaration.

server side. SOAP, however, does not support these object-oriented concepts [21]. Instead a general function is used where the *loginBusinessID* is explicitly given as a parameter.

We extended the VPL with the possibility to specify conditions of the form **if caller** = *param*, where the keyword **caller** represents the ID of the caller of a Web service and *param* is an operation parameter. The caller of a Web service is identified by an integer, i.e., only parameters of type integer can be used in the condition **if caller** = *param*. This is a first attempt sufficient for the Video Central example. If a parameter x_i of an operation $op(x_1, .., x_i, ..., x_n)$ is not restricted (i.e., all values are allowed in an operation call), we denote this by $op(x_1, ..., \_, ..., x_n)$. If there is no condition for the parameters of $op(x_1, .., x_n)$ in a view, the operation can be called with all possible parameter values. In this case we simply write the operation name *op* without parameter list (e.g., *processRegisterProcess* in view `BusinessRegistration`).

The view `CustomerInfraction` gives the permission to call the Web service operations *processAddRequest* and *processQueryRequest*, again only for the customers of the video store.

---

view CustomerRentedListFull **controls** CustomerRentedList
                      restricted to staff {
        processAddRequest(loginBusinessID,_,_,_) **if caller** = loginBusinessID

        processQueryRequest(loginBusinessID,_,_) **if caller** = loginBusinessID
}

view CustomerRentedListRestricted **controls** CustomerRentedList {
        processQueryRequest(_,_, customerGUID) **if caller** = customerID
}

Fig. 4. The VPL view declaration.

There are different access requirements for the roles `staff` and `customer` with respect to the Web service CustomerRentedList. A staff member can call both operations *processAddRequest* and *processQueryRequest*, but a customer can call *processQueryRequest* only. The view `CustomerRentedListFull` is restricted to the role `staff` and gives the permission to call both operations. The view `CustomerRentedListRestricted` permits only to call *processQueryRequest* and is not restricted to a certain role, but to certain parameters. The operation can be called only if the **caller** is the customer for which the rented list shall be checked.

For the Web service WishList, we have again different views for customers and staff members. Staff members can add, remove, and query the wish list of all their customers. A customer can add, remove and query only his/her own wish list. This is reflected in the view `WishListFull` for the role `staff` and view `WishListRestricted` for the role `customer`. The Web service MovieSearch can be used by staff members and customers without any restriction (see fig. 5).

---

view WishListFull **controls** WishList **restricted to** staff {
    processAddRequest(businessGuid,_,_,_) **if caller** = businessGuid

    processQueryRequest(businessGuid,_,_,_) **if caller** = businessGuid

    processRemoveRequest(businessGuid,_,_,_) **if caller** = businessGuid
}

view WishListRestricted **controls** WishList **restricted to** customer{
    processAddRequest(_,_,customerGuid,_) **if caller** = customerGuid

    processQueryRequest(_, _, customerGuid,_) **if caller** = customerGuid

    processRemoveRequest(_,_,customerGuid,_) **if caller** = customerGuid
}

view MovieSearch **controls** MovieSearch {
    processRequest }

Fig. 5. The VPL view declaration.

Initially only the view `BusinessRegistration` is assigned to a role, namely to `staff`. Therefore, users in role `staff` can access the Web service Business-Registration but they cannot access any other Web service. Customers can not access any Web service. Customer-specific Web services become available not before a video store has registered with Video Central. After the video store registered with Video Central, the views to access the Web services are assigned to the roles. The dynamic assignment and removal of views (and so of authorizations) to/from roles is specified in *VPL schemas* introduced by the keyword **schema** followed by the schema name and an **observes** clause that specifies the Web service for which the schema is defined. The assignment (removal) of views is triggered by the execution of an operation of a Web service. After the operation name *op*, we specify by **assign** $V_1, ..., V_N$ **to** R that the views $V_1,...,V_N$ are assigned to role R after calling the operation *op*. We specify by **remove** $V_1, ..., V_N$ **from** R that the views $V_1,...,V_N$ are removed from R after calling *op*. Fig. 6 depicts the schema of the Video Central example, which specifies the view assignment after a video store has registered with Video Central.

4   Implementation – Enforcing the Policy

We show in this section the infrastructure to enforce an access control policy specified in VPL. This infrastructure is integrated into the Raccoon infrastructure [5] which enforces VPL policies in CORBA environments. We start with an introduction of Raccoon and show afterwards how we have integrated SOAP messages.

```
schema BusinsessRegistration controls BusinessRegistration {
    processRegisterRequest
            assigns CustomerRegistration, CustomerInfraction,
                    CustomerRentedListFull, WishListFull, MovieSearch to staff

            assigns CustomerRentedListRestricted,
                    WishListRestricted, MovieSearch to customer
}
```

Fig. 6. The VPL schema declaration.

4.1   Raccoon Infrastructure

The Raccoon infrastructure consists of a deployment tool which processes VPL policies and stores view and role definitions in repositories (role and policy server) that can be managed using graphical management tools. Access decisions are made on the basis of policy information that is supplied by these repositories.

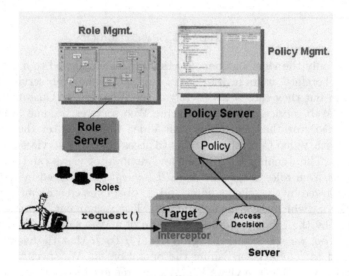

Fig. 7. Security infrastructure.

Figure 7 shows the main parts of the Raccoon infrastructure. A role server contains all the role certificates of a user. When a client authenticates at the system, he/she gets all their role certificates. The role certificates are transmitted when a client calls a server operation. This call is intercepted by a CORBA interceptor which forwards the client information to an access decision object. This access decision object decides on the basis of the given roles and the policy if the client is permitted to call the operation. The current policy can be requested on the policy server. If the policy permits to call the operation for the client, the interceptor forwards the request to the servant. If the client is not permitted to call the operation, the request is denied.

Graphical management tools support the management of access control. There is a tool for the definition of roles and the user role assignment, a tool for the definition of views and a tool for the definition of policies, i.e., the relation of views to roles. Modifications made in these tools become immediately valid and are enforced in the distributed system.

4.2   Access Control Enforcement in Web Services

We use Raccoon for the management and the enforcement of VPL policies in Web service environments. The idea is to intercept SOAP messages and to delegate the access control decision to Raccoon. Depending on the Raccoon decision, the SOAP message is forwarded or rejected. Figure 8 shows the integrated architecture. We use HTTPS as communication protocol, since messages are encrypted and client certificates are transported on the server side.

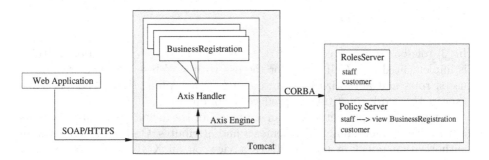

Fig. 8. Security infrastructure.

Deployment of Web Services
The Web services are deployed on the Web server. We use the Apache Tomcat Web Server [2] together with the Axis SOAP implementation [1] in order to take advantage of the concept of Axis *handlers*. A handler is a component that acts on a specific part of a SOAP message; for example, a handler can be in charge of performing authentication on the message's sender before allowing it to be processed by the service provider.

Policy Deployment
The VPL policy for the Web services is deployed in the Raccoon infrastructure. Raccoon is a CORBA-based application and the deployment of the VPL policy needs the CORBA interface repository. The interfaces defined in the Interface Definition Language (IDL) are derived from the WSDL document of the Web services. This transformation in IDL can be done by an XSL stylesheet. For example, WSDL *portTypes* are IDL interfaces, WSDL operations are IDL operations, WSDL *<input>* elements for operations are IDL **in** parameters and WSDL *<output>* elements are IDL **out** parameters.

Axis Handler for Access Decision

We implemented a handler on the server side which is located before the Web service, i.e., the SOAP message must pass this handler before it reaches the service. The handler serves as CORBA client to communicate with the CORBA-based Raccoon infrastructure, i.e., the Raccoon role and policy server. When a SOAP message passes the handler, the handler extracts the user information (e.g., certificates) and the requested method name and the parameters from the SOAP message. This certificates are used to get the role certificates of the user from the Raccoon role server. The role server stores the relation between user certificates and roles. The policy server contains the views and the view-role association, so that the handler can determine, on the basis of the client roles, if the access to the requested Web service operation is permitted or denied. If access is denied, an exception is thrown. Otherwise, the SOAP message is transmitted to the Web service.

5   Related Work

In [3] role-based access control (RBAC) is applied to Web applications. RBAC is implemented as a CGI script for the use with a Web server. The creation of users, roles and authorizations are created by an Admin Tool. Thus, in some aspects this work constitutes a predecessor of our work.

Damiani et. al present in [8,7] an approach for the definition of authorizations at the level of individual XML elements and attributes. On the basis of such an authorization policy, a tool produces a view on an XML document for each requester, showing the XML elements and attributes for which the requester has a permission. In contrast to our approach, where a client can see all Web services but get an exception if a denied service is called, Damiani et. al hide the denied services. Moreover, their approach misses a complete management environment, the underlying access control model does not provide dynamic right changes nor the concept of roles and group definition.

Sirer and Wang present in [18] an approach for formal specification and enforcement of security policies on Web services. The specification language is based on temporal logic. A policy is processed by an enforcement engine which produces platform-specific code that is integrated into the Web server. This approach, however, is difficult to handle in dynamic environments (e.g., changing access control requirements). An authorization change requires to write a new policy, to generate new code, and to integrate it in the Web server. In our approach dynamic right changes can be done by graphical management tools and policy modifications are immediately enforced without changing the web application. Moreover, the policy language in [18] focus more on the specification of sequencing actions by inserting predicates and implications. Actions are URL invocations initiated by clients and server-side script executions.

The IONA Security Framework (iSF) [20] provides security service adapters for Web Services, J2EE and CORBA applications allowing interoperable security enforcement. In contrast to our appraoch, however, the iSF does not support the designer or administrator with a declarative description language as the VPL. Dynamic right changes specified in VPL schemas and a permission management by views are not possible, either.

6   Conclusion and Future Work

We used the View Policy Language (VPL) to specify access control requirements in Web services. The VPL and the corresponding access control model originate from CORBA-based applications. Extensions of the VPL were necessary to cover all requirements occurring in Web services. We implemented an infrastructure to enforce an access control policy in Web-based applications. We also provide deployment and management tools for Web service security management.

The VPL can be used as a front-end for XACML specifications. We have to investigate the mapping from VPL to XACML in more detail to see if all VPL features can be mapped and if so, how this mapping should look like. Future work will concern also the mapping of the Raccoon infrastructure to the XACML model. This would provide interoperability with other systems, such as jiffyXACML or Sun's XACML implementation.

References

1. Apache. Axis. http://ws.apache.org/axis/.
2. Apache. Tomcat. http://jakarta.apache.org/tomcat/index.html.
3. J. Barkley, A. Cincotta, D. Ferraiolo, S. Gavrila, and D. Kuhn. Role-based Access Control for the World Wide Web. In *Proc. of the 20th National Information System Security Conference*, 1997.
4. G. Brose. *Access Control Management in Distributed Object Systems*. PhD thesis, Freie Universität Berlin, 2001.
5. G. Brose. Raccoon – An infrastructure for managing access control in CORBA. In *Proc. Int. Conference on Distributed Applications and Interoperable Systems (DAIS)*. Kluwer, 2001.
6. G. Brose. Manageable Access Control for CORBA. *Journal of Computer Security*, 4: 301–337, 2002.
7. E. Damiani, S. De Capitani di Vimercati, S. Paraboschi, and P. Samarati. Fine Grained Access Control for SOAP E-Services. In *Proc. of 10th WWW Conference*, 2001.
8. E. Damiani, S. De Capitani di Vimercati, S. Paraboschi, and P. Samarati. A Fine-Grained Access Control System for XML Documents. *ACM Transactions on Information and System Security (TISSEC)*, 5(2), 2002.
9. IBM.   *IBM Video Central for e-business tutorial, Version 7.2*, 2002. http://www-106.ibm.com/developerworks/webservices/demos/videocentral/.
10. jiffySoftware. jiffyXACML. http://www.jiffysoftware.com/xacml/index.html, April 2003.
11. Microsoft. .Net Framework. http://www.microsoft.com/net/.
12. OASIS. *Security Assertion Markup Language (SAML) v1.0 Specification*, November 2002.

13. OASIS. *Web Services Security: SOAP Message Security, Working Draft 11*, March 2003.
14. OASIS. *XACML 1.0 Specification*, February 2003.
15. OMG. *Common Object Request Broker Architecture: Core Specification V.3.0.2*, December 2002.
16. R. Sandhu, D. Ferraiolo, and R. Kuhn. The NIST Model for Role-Based Access Control: Towards A Unified Standard. In *Proc. of the 5th ACM Workshop on Role-Based Access Control*. ACM, July 2000.
17. Ravi S. Sandhu, Edward J. Coyne, Hal L. Feinstein, and Charles E. Youman. Role–based access control models. *IEEE Computer*, 29(2): 38–47, February 1996.
18. E. G. Sirer and K. Wang. An Access Control Language for Web Services. In *Proc. of 7th ACM Symposium on Access Control Models and Technologies*, pages 23–30. ACM Press, 2002.
19. Sun. *Sun's XACML Implementation*, 2003. http://sunxacml.sourceforge.net/.
20. IONA Technologies. Enterprise Security in Web Services – White Paper, 2002.
21. S. Vinoski. Web Services Interaction Models. *IEEE Internet Computing*, pages 89–91, May/June 2002.

A Gateway to Web Services Security – Securing SOAP with Proxies

Gerald Brose

Xtradyne Technologies
Schönhauser Allee 6-7, 10119 Berlin, Germany
gerald.brose@xtradyne.com

Abstract. Integrating applications and resources using Web Services increases the exposure of critical resources. Consequently, the introduction of Web Services requires that additional effort be spent on assessing the corresponding risks and establishing appropriate security mechanisms. This paper explains the main challenges for securing Web Services and summarizes emerging standards. The most important of these, WS-Security, defines a message-based security model for SOAP that is suitable for achieving end-to-end security in environments with multiple trust domains. We propose one particular, gateway-based approach to implementing Web Services security, and compare it to other approaches.

Keywords: Web Services, SOAP message security, security architecture, WS-Security, SAML.

1 Introduction

While Web Services are expected to significantly lower the cost of integrating applications and resources — e.g., in *Enterprise Application Integration* (EAI) or Business-to-Business (B2B) settings — there are still many different definitions for the term. An abstract view on Web Services as a component technology, e.g., is the *Web Services Invocation Framework* (WSIF) [DMSW01,KKL03]. For the purposes of discussing security, we take a more narrow approach and simply observe that the kind of Web Services that are used today rely on only two main technical components, viz. SOAP [W3C00] over HTTP as a messaging protocol and the *Web Services Description Language* (WSDL) [W3C01] as declarative language for service interfaces. UDDI [OAS02] is often mentioned as the third main cornerstone of Web Services, but it is not as widely used as the other two, and it is unclear if it will see widespread acceptance on a global scale. We don't consider UDDI here.

The expectation that Web Services will increasingly be used to integrate enterprise resources and applications calls for a thorough investigation of its security implications. Security is an issue because integrating more applications and resources implies an increased degree of exposure to accesses that have not been possible before. This increased exposure is also reflected in an increased risk of damage to these resources. Security is hence a fundamental prerequisite for the acceptance of Web Services in production environments – at least if organizational and trust boundaries have to be crossed.

M. Jeckle and L.-J. Zhang (Eds.): ICWS-Europe 2003, LNCS 2853, pp. 101–108, 2003.
© Springer-Verlag Berlin Heidelberg 2003

However, securing Web Services is a challenge because existing security technology does not apply well to the message-based style of Web Service interactions. First, typical perimeter security mechanisms (firewalls) are effectively bypassed with SOAP over HTTP(S) as soon as HTTP messages are allowed to cross the domain boundary at all. It is obvious that additional security mechanisms are required to provide finer-grained control than this all-or-nothing approach. Second, connection-based security mechanisms such as SSL are not sufficient as they provide only point-to-point protections to messages, i.e., between the connection endpoints directly involved in the transmission of a message. However, Web Services are specifically designed to support settings where messages traverse multiple intermediaries and thus multiple transport connections, so SSL cannot be used to achieve end-to-end security. Since the most widely deployed security measures are not sufficient in a Web Services world, new technology is required.

The remainder of this paper is structured as follows: Section 2 summarizes the most important security specifications that apply to SOAP security. Section 3 discusses the alternatives for implementing SOAP message security according to these specifications and proposes a gateway-based implementation approach, and section 4 presents a concrete example for this approach.

2   Specifications and Emerging Standards

The security decisions that need to be made in message-based interactions are the following:

- Where does this message originate from? (authentication)
- May this message be sent to this destination? (authorization)
- Has this message (or parts of it) been modified? (integrity)
- Has this message (or parts of it) been read? (confidentiality)

Note that it is important to carefully distinguish between the current channel over which a message arrives and the actual principal where the message originated [WABL94]. The communication partner at the other end of the transport channel may just be forwarding a message that it received previously and may thus not be the actual origin of the message. With message-based systems, this is somewhat more apparent than in invocation-based distributed systems, where the distinction between a caller and a subject on whose behalf a call is made (delegation) is often subtle and difficult to make.

Also note that the additional security requirement of *availability* is not listed separately above but understood to be covered by access control (authorization). This implies a simple definition of availability as the absence of denial-of-service through excessive service usage by an attacker. We cannot positively guarantee availability in a simple store-and-forward message system, however, because the sender of a message has no means to make sure his message ever reaches the target. Additional application-level protocols would be required here but this does not blend well with the overall Web Services goal of achieving loose coupling between interaction partners. Therefore, availability is not considered a security requirement in its own right here.

The SOAP messaging layer does not offer security mechanisms to support any of the security decisions listed above, nor does the underlying HTTP layer.[1] Existing security technology in the underlying transport layer, i.e., SSL/TLS, does provide means for public key authentication and protection of the confidentiality and integrity of data in transit. As pointed out above, SSL/TLS can only provide security between directly communicating parties, i.e., in a point-to-point fashion. In such a more general scenario with intermediaries and without end-to-end protection, both the sender and the receiver would need to trust that no intermediary in the communication path violates their security requirements, e.g., by storing and later replaying messages. This may be an acceptable assumption in internal EAI projects, but it is not acceptable in B2B applications.

Note that the same problems also exists with other transport protocols for SOAP, such as SMTP. Because the transport protocol layer underneath SOAP does not offer it, end-to-end protection of messages must either be implemented within applications, or it can be provided by middleware above the SOAP layer, as indicated in figure 1.

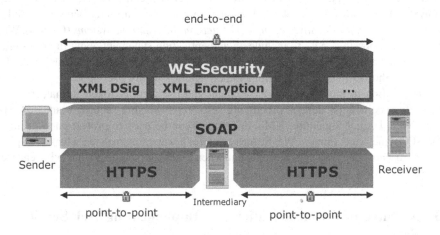

Fig. 1. Protocol layers and security.

Because this is a recurring requirement for many applications, the WS-Security [OAS03c] specification proposes a message-based security model for SOAP to address the problems outlined above. Figure 1 illustrates how WS-Security combines with SOAP, HTTP, and SSL, and how it relates to XML Digital Signature and Encryption. The "..." denote extensibility, so other technology or standards can be used with WS-Security. The figure depicts one conceptual SOAP messaging layer on top of one or more HTTP connections between the sender, any intermediaries, and the final receiver of the SOAP message.

The WS-Security specification explicitly addresses end-to-end message security in application environments where messages cross organizational and trust boundaries. Technically, this is achieved through the definition of an XML security header format so that each SOAP message can contain (or reference) the security information about

---

[1] With the exception of HTTP basic authentication, which supports the transmission of user ID and password.

itself that is required for making security decisions. Security information is expressed as *security tokens*, which assert security claims. The security tokens that may need to accompany a message can include a wide variety of signed or unsigned application-specific, textual and binary data, such as user names, Kerberos tickets, X.509 certificates, encryption and/or signature keys. For example, a message may contain a digital signature over a certain part of the message body and the public key necessary to verify the signature, so that each recipient of the message can determine that the message was not tampered with in transit.

The WS-Security core specification defines only two token formats, a username format and a binary token format, but it is extensible to use additional formats. A prime candidate for security tokens is the the *Security Assertion Markup Language* (SAML) [OAS03a]. SAML expresses any security information in XML syntax as *assertions* by an issuer about a subject. SAML assertions can state that a subject was authenticated (authentication assertion), authorized (authorization assertion), or that a subject possesses a certain attribute (attribute assertion), e.g., a role membership. A standard profile [OAS03b] for SAML assertions as WS-Security tokens is currently being specified at the *Organization for the Advancement of Structured Information Systems* (OASIS). With SAML, it is possible, e.g., to include an authentication statement about the message's origin that was made by one vendor's product, and then use that statement as a basis for making authorization decisions with another vendor's security service.

In addition to the SOAP header element and the security token format, the WS-Security specification defines processing rules for two other security standards, viz. how XML Digital Signature, XML Encryption can be used to protect parts or all of the SOAP message. Finally, WS-Security defines a way of expressing when a recipient should discard stale messages, i.e., the time when a message should no longer be regarded as fresh.

3   Architectural Considerations for Implementing Web Services Security

The specifications outlined above do not, of course, imply any specific architectural approaches for possible implementations. A straightforward approach for providing security is to supply application developers with appropriate libraries so that applications can be programmed to perform security controls. As an example, Microsoft provide libraries called *Web Service Enhancements* [Cor] as an extension to its Visual Studio .NET environment. However, this approach places the burden of correctly enforcing security on the application developer rather than on the security infrastructure and security administrators, which requires a significant amount of expertise from developers.

This library approach may be combined with security services provided by the server-side run-time environment, i.e., application server products. The server administrator would configure security policies to be enforced by the application server, which would rely on client applications to provide security information (credentials) in a suitable format for the security infrastructure. In this case, the burden is on the client-side toolkits to appropriately use security libraries, e.g., to create (or obtain form third-party products) and insert SAML assertions that contain authentication statements into outgoing messages. If an application consists of services deployed on multiple, heterogeneous application servers, these platforms will have to be managed individually, typically using separate management infrastructure and concepts for each vendor's products.

As an elegant and simple-to-deploy approach that does not have these disadvantages, we propose an application-level security gateway ("SOAP security proxy") as an implementation approach. SOAP security proxies can be transparently integrated into existing Web Services infrastructures and do not require changing existing applications. Operating at the application level, they can perform security checks such as XML schema validation and content filtering that are not possible at the transport level. Additionally, SOAP security proxies provide typical application-layer security functions such as role-based access control, and auditing. Based on open standards such as SAML, these components can interoperate with other enterprise security products. Like application-level proxies for other protocols (IIOP, SMTP, HTTP), SOAP security proxies complement rather than replace existing packet filters. Packet filters must be configured to allow traffic to these proxies which they can now trust to be analysed and restricted according to application-level policies.

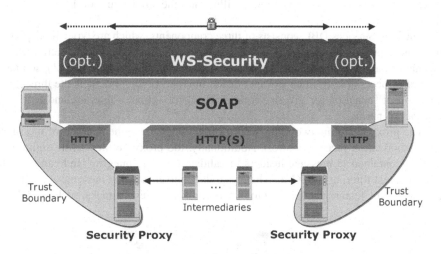

Fig. 2. Dual proxy scenario.

The main advantage over library-based solutions as provided by application servers or SOAP toolkits is the reduced administrative overhead. A SOAP security proxy component can be managed as a central component, so the gateway approach thus serves to simplify deployment and integration, and helps unify security management. This advantage becomes more apparent when the number of different server-side platforms is large.

Application clients requiring security management or the distribution of credentials necessitate decentralized management efforts, but this effort can be reduced by the use of a *client-side* SOAP proxy. Such a proxy would be placed within the trust domain of the application clients and can insert security information such as SAML assertions or digital signatures to outgoing messages. This situation is outlined in figure 2.

The advantages of such an approach to the creation of security information and its insertion in messages are most prominent in B2B scenarios where partners want to co-operate without having to trust each other completely. In the example of a manufacturer-supplier scenario, both parties may have large IT infrastructures relying on disparate technologies and standards (programming languages, server architectures, user management, etc.). To align one party's IT with its partner's may become prohibitively expensive if all client-side software has to be modified and new credentials distributed. In this setting, a centralized security gateway that will authenticate clients, map credentials, and add these to outgoing messages can provide significant cost saving benefits because it does not require any software modifications or distribution of credentials.

4   Example

As a concrete example for an implementation of the gateway approach outlined above, this section presents Xtradyne's *Web Services Domain Boundary Controller* (Web Services DBC, WS-DBC) [Xtr03]. Figure 3 illustrates the architecture of the implementation.

The Web Services DBC consists of three components, which are typically deployed in separate parts of the network. The proxy component is the actual security enforcement mechanism and would typically be located in the demilitarized zone (DMZ), so that it is directly accessible from an extranet or the Internet. Figure 4 depicts the three main deployment scenarios for a Web Services DBC, viz. intranet, Internet, and federated extranet scenarios.

The proxy performs two main security functions, viz. authentication of messages and authorization (access control). Additionally, the proxy verifies XML digital signatures contained in message headers to validate message integrity, and can perform XML content filtering and XML schema validation to ensure that message content is as expected. This feature can be used to thwart application-level attacks, such as SQL in-

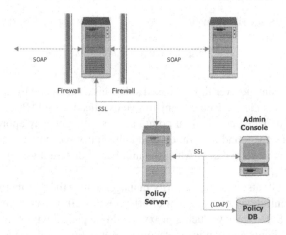

Fig. 3. Web Services DBC architecture.

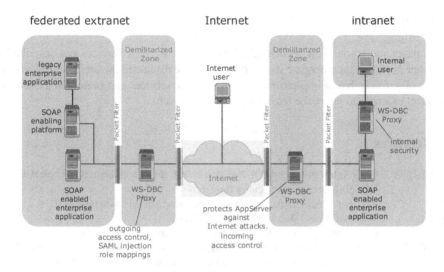

Fig. 4. Web Services DBC deployment scenarios.

jection [Anl02]. Finally, the proxy sends out notifications for security-critical events for auditing purposes, and can create SAML assertions that are added to outgoing messages.

To make security decisions, the proxy consults the policy server for policy information. Since the proxy is a performance-critical component, Xtradyne's implementation realizes the proxy as a highly optimized, native C++ implementation for high throughput rather than as a Java servlet that runs embedded in a Web server.

The security policy server is used to configure the proxy component and to hold the security policies. It is therefore a highly sensitive part of the security architecture: if an attacker can compromise the policy server and reconfigure the proxy or manipulate policies, no security can be guaranteed for the resources protected by the proxy. It is hence advisable not to expose the security server in the DMZ but to deploy it in a more restricted network domain.

The security policy server answers policy requests from the proxy and receives event notifications for auditing. User, group, and role information as well as access and audit policies are stored in either flat files on the policy server, or in a remote LDAP repository.

The administration console, finally, is a Java implementation that provides administrators with a powerful and convenient user interface for managing the security infrastructure. It displays configuration and policy information, and shows event notifications. The GUI also supports convenient exposure of secure Web Services through the import of WSDL descriptions. For services imported in this way, the administration console extracts a template security policy from the WSDL description, which then needs to be refined by administrators. The WSDL description is modified during the import to contain the proxy address instead of the original service address, so that client that obtain the WSDL for a secure service from the proxy will automatically receive the "proxified" addressing information.

The administration console relies on a secure CORBA transport (IIOP over SSL) to communicate with the security policy server. The security server uses the same transport to talk to the WS-DBC proxy.

5 Summary

This paper summarized the security challenges posed by Web Services and described a number of important emerging standards in field. We discussed the architectural advantages of gateway-based implementations of security services and presented a concrete product example to prove the feasibility of the approach.

References

[Anl02]   Chris Anley. Advanced SQL injection in SQL server applications. Technical report, NGSSoftware Insight Security Research, http://www.ngssoftware.com/papers/advanced_sql_injection.pdf, 2002.

[Cor]   Microsoft Corp. Web services enhancements. http://msdn.microsoft.com/webservices/building/wse/default.aspx.

[DMSW01]   Matthew J. Duftler, Nirmal K. Mukhi, Aleksander Slominski, and Sanjiva Weerawarana. Web services invocation framework (WSIF). In *OOPSLA 2001 Workshop on Object-Oriented Web Services*, October 2001.

[KKL03]   D. König, M. Kloppmann, F. Leymann, G. Pfau, and D. Roller. Web Services Invocation Framework: A step towards virtualizing components. In *Procs. XMIDX 2003*, February 2003.

[OAS02]   OASIS. UDDI version 2.04 API specification 1.0. OASIS Committe Spec., http://uddi.org/pubs/ProgrammersAPI-V2.04-Published-20020719.htm, July 2002.

[OAS03a]   OASIS. Assertions and protocol for the OASIS Security Assertion Markup Language. Committee Specification, May 2003.

[OAS03b]   OASIS. Web services security: SAML token profile. OASIS TC Working Draft 6, February 2003.

[OAS03c]   OASIS. Web services security: SOAP message security. OASIS TC Working Draft 12, April 2003.

[W3C00]   W3C. Simple object access protocol, version 1.1. W3C Note, http://www.w3.org/TR/SOAP, May 2000.

[W3C01]   W3C. Web services description language v1.1. W3C Note, http://www.w3.org/TR/wsdl, March 2001.

[WABL94]   Edward Wobber, Martin Abadi, Michael Burrows, and Butler Lampson. Authentication in the Taos operating system. *ACM Transactions on Computer Systems*, 12(1): 3–32, February 1994.

[Xtr03]   Xtradyne Technologies. Web Services Domain Boundary Controller. http://www.xtradyne.com/products, 2003.

Conflict Resolution in Web Service Federations

Veruska R. Aragão and Alvaro A.A. Fernandes

Department of Computer Science
University of Manchester
Manchester M13 9PL, UK
{v.aragao,a.fernandes}@cs.man.ac.uk

Abstract. Web services are expected to become the foundation of highly-dynamic distributed business computing architectures. By building upon the Internet-based technologies that changed the face of business computing over the last decade, web services are a significant step towards a truly universal infrastructure for e-business. Focusing on the case of opportunistic virtual enterprises, this paper first considers the widely-held view that they can be modelled by web service federations and then highlights the fact that, in that case, similar problems to those faced in attempts to federate databases will also stand in the way of virtual enterprise formation. A lightweight, unobtrusive approach is described to improve the chances that web service federations can be formed unimpededly, thereby reducing the cost of virtual enterprise formation and operations. Therefore, the paper contributes an enabling technology to facilitate an important, and highly dynamic, kind of e-business.

Keywords: Web services, Virtual Enterprises, Dynamic business process adaptation and composition, Mediation middleware, Rule-based conflict resolution of heterogeneities.

1 Introduction

The greatest promise of the web services approach [8] to business computing is that it will make it significantly easier for businesses to orchestrate different services (possibly from different, autonomous providers) into complete business processes that can be enacted over an Internet-based fabric.

The kind of enterprise that such business processes would give rise to have been called *virtual enterprises* (VEs) [13,17]. VEs can be understood as a federation of business processes. The federation is the outcome of an organizational process by which different individual, autonomous enterprises pool together their complementary competences. This complementarity gives rise to a new, composite enterprise whose pooled business competences allow it to pounce on business opportunities unattainable by its members in isolation.

This organizational process can be modelled fairly directly under the web services approach, as follows. Assuming competences to be organizationally captured in business processes, web services can be seen to capture and expose the

M. Jeckle and L.-J. Zhang (Eds.): ICWS-Europe 2003, LNCS 2853, pp. 109–122, 2003.
© Springer-Verlag Berlin Heidelberg 2003

latter concretely. In the context of VE formation, publishing a web service onto a public registry corresponds to submitting the competences it embodies to a pool of candidates. The federation process from which a VE arises is captured in two steps: firstly, all the web services that comprise the desired configuration of competences need to be found in public registries; secondly, such a configuration is given computational expression as a workflow in some web service orchestration language. Once the federation is formed, the operation cycle of the new organization corresponds to the enactment of the composite workflow characterizing the complete business process which the federation was formed to offer.

Computationally, the requirements for the web services approach include:

1. each provider should be in a position to deliver web services quickly and at an economical cost, in full awareness that the federation may be disassembled quickly;
2. each provider benefits the most if the web service is kept stable (i.e., requires no adjustment for participation) while still allowing that web service to participate in many other federations both at once and over time.

The web services technologies currently available [18] can be said to satisfy Requirement (1) above, but not Requirement (2). Web services build on widely-adopted Internet standards and are themselves standardized with a very light hand. In this way, many impediments to quick phase-in and phase-out are removed, and participation costs are kept comparatively low. However, in the scenarios covered in this paper, because the returns may be over short periods only, the ability of web services to participate *without change* in many federations both at once and over time is highly desirable. Unfortunately, this cannot be ensured by standardization alone. There are impediments for the federation of stable components whose removal requires not just standardization, but *mediation* [19,20] as well.

Given the view proposed here of VEs as federations of computational resources embodied in web services, it turns out that the well-studied impediments described in [9,10] to federating data resources [3] can be used to show both why standardization alone does not suffice to fulfill Requirement (2) above and what kind of solution is needed, as follows. Consider this: databases that adhere to the standard represented by the relational data model are not thereby protected from impediments to federation. As shown in [10], many forms of schematic and data heterogeneities conspire against participation without change of a particular database in many database federations. Since it is as undesirable to redesign and re-implement a database for each federation as it would be for a web service, solutions for schematic and data heterogeneities have always been eagerly sought. One effective and efficient approach to heterogeneity problems in database federations involves the definition of views over the data [12]. Such views act as mediators between the reality of an autonomous member database and the needs of each of the federated databases of which it is a member [9].

The remainder of the paper is structured as follows. Section 2 introduces an application scenario to illustrate issues, challenges and solutions. Section 3 describes a taxonomy of heterogeneities that are likely to arise in web service federations. Then, in Section 4, the contributions of the paper are presented, viz., an approach to the resolution of the heterogeneity conflicts described in Section 3. Section 5 considers related work, and, finally, Section 6 draws some conclusions.

2   Application Scenario

Consider the business scenario shown as an extended data flow diagram in Figure 1. It shows three small, specialist providers (viz., PDP, ET and TS) whose web services (among others not shown) are being orchestrated into a customer-facing web service federation that computationally captures a VE called PET.

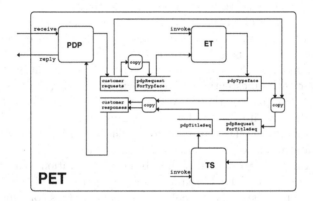

Fig. 1. The PET Virtual Enterprise

   PDP specializes in pulling together the various skills that go in the the production design of television programs. ET specializes in the design of bespoke, one-off, copyrighted electronic type faces. TS specializes in the design of title sequences. The business opportunity behind PET was spotted by PDP, viz., a contract for the production design of a new television series in which the use of sophisticated, distinctive electronic typography plays a major role. PDP, therefore, proposed to ET and TS (and possibly others not shown) the formation of the PET VE for the duration of the production design process. The PET virtual enterprise starts when PDP, which leads the VE, receives a request from a customer to produce a new television program. Thus, PDP invokes ET to produce the typeface for that program. As soon as ET creates the typeface PDP invokes TS to produce the title sequence of the program using the typeface delivered. It is assumed that PDP invokes other services to complete the production of the new television program. However, the services described here are enough to point out the relevant issues in our discussion.

   This paper assumes that business opportunities have short windows of opportunity and lead to short lifespans, therefore, in practice, companies such as the above are likely to be involved in many such VEs at any one time, routinely changing exactly which VEs they are currently members of and for how long, although, for simplicity, this multiple participation is not shown in Figure 1[1] The WSDL [5] documents published by PDP and ET are given in Figures 2 and 3, respectively (TS's is omitted for reasons of space).

They reveal several barriers for integration, i.e., they contain conflicts that require resolution before the described services can be orchestrated into the desired VE. In general, such conflicts are unavoidable in practice, because the web service designers have many routes to implementation and must make choices. A conflict arises whenever such a commitment (e.g., to choice of names, or of types, etc.) by the implementer of a web service W differs from the corresponding commitments by the implementers of web services $W_1, \ldots, W_n$ that might bind to W. So, while at a higher level of abstraction (i.e., the design level) two highly cohesive services can be integrated, concretely they cannot couple. A resolution mechanism is required that reconciles the two concrete choices by mapping either one to the other, thereby smoothing out what is, in essence, irrelevant detail that only becomes significant due to its standing in the way of orchestration. For example, in Figures 2 and 3, a type face specification by PDP (i.e., typefaceSpecs) has inessential variations with ET's (i.e., typeface). Conflicts such as these may prevent the ET web service to be found in web service registries by PDP. Even if it is found, as is being assumed, some conflict resolution is still required before PDP can bind to it. The research challenge is to decide how, where and when to effect this conflict resolution.

Since this paper is concerned with web service federation as a computational model for opportunistic VEs, both publishing and matching of WSDL documents are assumed to have been carried out, as preliminary steps corresponding to VE formation. Thus, the challenge is, more specifically, that of resolving heterogeneity conflicts during the enactment of the workflows that express the VE. What is needed is an unobtrusive mechanism that prevents inessential implementation dissimilarities from defeating the essential design similarities that justified the attempt at orchestration. By unobtrusive is meant that, ideally, the conflict resolution mechanism should not be sucked into the orchestration itself, not should it require maintenance (in the form of re-design or re-implementation) of either party in the interaction that is being disrupted.

Web service federations lack an unobtrusive mechanism to express conflict resolution. The solution proposed here is inspired by the use of views for the same purpose in database federations. In Section 4, a restricted, well-behaved class of event-condition-action (ECA) rules [14] is defined that resolves a significant set of conflicts arising in web service federations.

---

[1] The web service federation in Figure 1 is expressed in the BPEL4WS web orchestration language, (for the BPEL4WS specification, see [http://www-106.ibm.com/developerworks/webservices/library/ws-bpel/]) in an extended version of this paper

```
<?xml version="1.0" encoding="ISO-8859-1"?>
<definitions targetNamespace="http://www.productionDesigns.com"
  xmlns="http://schemas.xmlsoap.org/wsdl"
  xmlns:soap="http://schemas.xmlsoap.org/wsdl/soap/"
  xmlns:xsd="http://www.w3.org/2001/XMLSchema">
  xmlns:tns="http://www.productionDesigns.com"
  <types>
    <xsd:schema>
      <xsd:element name="typeface"     type="xsd:string"/>
      <xsd:element name="titleSeqSpecs" type="xsd:titleSeqSpec"/>
      <xsd:element name="titleSeq"      type="xsd:string"/>
      <xsd:element name="prodSpecs">
        <xsd:complexType>
          <xsd:sequence>
            <xsd:element name="typefaceSpecs" type="typefaceSpecs"/>
            <xsd:element ref="titleSeqSpecs"/>
          </xsd:sequence>
        </xsd:complexType>
      </xsd:element>
      <xsd:element name="prodDesign">
        <xsd:complexType>
          <xsd:sequence>
            <xsd:element ref="typeface"/>
            <xsd:element ref="titleSeq"/>
            ...
          </xsd:sequence>
        </xsd:complexType>
      </xsd:element>
      <xsd:complexType name="typefaceSpecs">
        <xsd:sequence>
          <xsd:element name="varieties" type="typefaceStyle" />
          <xsd:element name="serif"    type="xsd:boolean" default="true"/>
          ...
        </xsd:sequence>
      </xsd:complexType>
      <xsd:complexType name="titleSeqSpecs">
        <xsd:sequence>
          <xsd:element ref="typeface" />
          <xsd:element ref="titleSeq" />
        </xsd:sequence>
      </xsd:complexType>

      <xsd:simpleType base="xsd:string" name="typefaceStyle">
        <xsd:enumeration value="bold"/>
        <xsd:enumeration value="italic"/>
        <xsd:enumeration value="slanted"/>
      </xsd:simpleType>
    </xsd:schema>
  </types>
  <message name="customerRequest">  <part name="prodSpecs"           element="prodSpecs"/>
  </message>
  <message name="customerResponse"> <part name="prodDesign"          element="prodDesign"/>
  </message>
  <message name="requestToET">      <part name="requestTypeface"     type="typefaceSpecs"/>
  </message>
  <message name="responseFromET">   <part name="typeface"            element="typeface"/>
  </message>
  <message name="requestToTS">      <part name="requestTitleSeq" type="titleSeqSpecs"/>"
  </message>
  <message name="responseFromTS">   <part name="titleSeq"        element="titleSeq"/>
  </message>
</definitions>
```

Fig. 2. WSDL Document for the PDP Web Service

```xml
<?xml version="1.0" encoding="ISO-8859-1"?>
<definitions targetNamespace="http://www.electronicTypeface.com"
  xmlns="http://schemas.xmlsoap.org/wsdl"
  xmlns:soap="http://schemas.xmlsoap.org/wsdl/soap/"
  xmlns:xsd="http://www.w3.org/2001/XMLSchema">
  xmlns:tns="http://www.electronicTypeface.com"
  <types>
    <xsd:schema>
      <xsd:complexType name="typeface">
        <sequence>
          <xsd:element name="serif"     type="choices"/>
          <xsd:element name="styles"    type="typefaceStyle"/>
          <xsd:element name="lowerCase" type="xsd:boolean" default="false"/>
        </sequence>
      </xsd:complexType>
      <xsd:simpleType base="xsd:string" name="choices">
        <xsd:enumeration value="yes"/>
        <xsd:enumeration value="no"/>
      </xsd:simpleType>
      <xsd:simpleType base="xsd:string" name="typefaceStyle">
        <xsd:enumeration value="bd"/>
        <xsd:enumeration value="it"/>
        <xsd:enumeration value="slt"/>
      </xsd:simpleType>
    </xsd:schema>
  </types>

  <message name="propertiesTypeface"> <part name="designSpecs" type="typeface"/>
  </message>
  <message name="typeface">              <part name="characters" type="xsd:string"/>
  </message>

  <portType name="typefacePortType">
    <operation name="designTypeFace">
      <input message="tns:"propertiesTypeface"/>
      <output message="tns:typeFace"/>
    </operation>
  </portType>

  <binding name="etBinding" type="tns:typefacePortType">
    <soap:binding style="rpc" transport="http://schemas.xmlsoap.org/soap/http"/>
    <operation name="designTypeFace">
      <soap:operation soapAction=""/>
      <input>
        <soap:body
          encodingStyle="http://schemas.xmlsoap.org/soap/encoding"
          namespace="urn:typeface" use="encoded"/>
      </input>
      <output>
        <soap:body
          encodingStyle="http://schemas.xmlsoap.org/soap/encoding"
          namespace="urn:typeface" use="encoded"/>
      </output>
    </operation>
  </binding>

  <service name="etService">
    <port binding="tns:etBinding" name="etPort">
      <soap:address location="http://et.resources.net:80/soap"/>
    </port>
  </service>
</definitions>
```

Fig. 3. WSDL Document for the ET Web Service

3   Web Services Heterogeneities

The application scenario in Section 2 is now used to illustrate how web service interactions, and hence the formation of opportunistic VEs, may be impeded by heterogeneities. This section presents a coarse classification of heterogeneities that are probable in web service federations. The classification is inspired by the one introduced in [9,10] for database federations. It assumes that the messages exchanged are SOAP messages [5] invoking WSDL-defined operations on values whose types are defined using XML Schema [5]. In the context of this paper, the heterogeneities of interest are those that manifest themselves in SOAP messages (since the conflict resolution mechanism described in Section 4 acts on those), although there is no reason why the approach could not be deployed with greater scope. The heterogeneities that arise in this context can be categorized into *description-level heterogeneities* and *value-level heterogeneities*.

Description-Level Heterogeneities arise when two web services describe differently one or more of the elements in the message they exchange. They can be further split into *name*, *type*, and *cardinality* heterogeneities.

Name Heterogeneity occurs when two elements with the same semantics are assigned different concrete names or when the same concrete name is given to two elements with different semantics. In the former case, the implementors assign different labels to the same design concept, thereby impeding federation which would be unproblematic otherwise. In the latter case, the implementors assign the same label to different design concepts, thereby misrepresenting real federation impediments. As an example of the first case, PDP uses the name varieties in Figure 2 for what ET calls styles in Figure 3. Both names denote the same concept, and hence, the same set of values. As an example of the second, PDP might assign the name price to an attribute recording price alone while ET assigns it to an attribute recording price plus tax. Resolving such conflicts is necessary for the VE to function.

Conflict resolution in web service federations can be done in two contrasting ways. The first way is disruptive and involves maintenance intervention in the implementation of services. It is currently the only one available (for this and the other conflicts described in the remainder of this section). The second way is contributed by this paper: it is based on non-disruptive mediation and allows the implementation of services to remain as they are. In the first way, the participants agree which one among them is going to adopt the other's preferred description. One might think that all that would remain would be to change the WSDL document. However, this may open up previously resolved conflicts in other VEs that this VE member may be involved in: those other VEs rely on the WSDL as it stood before this conflict arose. Because of this, it is necessary to import, as additional internal logic, into the web service the reconciliation of the heterogeneity (roughly, a branch for each such conflict in a case analysis). Besides going against best practice in software design (which recommends keeping cohesion levels highs and coupling levels low), this approach is likely to be costly, time consuming and risky (insofar as every maintenance episode risks injecting faults into the implementation). The second way of resolving such conflicts, as well as those in the remainder of this section, is made possible by the contributions reported in this paper and is described in detail in Section 4.

Type Heterogeneity occurs when two elements with the same semantics are assigned different concrete (built-in or used-defined) types or when the same concrete type is assigned to two elements with different semantics. As an example of the first case, in the scenario in Section 2, PDP and ET assign different concrete types to represent the *serif* abstract type. The former uses the `boolean` built-in XML Schema type while the latter goes for a user-defined type with domain {`yes, no`}.

Cardinality Heterogeneity occurs when different numbers of elements are used to describe what is, semantically, the same information. One special case is *arity heterogeneity*, another special case arises by the interplay of XML Schema constraints such as `minOccurs` and `maxOccurs`.

As an example of arity heterogeneity, in the scenario in Section 2, modulo name heterogeneity, ET requires three elements to specify a type face, viz, {`styles, serif, lowercase`}. However, PDP makes no provision for the specification of a `lowercase` element. Thus, from the viewpoint of ET there is one element missing in PDP-originated type face specifications.

Value-Level Heterogeneities arise when two web services define differently one or more of the values in the message they exchange even as they are homogeneous at the description level. They can be further split into *representational* and *interpretational* heterogeneities.

Representational Heterogeneity occurs when the same datum is concretely represented differently. As an example, in the scenario in Section 2, PDP represents the style *bold* with the string `bold`, while ET represents it with `bd`.

Interpretational Heterogeneity occurs when a different interpretation is given to the same concretely represented value. As an example, PDP may interpret `size` to be in pica, while ET may interpret it to be in points (where there are twelve points in a pica).

4   Resolution of Heterogeneity Conflicts

For the cases considered in this paper, the state of the art is that when conflicts arise in web service federations, their resolution requires maintenance intervention in the implementation of services. Especially In the case where one web service must participate in many federations, it is unlikely that the interface exposed by that web service will be exactly as expected by its potential users. The web services approach postulates that once the interface is obtained, the potential user is responsible for abiding by the service description embodied in the corresponding WSDL document. In other words, the requester has to factor into the code of the client application the generation of conformant messages to the server web service. However, in cases where opportunities are volatile, and hence the cost of quick client adjustment is high, unless there is an unobtrusive adjustment mechanism, business will be lost. If there were a mechanism that allowed, without code maintenance, either the server to adjust to many clients or a client to adjust to many servers (or both), then web service federations would be more suited still for modelling dynamic, opportunistic VEs. This section describes exactly such an unobtrusive and non-intrusive mechanism to overcome the heterogeneities described in Section 3.

The mechanism is concretely implemented as a mediator component in the SOAP engine (e.g., Apache Axis [7]) that underpins web service invocation. It is referred to as a *personalization framework* insofar as it allows the adjustment of concrete interaction events so as to take into account specific characteristics of the interacting parties. In this way, it is analogous to the concept of a *view* in database settings, whereby a particular user can be provided with specific retrieval possibilities that, ultimately, may be exclusive to them. This analogy indicates that, as shown below, the use of views for conflict resolution in database federations can be emulated by personalization rules in web service federations.

The specification of personalization processes takes the form of a set of personalization rules. Such rules are processed by a personalization engine that is placed as the first component in the global handler chain (see Figure 4) for incoming messages (or the last for outgoing messages) within the SOAP engine of the party whose wish it is to personalize some (or all) of its interactions. In the specific context of this paper, personalization rules express conflict resolution strategies, and personalization engines act as mediators that allow the services exposed by an organization to remain unmodified even as they face many different heterogeneity conflicts across many different VE configurations.

Personalization Rules. A personalization rule is an event-condition-action (ECA) rule (see [14] for a comprehensive collection of research papers on the topic). An ECA rule has the general form: on ⟨event⟩ if ⟨condition⟩ do ⟨action⟩.

In a personalization rule, an *event* occurs when a SOAP message is received by the targeted SOAP engine in the host. Syntactically, an event is either the constant **true** or an XPath [5] expression that queries the header of the SOAP message (for features in the interaction such as its purpose, its originator, the date, the time, etc.). Semantically, an event causes a rule to *trigger* if it is **true** or else the XPath expression returns a non-empty result.

Once a rule is triggered, its *condition* is evaluated. Syntactically, a condition is either the constant **true** or an XPath expression (possibly compound, using the standard Boolean connectives) over the system environment that is visible through the host SOAP engine (including, e.g., the host organization's database systems). Semantically, a condition causes a rule to *fire* if it is **true** or else the XPath expression returns a non-empty result.

Once a rule is fired, its *action* is executed. Syntactically, an action is an XSLT [5] program. Semantically, an action changes the body of the incoming SOAP message and hands over the message, thus personalized, to the next handler in the chain.

Personalization Engines. The Axis SOAP Engine is designed as chain of *handler chains*. There are three standard handler chains for requests and three for responses: they are paired to deal, respectively, with matters of *transport*, matters

that are *global* to all web services, and matters that are specific to a *service*. At
the sink of a request and at the source of a response lies the *target web service*.
This is depicted in the top part of Figure 4. The role of each chain is to provide a
sequence of opportunities for manipulation of incoming and outgoing messages.
The personalization engine proposed here is implemented as an additional handler chain that is deployed as prefix chain of the standard global handler, on the
way in, and as a suffix chain, on the way out. In the top part of Figure 4, the
personalization engine is depicted as shaded bands.

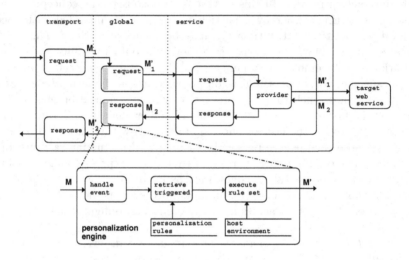

Fig. 4. A SOAP Engine with Personalization

The bottom part of Figure 4 shows the internal structure of the *personalization engine* (the shaded bands) as a handler chain deployed inside the global
handlers. The **handle event** component receives the original SOAP message
M, identifies the sender and appends this identification to the message context.
The **retrieve triggered (rules)** identifies, within the rules associated with
the sender, those whose event part match the message received (or are event-
independent, i.e., have the event part equal to `true`).

The matching is effected against an underlying XPath-compliant store (e.g.,
Apache Xindice [6]).

The retrieved triggered rules are passed on to the `execute rule set` component. Note that because the event part simply denotes the arrival of a message
from a sender, the evaluation of the rule set cannot generate new events. This,
in turn, means that, at the evaluation stage, the ECA rules become *productions*
(i.e., CA rules), losing their event part. Thus, a CA-rule evaluation engine (e.g.,
JESS [11]) suffices to evaluate them. It is the execution of the rule set that effects
personalization of the original message M into its personalized version M'. The
rule engine proceeds in the classical way, except that a condition is evaluated by
matching the XPath expression that captures it against (a suitable representation of the relevant features of) the host environment and an action is performed

```
<personalizationRule> <!-- - - - - - - - - - reconciling name heterogeneity -->
  <on> //interaction[sender="http://www.productionDesigns.com"]   </on>
  <if> //varieties  </if>
  <do>
    <xsl:stylesheet version="1.0"
                    xmlns:xsl="http://www.w3.org/1999/XSL/Transform">
      <xsl:output indent="yes" method="xml"/>
      ...
      <xsl:template match="varieties">
        <xsl:element name="styles">
          <xsl:value-of select="."/>
        </xsl:element>
      </xsl:template>
    </xsl:stylesheet>
  </do>
</personalizationRule>
<personalizationRule> <!-- - - - - - - - - - reconciling cardinality heterogeneity -->
  <on>    //interaction[sender="http://www.productionDesigns.com"]   </on>
  <if>    not(//lowercase) </if>
  <do>
    <xsl:stylesheet version="1.0"
                    xmlns:xsl="http://www.w3.org/1999/XSL/Transform">
      <xsl:output indent="yes" method="xml"/>
      ...
      <xsl:template match="serif">
        <xsl:copy-of select="."/>
        <xsl:element name="lowercase">false</xsl:element>
      </xsl:template>
    </xsl:stylesheet>
  </do>
</personalizationRule>
<personalizationRule> <!-- - - - - - - - - - reconciling type heterogeneity -->
 <on>
 //interaction[sender="http://www.productionDesigns.com"]
 </on>
 <if>
 //serif
 </if>
 <do>
  <xsl:stylesheet xmlns:xsl="http://www.w3.org/1999/XSL/Transform" version="1.0">
   <xsl:output method="xml" indent="yes"/>

   ...
   <xsl:template match="serif[text()='true']">
    <xsl:element name="serif">yes</xsl:element>
   </xsl:template>

   <xsl:template match="serif[text()='false']">
    <xsl:element name="serif">no</xsl:element>
   </xsl:template>

   <xsl:template match="serif[text()='1']">
    <xsl:element name="serif">yes</xsl:element>
   </xsl:template>

   <xsl:template match="serif[text()='0']">
    <xsl:element name="serif">no</xsl:element>
   </xsl:template>

  </xsl:stylesheet>
 </do>
</personalizationRule>
```

Fig. 5. Resolving Conflicts with Personalization Rules

by executing the XSLT program that captures it. The goal is to transform M into M'. Notice, for example, that there is no need to side-effect the host environment. Once the personalization stage is completed, M' is handed over to the classical Axis chains.

The resolution of heterogeneity conflicts such as described in Section 3 can be expressed using personalization rules, as the examples in Figure 5 illustrates.

One of the advantages of the approach proposed in this paper is that personalization engines can be deployed at the SOAP engines of either (or both) the interacting parties. Assume now that the personalization framework is deployed at ET and affects the arrival of requests that are sent to its services. Thus, when the request for a typeface arrives from PDP in the form of a SOAP message, the personalization engine identifies this and stamps the message appropriately. Then, the engine retrieves the rules pertaining to ET whose event is either true or an XPATH expression that matches the header of the SOAP message. Assume that the header of the SOAP message flowing from PDP to ET is such as to cause the XPath expressions on the event part of the rules in Figure 5 to be triggered.

If the condition of a triggered rule is either true or an XPath expression that matches its target, then it will fire. Figure 2 shows that the PDP message requesting ET to design a typeface will contain a varieties node. Thus, the XPath expression in the condition part of the personalization rule in Figure 5 for reconciling name heterogeneity will match and the rule will fire. The personalization rule for reconciling cardinality heterogeneity will also fire, because the SOAP message flowing from PDP to ET will not contain a lowercase node. Finally, the personalization rule in Figure 5 for reconciling type heterogeneity will also fire because of the match with a serif node.

Since the rules in Figure 5 have all fired, the XSLT programs in their action parts are executed. The first personalization rule in Figure 5 maps the varieties node in the original message M into a styles node in M', the personalized one, thereby resolving the name conflict between PDP and ET. The second personalization rule resolves the cardinality conflict by introducing, just below the serif node, a lowercase node and setting its value to false which is the default specified in the WSDL document for the service. Finally, the third personalization rule in Figure 5 resolves the type conflict by changing the type of the serif node, which is of type boolean in PDP to the ET-defined type choices. Thus, 'true' and 1 (which are the representations for a true value in XML Schema) are mapped to yes, whereas 'false' and 0 are mapped to no.

5   Related Work

The approach described in this paper is best understood in the context of research on web service composition, where the resolution of heterogeneities between web services becomes a focus of attention.

eFlow [4] is a platform to specify, enact and monitor e-service composition. Among other features, it can personalize process instances to a specific instance (or set of instances). Personalization relies on condition-action rules to modify the schema of the process at run time, relying for that on the users' understanding of the process schema. This raises significant risks, not incurred in our approach. Our approach uses personalization as a way to cope dynamically with changes in services and maximize business opportunities, whereas eFlow uses personalization to cope with specific and exceptional situations. It is doubtful whether eFlow would be sufficiently agile and lightweight to underpin opportunistic VEs as targeted by our approach.

The approach in [16] uses a mediator to reconcile interfaces provided by a server with those assumed by a client. It suggests that this process could be applied in the context of web services using XSLT to effect transformations in SOAP messages flowing between web services, as is done in this paper. However, the infrastructure sketched in [16] is, in comparison, very large and very heavy. Also, to the best of our knowledge no precise, detailed, web service-based design, let alone an implementation, exists of it. It is doubtful whether the approach in [16] would be sufficiently agile and lightweight to underpin opportunistic VEs as targeted by our approach.

WebTransact [15] is a framework to enable web service composition using mediator services. These mediator services are wrappers which aim to provide applications with a homogeneous view of heterogeneous web services. Each mediator service is associated with one or more remote service and maps the web service description (provided in WSDL and WSTL, their homegrown web service transaction language) to the target form. While our approach expresses mediation as restricted, well-behaved ECA rules, WebTransact requires much more unrestricted wrappers (and hence more error-prone and more costly to develop and deploy). Also, while our approach uses no non-standard formalism (since XML, XPATH, XSL, WSDL and SOAP are W3C-sponsored and no dependency on BPEL4WS exists), WebTransact uses WSTL, which is homegrown. Finally, note that our approach deploys the mediation component inside the SOAP engine and hence implies minimal effort and minimal disruption, whereas WebTransact must deploy its wrappers visibly (and hence, comparatively obtrusively).

6   Conclusions

This paper has taken inspiration on past work on federating databases to address the issue of conflict resolution in web service federations and constitutes an evolution and an application of our recent work on personalization [2] and web service federation [1]. The paper has contributed a lightweight, unobtrusive approach to the resolution of such conflicts. The personalization framework described here allows either the server to adjust to many clients or a client to adjust to many servers (or both) without code maintenance to the web services themselves. The availability of this mechanism makes web service federations more suited still for modelling dynamic, opportunistic VEs. The approach has been implemented as described and the first evaluation results confirm the intuition that our contributions constitute an enabling technology to facilitate the formation and operation of agile, highly dynamic, opportunistic VEs.

References

1. M. A. T. Aragão and A. A. A. Fernandes. Characterizing Web Service Substitutivity with Combined Deductive and Inductive Engines. In *Advances in Information Systems, Second International Conference, ADVIS 2002*, pages 244–254, 2002.
2. V. R. Aragão, A. A. A. Fernandes, and C. A. Goble. Towards an Architecture for Personalization and Adaptivity in the Semantic Web. In *Third International Conference on Information Integration and Web-Based Applications and Services*, pages 139–149, 2001.
3. M. W. Bright, A. R. Hurson, and S. H. Pakzad. A Taxonomy and Current Issues in Multidatabases Systems. *IEEE Computer*, 25(3): 50–60, 1992.
4. F. Casati, S. Ilnicki, L. Jin, V. Krishnamoorthy, and M.-C. Shan. Adaptive and Dynamic Service Composition in eFlow. Technical report, HP Laboratories Palo Alto, 2000.
5. W. W. W. Consortium. W3c technical reports and publications. http://www.w3c.org/TR/.
6. T. A. S. Foundation. Apache xindice. http://xml.apache.org/xindice/.
7. T. A. S. Foundation. Axis. http://xml.apache.org/axis/.
8. K. Gottschalk, S. Graham, H. Kreger, and J. Snell. Introduction to Web Services Architecture. *IBM Systems Journal*, 41(2): 170–177, 2002.
9. W. Kim, I. Choi, S. Gala, and M. Scheevel. On Resolving Schematic Heterogeneity in Multidatabase Systems. *Distributed and Parallel Databases*, 1(3): 251–279, 1993.
10. W. Kim and J. Seo. Classifying Schematic and Data Heterogeneity in Multi-database Systems. *IEEE Computer*, 24(12): 12–18, 1991.
11. S. N. Laboratories. Jess. http://herzberg.ca.sandia.gov/jess/.
12. A. Y. Levy. Logic-Based Techniques in Data Integration . In J. Minker, editor, *Logic-Based Artificial Intelligence*. Kluwer, 2000.
13. N. Nayak, K. Bhaskaran, and R. Das. Virtual Enterprises – Building Blocks for Dynamic e-Business . In *Proc. IT for Virtual Enterprises*, pages 80–87. IEEE Press, 2001.
14. N. W. Paton, editor. *Active Rules in Database Systems*. Springer, 1998. ISBN 0-387-985298.
15. P. F. Pires, M. Benevides, and M. Mattoso. Building Reliable Web Services Compositions. In *International Workshop Web Services Research, Standardization, and Deployment*, pages 551–562, 2002.
16. G. Smith. Component Adaptation of Web Services. In *13th Australian Software Engineering Conference*, Canberra, Australia, 2001.
17. A. Umar and P. Missier. A Framework for Analyzing Virtual Enterprise Infrastructure. In *Proc. RIDE-VE'99 Workshop on IT for Virtual Enterprises*, pages 4–11. IEEE Press, 1999.
18. WebServices.Org. http://www.webservices.org/.
19. G. Wiederhold. Mediators in the Architecture of Future Information Systems. *IEEE Computer*, 25(3): 38–49, 1992.
20. G. Wiederhold and M. Genesereth. The Conceptual Basis for Mediation Services. *IEEE Expert*, 12(5): 38–47, 1997.

Web Services Based Architectures to Support Dynamic Inter-organizational Business Processes

Rainer Schmidt

Department of Computer Science
University of Applied Sciences
Beethovenstraße 1
73430 Aalen
Rainer.Schmidt@fh-aalen.de

Abstract. Dynamic inter-organizational business processes are necessary to enable the flexible creation of partnerships in areas such as e-commerce and supply-chain-management. Although many information system architectures for the support of static inter-organizational business processes exist, such architectures are still not available for supporting dynamic inter-organizational business processes. In this paper the special requirements created by dynamic inter-organizational business processes will be analyzed and the contributions of existing approaches and web services evaluated. Based on the paradigm of the composite application, an architecture designed to support dynamic inter-organizational business processes has been developed and will be introduced.

Keywords: Dynamic Inter-organizational business process, composite application

1 Introduction

Successful enterprises must be able to cope with quickly changing market requirements and keep pace with the accelerated speed of economic change in areas such as e-commerce, e-procurement, supply-chain-management, etc. Enterprises, for example, must continually seek out new suppliers, which provide better products, or be willing to cooperate with new partners to develop more efficient supply chains. Each new partnership implies the creation or adaptation of business processes that cross organizational boundaries, and are best identified as "dynamic inter-organizational business processes". The dynamic inter-organizational business processes entail a permanent building and dismantling of partnerships, which is the key difference between them and (static) inter-organizational business processes, which have existed since the 1960s and have been based on technologies such as EDI [EDI]. The change from static to dynamic inter-organizational processes is further promoted by the appearance of technologies that allow for the dynamic coupling of information and application systems. The Internet, the World Wide Web and, ultimately, Web Services [W3C] provide transparent access to services in distributed and heterogeneous environments. Web services based languages such as BPEL4WS [BPEL] offer the specification of business processes using web services. However, an architecture

M. Jeckle and L.-J. Zhang (Eds.): ICWS-Europe 2003, LNCS 2853, pp. 123–136, 2003.
© Springer-Verlag Berlin Heidelberg 2003

which describes how to create process instances of dynamic inter-organizational processes, and how to execute them, still does not exist.

There is a plenty of research which covers the support of inter-organizational processes (also named cross-organizational processes, cross-enterprise processes etc. see "3 Existing Approaches for the Support of Static Inter-organizational Business Processes" later in this text). However, these approaches refer to static inter-organizational processes and not to dynamic ones. In order to analyse the requirements of dynamic inter-organizational business processes and to propose an architecture to support them, this paper will proceed as follows: first, basic terms and concepts in the area of business processes will be defined. Then, the requirements for the support of dynamic inter-organizational business processes will be identified. Using these requirements, existing approaches will be examined to determine whether they can provide at least partial solutions. This analysis is the basis for the development of an architecture to support dynamic inter-organizational business processes.

2 Basic Concepts of Business Process Support

A business process is a bundle of activities, which requires one or several inputs and which creates value for the customer. [HaCh93]. A business process is formalized using a business process model, as illustrated in Fig. 1. The business process model defines a set of elements which represent the parts of the business process. It can be seen as a kind of language description containing words and rules about how to combine words to phrases. In most cases this 'language' consists of graphical elements and rules on how to connect them.

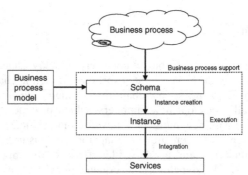

Fig. 1. Business process support

Using the elements and rules of the business process model, the real business process is formalized as business process schema (or schema for short). The business process schema abstracts the individual execution of the business process instance. Basically the schema defines the sequence of activities to be completed by the business process and the rules for carrying out certain activities in certain defined circumstances. For example a schema of an order processing defines the activities to be performed to process the order and rules i.e. "Reject the order if the ordered product is out of stock".

The business process schema is the template for creating business process instances. Business process instances (or instances for short) represent the concrete processing of an order, e.g. the processing of order number 4711. During execution of the business process instance, services are used to perform activities and to access data. The creation of instances and their execution is called, 'support of business processes'.

2.1 Requirements for the Support of Dynamic Inter-organizational Business Processes

Dynamic inter-organizational business processes are processes that are distributed over several organizations and show a high fluctuation of partners. The set of organisations participating in the definition and execution of business process is dynamic and not static. Organizations participate in the execution of a dynamic inter-organizational business process by executing one, or more, sub-processes and providing services for process execution even for sub-processes executed by other organizations. To clarify these points, we will introduce the scenario that is illustrated in Fig. 2. The scenario contains a mechanical engineering firm and an electronic control systems manufacturer that combine their core competencies. The mechanical engineering company profits from making their products more 'intelligent' with the integration of electronic control systems. The company for the production of electronic control systems gains access to new markets.

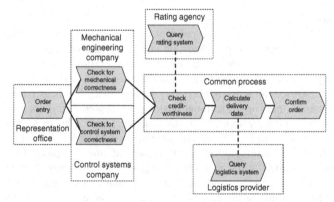

Fig. 2. Scenario for dynamic inter-organizational business processes

As both companies do not have infinite financial resources, they rely on representation offices to acquire orders. Only one of these representation offices is shown in Fig. 2. Acquired orders are sent to both companies to verify the technical details of the order from both mechanical engineering and the control systems perspectives. Then, an external rating agency is consulted in order to verify customer creditworthiness. This is done by querying the rating agencies rating system. The delivery date is calculated by querying the logistics system of an appropriate logistics provider. Lastly, an order confirmation is sent out (potential exceptions, e.g. a bad credit ranking are yet not covered). Six requirements for the support of dynamic inter-organizational business processes can be identified:

Process Autonomy

Process autonomy is defined as the capability of autonomously defining and executing business processes. Since the participating organizations of a dynamic inter-organizational business processes change quickly, all participants should be assured to retain their capability to define and execute business processes, even when they leave such a partnership. All participants must be able to enter into newer partnerships quickly. In the scenario, process autonomy would be destroyed by using a centralized business process support system installed at the mechanical engineering company. As process schemas and service descriptions are centralized at the mechanical engineering company, the control systems company loses the rapid response ability to switch to another partner.

Flexibility

Dynamic inter-organizational business processes are subject to more changes than static inter-organizational business processes since greater potential sources of change requests exist. Therefore, the support of dynamic inter-organizational business processes must be highly flexible.

Scalability

In order to react to market changes it must be possible to provide quick support for additional business processes or to augment the instances of an existing business process significantly. Therefore, scalability is an important requirement of supporting dynamic inter-organizational business processes.

Service Autarchy

Service autarchy is defined as the capability of independently associating the services needed to support business processes or sub-processes of them. Service autarchy guarantees that each organization participating in a certain business process can use the necessary services to execute their business processes without the involvement of a third party. Service autarchy is necessary to cope with business partner fluctuation typical to dynamic inter-organizational business processes. Only when it is possible to quickly change a service provider is it possible to change a business process quickly. In the scenario shown in Fig. 2, service autarchy would be lost by using a centralized Enterprise Application Integration (EAI) system at one company. For example, an EAI-system is installed at the mechanical engineering company. Services s1 and s2 provided by the rating agency and the logistics provider are centrally integrated. This means that they can not be directly accessed; every usage of the services would have to pass through the EAI system. This could be disastrous when the controls systems company switches to another partner because access to the services would be lost.

Service Extensibility and Integration

Because dynamic inter-organizational business processes are subject to continual change, the set of services necessary to enable them is highly dynamic as well. New services must be continually integrated due to changes in the business processes. Therefore, an architecture to support inter-organizational business processes must be capable of integrating new and previously unknown services. The services may be highly-distributed and heterogeneous, because different organizations use different infrastructures. Service extensibility and integration describes the possibility of quickly and transparently switching from a service, referred to as s2, and provided by the old logistics, to the service s3 provided by the new logistics service. Service s3 may be implemented in a totally different way than s2.

Asynchronous Service Eevolution

When dealing with dynamic inter-organizational business processes, services evolve independently. There is no centralized institution coordinating the evolution of services. In the scenario, illustrated in Fig. 2, the rating agency could introduce new and enhanced versions of its rating service s1 called s1'. This should not influence the established business process in any way. Asynchronous service evolution is defined as the capability to cope with services which evolve independently and without central coordination.

The requirements for supporting dynamic inter-organizational business processes can be divided into two groups. Process autonomy, flexibility and scalability are process oriented requirements. They deal with the definition, management and execution of business processes. The second group are service oriented requirements, which include service autarchy, service extensibility and integration and asynchronous service evolution.

3 Existing Approaches for the Support of Static Inter-organizational Business Processes

The support of (static) inter-organizational business processes is a frequently mentioned topic with many concepts. To identify possible contributions to the support of dynamic inter-organizational business processes, a selection of approaches will be examined using previously identified requirements.

The first group of approaches tries to create a support for inter-organizational business processes based on CORBA [OMG] such as [VoWe99]. The most advanced approach is the WorCos-concept [Schu99]. The primary goal of the WorCos-concept is the support of business processes on the basis of a workflow service, which is integrated into the Object Management Architecture (OMA) [OMG]. In [SBMW96] and [Böhm97], a proposal for a CORBA-Facility [OMG] is made. WorCos is a purely object-oriented approach. Business processes, are represented as CORBA objects, created by compilation. The objects contain nearly the complete functionality to execute a specific business process, such as role associations, process state and meta data. Therefore, the execution of business process instances is centralized in these objects. The Mentor project [WoWe97], [WeMW98] is aimed at supporting business processes organization-wide. The fundamental idea of the 'Mentor Project' is to model business processes in the form of state and activity charts [Hare88]. In this manner, different schemas can be easily distributed and executed. However, the execution of the business process instances is centrally managed. The Meteor- and Meteor2-Projekt [Wang95] creates a fully distributed process support for company wide business processes based on CORBA. Integration into the WWW is described in [DKMS96], [MPSK98]. In Meteor, business processes are represented in a Workflow Intermediate Language (WIL). This specification is used to generate task managers which control parts of a business process. Task managers are independent execution units, which may be distributed throughout an organization.

When the approaches listed above are carefully analyzed, two basic architectures can be identified. They are called, direct and indirect instance creation. In the direct instance creation architecture process instances are created directly from the process schema, and no intermediate structure exists. The process instances are created by interpreting the process schema as shown in Fig. 3. The engine which interprets the process schema also integrates services, e.g. s1 and 2. This architecture can be found in the Mentor approach.

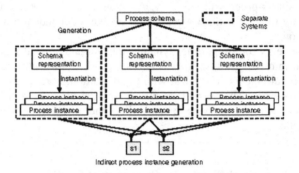

Fig. 3. Direct and indirect process instance creation

High flexibility is the primary advantage of the direct instance creation. Changes to the process schema can be immediately implemented because the schema is interpreted. However, this advantage is acquired by accepting the disadvantage of limited scalability since the interpretation is centralized and cannot be distributed. Since every step in the execution of the business process requires the involvement of the interpreter a central bottleneck is created. Furthermore, the existence of a centralized engine obliterates the process autonomy and service autarchy. Changes to sub processes can only be implemented by interacting with the centralized interpretation engine, which also integrates all the services used during process execution. The interpretation also impedes service extensibility and integration, since the interpretation engine is not designed in an extensible way. The same applies for asynchronous service evolution.

The other basic architecture - indirect instance creation - is also illustrated in Fig. 3. Here, process instances are created in two steps. In the first step, a so-called schema representation is generated. It is a template used for the automatic generation of process instances called instantiation. In the second step, the schema representation is used to create business process instances, which can be executed independently. Both instantiation and execution can be separated from the generation of the schema representation. Furthermore, services such as s1 and 2 have, for example, have not to be centrally integrated.

Indirect instance creation can be found in the Meteor and WorCos approaches. In WorCos, the schema representation consists of an object class created from the process schema. The instance creation is done in WorCos by creating instances of the object class. The use of two steps to create process instances is the reason for the high scalability of the indirect instance creation. The creation of a schema representation can be separated from instance creation and execution. By copying the schema representation and distributing it, process instances can be executed on a multitude of systems. Thus a high scalability is achieved because many process instances are executed in parallel on separate systems. However, indirect instance creation offers only limited flexibility, as changes to the process schema cannot be implemented incrementally. Process autonomy can be achieved by creating separate (sub-) schema representations for each sub process. In this way process autonomy can be achieved. Service extensibility and integration are impeded by the generating mechanism for the schema representation. The set of services is fixed, with the integration capabilities limited. The same applies for the asynchronous service evolution. Finally, the requirement of service autarchy is orthogonal to the concept of the indirect instance creation. By comparing the direct and indirect creation of process instances it can be easily seen, that there is a dilemma between flexibility and scalability. Direct approaches provide flexibility but limited scalability; indirect approaches provide scalability but only limited flexibility.

3.1   Web Services

Web Services [W3WS], [GrSi02] provide transparent access to services in a highly distributed, heterogeneous and dynamic environment. This achievement has been a goal within the field of computer science research for a long time. Web services realize the concept of a component as software unit, which is transparently accessible and makes explicit all context dependencies [Szyp96], [ScCi96]. An essential ingredient for the success of web services is the so-called, loose coupling of services. The implementation of loosely coupled services can be exchanged at run-time without side effects for the web service user. Loose coupling is crucial for service autarchy, because such services can be quickly integrated or sorted out. Furthermore, the name space concept already introduced with XML [XML] is very useful for coping with asynchronous service evolution by creating a decentralized versioning mechanism. Different versions of a web service are differentiated by different name spaces. The basic Web Services technologies provide no direct business process support. When they are combined with the architectures identified so far, the direct and indirect instance creation, only an improved service integration and support for service evolution is achieved. Therefore, applying Web Services to those architectures is not a remedy for the fundamental deficiencies found in these approaches.

3.2   Web Services Based Approaches for Business Process Support

Soon after the definition of basic Web Services technologies such as SOAP [W3C] it became more and more obvious that web services also have to provide concepts for orchestrating and coordinating web services in order to support business processes.

The Business Process Execution Language for Web Services (BPEL4WS) [BPEL] is based on WSFL and XLANG. It allows the specification of business processes and the definition of web services to be used in executing a specified business process [LeRo02].

BPEL4WS, WSFL and XLANG are language definitions which provide a set of elements and rules to describe business processes. Therefore, they can be thought of as a type of business process model. However, none of them provides concepts for executing and instantiating the defined schemas.

3.3   Execution Environments

A first approach for supporting the execution of business processes specified with the BPEL4WS is the IBM Business Process Execution Language for Web Services, JavaTM Run Time (BPWS4J) [BPWS4J]. The BPWS4J executes business processes using 3 documents. The process schema is represented in a BPEL4WS document. A WSDL-document [WSDL] specifies the interface that the business process provides to other business processes. A third document is used for specifying the web services used during execution [LeRo02]. BPWS4J creates process instances directly from the process schema by interpretation. Thus, BPWS4J is an approach using the direct instance creation. Therefore, the advantages and disadvantages of the direct instance creation approach also apply to BPWS4J. It is flexible, because process changes can be implemented immediately. However this flexibility is acquired in exchange for limited scalability.

3.4   Summary

The result of our investigations can be summarized as shown below in Fig. 4. Direct instance creation provides flexibility but fails to fulfil all other requirements. Indirect instance creation offers scalability and process autonomy, but does not provide service oriented requirements. Web services are not designed to support business processes directly. Therefore, it is not surprising that they fulfil only the service oriented requirements.

Process-oriented requirements

Direct instance creation	Indirect instance creation	
Flexibility	Scalability	Process autonomy

Service autarchy	Service extensibility and integration	Asynchronous service evolution

Web Services

Service-oriented requirements

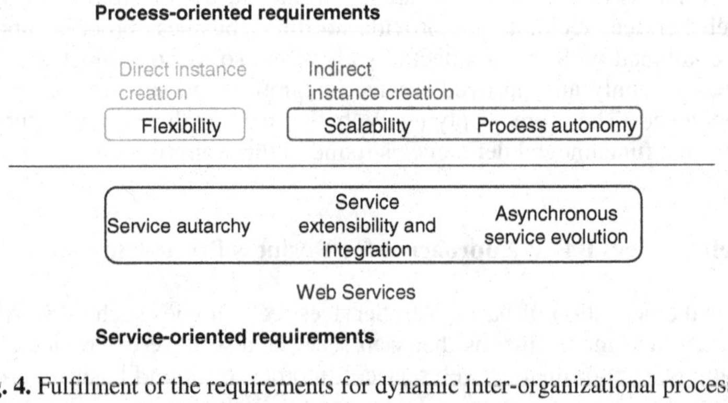

Fig. 4. Fulfilment of the requirements for dynamic inter-organizational processes

To create support for dynamic inter-organizational business processes by fulfilling all requirements, one has to combine the advantages of direct and indirect instance creation and combine them with the benefits gained from employing web services.

4 Support for Dynamic Inter-organizational Business Processes by Using Composite Applications

To create an architecture which escapes from the dilemma of trading off either scalability or flexibility and to fully make use of the advantages offered by web services, two different strategies are possible.

One strategy is to improve the scalability of direct instance creation architectures. For example, an attempt could be made to use several interpretation engines instead of only one. However, this does provide an answer to the fundamental problem that the 'flow of control' of the business process always returns to the interpretation engine. Therefore the centralized engine remains the bottleneck.

The other alternative is to use the indirect instance creation architecture and to make the schema representation incrementally adaptable, so that it can be quickly modified according to a changed business process. To achieve this, the paradigm for creating a schema representation has to be changed. Up until now, all the approaches resulted in the creation of a schema representation as a classical monolithic application. One has to go through a kind of edit-compile-link cycle to change the schema representation.

A paradigm which avoids these limitations is the composite application [Schm97]. Composite applications break with the thinking that applications and executables have to be one. A composite application is created by a set of interconnected and specialized services as shown in Fig. 5.

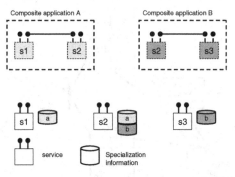

Fig. 5. Composite application

There is no central "executable" anymore which contains application functionality. All functionality remains in services which can participate in different composite applications. The services are integrated into composite applications via specialization. The specialization is done by applying specialization information to the services. The specialization information contains both parameterisation and connection information. Parameterisation information adapts the service to the individual needs of the composite application. The connection information contains information about the connection of the service with other services within the context of the composite application. The specialization information is not centrally stored but attached to the services. Therefore, every service "knows" what to do. An example is given also in Fig. 5. There are two composite applications A and B. They are created using three services s1, s2 and s3. Composite application A is created by using services s1 and s2 with the specialization information denoted as "a". The specialization information "a" of s1 contains the connection information representing the connection between s1 and s2. Furthermore, both services are parameterized. Composite application B is created by using services s2 and s3 using specialization information denoted with a "b". The paradigm of the composite application is used to create an incrementally adaptable and thus flexible schema representation. The starting point for this is the decomposition of processes and subprocesses into so-called representation elements. Representation elements can be easily identified by separating the business process functionality according into so-called aspect-elements [ScAs98]. Aspect elements are not further dividable; they are atomic parts of business processes which contain only functionality of one so called aspect [JaBu96]. Aspects are disjoint sets of elements of business process or workflow models. There are 5 basic aspects: the functional, control, informational, organisational and operational aspect [JaBu96]. The functional aspect describes how a business process is composed of sub-processes. The control aspect describes how activities are executed dependent on the result or completion of other activities. In the organizational aspect, the relation between the business process and the organization structure is established. The operational aspect describes external services to be used during the process. The data flow is covered in the informational aspect.

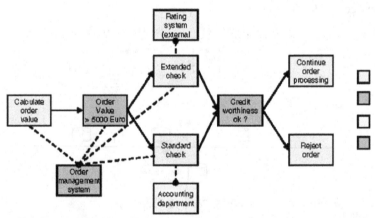

Fig. 6. Decomposition of business processes into representation elements

In order to illustrate the generation of a schema representation, a small fragment of a business process is transformed. The fragment defines, that above an order value of 5000 Euro, an extended check of the customer's credibility by querying an (external) rating system shall take place. Otherwise a standard check is done by the accounting department. The representation elements are coloured according to the aspect they belong to. The full lines indicate temporal connections. Two representation elements connected in this way are meant to be executed consecutively. Dotted lines indicate client-server relationships.

The first step to creating a composite application is the generation of representation elements from a business process schema provided as BPEL4WS document for example, as illustrated in Fig. 7. The second step for creating a composite application is to search for web services which can implement the representation elements. This may be done by querying a service repository such as UDDI [UDDI]. For each representation element, an appropriate service has to be found. In the scenario below, the service associated with the representation element is delineated below the representation element. In most cases, there is not a perfect fit; therefore, the search has to also include also services which can be properly adapted using specialization. Furthermore one service may fit well with several representation elements.

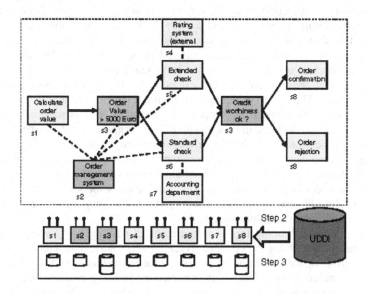

Fig. 7. Generation of a composite application

For example service s3 can be used to implement a check of whether the order value is greater 5000 euro and a check of whether a customer is credit-worthy. This is possible, because the service may be adapted via parameterization to the respective criterion. The first use of the service tests the criterion order value, the second checks the credit-worthiness. The same applies to service s8 which is used to implement both the order confirmation and potential order rejection.

In the third step, the specialization information is generated, as shown in Fig. 7. Appropriate parameterization information has to be provided to adjust the service to the individual needs of the business process. For example the order value which should initiate a detailed investigation of the customer's credit-worthiness can be adjusted. At the same time, connection information also has to be generated according to the connections of the representation elements in the business process. It is important to notice, that services s3 and s3 have 2 sets of specialization information because both are used twice. The types of use are differentiated using context identifications, which are issued by the antecedent service. For example s1 issues context identification 1, s5 and s6 issue context identification 2. In this manner, s3 will test the order value if it is called by s1 and test credit-worthiness if it is called by s5 or s6.

5 Conclusion

Dynamic inter-organizational business processes are crucial for enterprises which have to quickly adapt or create partnerships with other enterprises: Partners are replaced in existing partnerships and new partnerships are constantly being built. This fluctuation of business partners creates new or extended requirements. Two groups of requirements have been identified. Process oriented requirements concern the definition, management and execution of business processes: process autonomy, flexibility and scalability. The second group are service oriented requirements: Service autarchy, service extensibility, integration, and service evolution. The analysis of existing approaches has shown that neither direct, nor indirect instance creation can satisfy all requirements or preserve the benefits offered by web services. The direct instance creation architecture offers flexibility, but lacks scalability and process autonomy; the indirect instance creation architecture offers scalability and process autonomy, but lacks flexibility. The key to escaping this dilemma is to use a flexible and adaptable schema representation based on composite applications. In this way, it is possible to create an execution architecture for dynamic inter-organizational business processes, which is both flexible and scaleable. Process autonomy is fully achieved, as the composite application can be fragmented on a representation element level basis. The use of representation elements as a paradigm also assures that the process autarchy provided by web services is maintained. The same applies for service extensibility and integration. In addition the ability of web services for supporting the asynchronous evolution of services is also preserved.

The next steps will comprise the introduction of tracking and tracing mechanisms and the integration of legacy systems. Tracking and tracing mechanisms provide the capability to track the execution of business process instances and to create a log of the business process execution which is necessary in many business areas. The integration of existing applications systems poses the challenge that they contain functionality which does not separate aspects and even aspect elements. Therefore a system of wrappers and mediators has to be developed, which allows the integration of legacy systems.

References

[AALS]   W. M. P. van der Aalst: Process-oriented Architectures for Electronic Commerce and Interorganizational Workflow. Information Systems, 24(8), 2000

[BPEL]   Business Process Execution Language for Web Services, Version 1.0
ftp://www6.software.ibm.com/software/developer/library/ws-bpel.pdf

[BPML]   BPML.org. Business Process Modeling Language (BPML).

[BPWS4J]   http://www.alphaworks.ibm.com/tech/bpws4j

[Böhm97]   M. Böhm. Objektorientierte Implementierungstechniken für Workflow-Management-Systeme in OMA-konformen Architekturen. In [JaBS97].

[Chap96]   D. Chappell: Understanding ActiveX and OLE. Microsoft Press, Redmond, 1996.

[CiSc96]   O. Ciupke, R. Schmidt: Components As Context-Independent Units of Software. WCOP 96, Linz 1996. Special Issues in Object-Oriented Programming. Workshop Reader of the 10th European Conference on Object-Oriented Programming ECOOP96. Dpunkt.verlag, Verlag 1996.

[EDI]   http://www.unece.org/trade/untdid/welcome.htm

[GrSi02]   S. Graham, S. Simeonov et. Al.: Building Web Services with Java, SAMS Publishing, Indianapolis, Indiana, USA, 2002

[HaCh93]   M. Hammer, J. Champy: Reengineering the Cooperation, A Manifesto for Business Revolution. Harper Business, New York, 1993.

[Hare88]   D. Harel: On Visual Formalisms. Communications of the ACM, 31(5), Mai 1988, S. 514 – 530.

[JaBu96]   S. Jablonski, C. Bußler: Workflow Management - Modeling Concepts, Architecture and Implementation. London 1996

[Kicz96]   G. Kiczales: Aspect-oriented programming. ACM Computing Surveys, 28(4), December 1996.

[LeRo02]   F. Leymann, D. Roller: Business processes in a Web services world: A quick overview of BPEL4WS.
             ftp://www6.software.ibm.com/software/developer/library/ws-bpelwp.pdf

[MPSK98]   J. A. Miller, D. Palaniswami, A. P. Sheth, K. Kochut, H. Singh: WebWork: METEOR2's Web-Based Workflow Management System. Journal of Intelligent Information Systems (JIIS), 10(2), 1994, S. 185–215.

[OMG]   http://www.omg.org

[SBMW96]   W. Schulze, M. Böhm, K. Meyer-Wegener: Services of Workflow Objects and Workflow Meta-Objects in OMG-compliant Environments, OOPSLA 96, Workshop on Business Object Design and Implementation, San José, CA.

[ScAs98]   R. Schmidt, U. Assmann. Extending Aspect-Oriented Programming in Order to Flexibly Support Workflows. In Proceedings of the ICSE98 AOP Workshop, Kyoto, Japan, April 1998, S. 41 – 46

[Szyp96]   Proceedings and Summary of ECOOP'96 Workshop: Component-oriented Programming (WCOP 96), 10th European Conference on Object-Oriented Programming, Linz, Austria, July 1996.

[Schm97]   R. Schmidt: Component-based systems, composite applications and workflow-management. In Proceedings Workshop Foundations of Component-Based Systems, Zürich, Schweiz, 26. September, 1997, S. 206 – 214.

[Schu99]   W. Schulze: Ein Workflow-Management-Dienst für ein verteiltes Objektverwaltungssystem. Dissertation, TU Dresden 1999.

[Snel02]   J. Snell: Automating business processes and transactions in Web services
             ftp://www6.software.ibm.com/software/developer/library/ws-autobp.pdf

[Szyp98]   C. Szyperski: Component Programming, Beyond Object-Oriented Programming. Addison Wesley, New York, 1998.

[W3C]   www.w3c.org

[W3WS]   http://www.w3.org/2002/ws/

[Wang95]   X. Wang: Implementation and Evaluation of CORBA-Based Centralized Workflow Schedulers. Master's thesis. University of Georgia, August 1995.

[WeMW98]   J. Weissenfels, P. Muth, G. Weikum: Flexible Worklist Management in a Light-Weight Workflow Management System. In Proceedings of EDBT Workshop on Workflow Management Systems, Valencia, 1998.

[WeKl02]   I. Wetzel, R. Klischewki: Serviceflow Beyond Workflow? Concepts and Architectures for Supporting Inter-Organizational Service Processes. 14th CAiSE. Springer Lecture Notes in Computer Science, Berlin, pp. 500–515, 2002

[WfMC]   Workflow Management Coalition: http://www.aiai.ed.ac.uk/project/wfmc/

[Wodt96]   D. Wodtke: Modellbildung und Architektur von verteilten Workflow-Management-Systemen. DISDBIS 31, infix Verlag, Sankt Augustin, 1996.

[WoWe97]   D. Wodtke, G. Weikum: A Formal Foundation for Distributed Workflow Execution Based on State Charts. In Proceedings ICDT 1997, S. 230 – 246.
[WSDL]   www.w3c.org/wsdl
[WSFL01]   F. Leyman, 'Web Services Flow Language', IBM Software Group specification, Mai 2001
[WWWK96]   D. Wodtke, J. Weissenfels, G. Weikum, A. Kotz-Dittrich: The Mentor project: Steps towards organizational-wide workflow management. In Proceed-ings 12th IEEE International Conference on Data Engineering, 1996.
[XML]   www.xml.org

AOP for Dynamic Configuration and Management of Web Services

Bart Verheecke, María Agustina Cibrán, and Viviane Jonckers

System and Software Engineering Lab
Vrije Universiteit Brussel
Pleinlaan 2
1050 Brussels, Belgium
{Bart.Verheecke,Maria.Cibran}@vub.ac.be,
vjoncke@info.vub.ac.be

Abstract. Web service technologies accelerate application development by allowing the selection and integration of third-party web services, achieving high modularity, flexibility and configurability. However, current approaches only allow this integration by hard wiring the references to concrete web services into the client applications. Moreover they do not provide any management support, which is fundamental for achieving robustness. We observe the need for the application to be independent of specific services and present the WSML, a management layer placed in between the application and the world of web services. In this paper we identify the requirements for this layer to realise the dynamic selection and integration of services, client-side management of services, and support for rules that govern the selection, integration and composition. We show how dynamic AOP is ideally suited to implement the core functionality of the WSML using the JAsCo dynamic aspect-oriented language to conduct the experiments.

Keywords: Web Services, Aspect Oriented Programming, Web Services Management, Dynamic Configuration, Hot-Swapping.

1 Introduction

Web services are modular applications that are described, published, localised and invoked over a network. In the relative short time that web services have been around, an impressive range of supporting tools has been developed that enable the creation and deployment of web services and the development of service oriented applications. Large platforms such as Java ONE and Microsoft.NET provide the key technologies, build around W3C standards such as SOAP [1], WSDL [2] and UDDI [3], and allow publishing, looking up and consuming services in a straightforward manner.

However, the approaches typically used to integrate services in client applications are very static and do not allow any dynamic adaptations of the web services themselves or the way they are used. As stated in [4], this leads to unmanageable applications that cannot adapt to changes in the business environment (e.g. a service that is abandoned or changed, a new service that becomes available on the market, etc).

M. Jeckle and L.-J. Zhang (Eds.): ICWS-Europe 2003, LNCS 2853, pp. 137–151, 2003.
© Springer-Verlag Berlin Heidelberg 2003

A second obstacle is that by generating hard-wired proxy-classes, and as such treating the services as regular software components, the specific requirements of services are completely ignored. Services are organisationally fragmentized, can be asynchronous and latent, can become unavailable due to unpredictable network conditions and thus require more overall management [5]. To deal with these issues in order to create more robust applications, code has to be written manually and repeated for each service. This way, the code is duplicated, scattered all over the application and becomes an obstacle for future maintenance.

A third limitation encountered is that services can only be selected based on the functionality they offer. The web service documentation provided in WSDL-format does not support the explicit specification of non functional requirements such as constraints based on Quality-of-Service and management statements, classes of service, access rights, pricing information, SLA's (Service Level Agreements) and other contracts between web services. Explicitly specifying these non-functional requirements at the service side in a precise and unambiguous way would allow the composition and integration of services to occur in a more intelligent and customized manner. This way, applications are able to specify criteria to be considered at service selection time to integrate those services that best fit the application requirements.

In this paper we present a management layer called **Web Services Management Layer (WSML)**, which is placed in between the application and the world of web services. This intermediate layer allows: dynamic selection and integration of services into an application, client-side management of the service, and support for rules that govern the selection, integration and composition.

The focus of this paper is to identify the requirements for a technological platform to realise the WSML. We show how dynamic *Aspect Oriented Programming* (AOP) [6,7] is ideally suited to build the core functionality of this management layer. To deal with the dynamic nature of the service environment we suggest the use of a dynamic aspect-oriented programming language called JAsCo [8,9]. In the next section we identify the requirements pursued for the WSML and analyse how state-of-the-art approaches fail in achieving them. In section 3 we explain the basic architecture of our solution and the objectives achieved. A following section describes the need for AOP and gives an overview of the characteristics of JAsCo. In section 5 we show how JAsCo is ideal to implement the core functionality of the WSML and provide code examples. Finally, we present related and future work in section 6 and conclude in section 7.

2   Requirements for WSML

Web services constitute a promising middleware technology. However, we believe there are some important management issues that still need to be addressed. Today, the technology only provides standardised connection mechanisms, but this might not be sufficient to drive its world wide adoption. We identify the following challenges that have to be taken into account:

- **Composition of Web Services:** the real strength of web services lies in the concept of combining and orchestrating them in order to deliver added-value services. However, this leads to the question of how to dynamically (i.e. at runtime) integrate a service in the consuming application. How can the required service be found and plugged in? How can one deal with different services delivering similar functionality? How can compositions of services be made that were not anticipated at design time of the application?

- **Multi-Partner Processes:** consuming web services means that processes of several business partners situated on different locations are being integrated with each other. This raises significant management issues (e.g. organisational fragmentation of the application) and technical consequences (e.g. much longer processing times, security issues, AAA, etc).

- **Dependencies:** an application that integrates with external services becomes dependent on them. Failure of the service will have a negative impact on the execution of the application.

- **Flexibility:** since the context is an ever-changing business environment, the application must be flexible enough to deal with changes in the functionality, displacement or use of web services.

If we look at the current approaches of how web services are integrated in applications, we see that these issues are not addressed at all, or if so only partly: in the **Wrapper Approach** each web service is wrapped and treated as an internal software component (see figure 1). State-of-the-art tools like MS Visual Studio.NET and BEA WebLogic adopt this mechanism [10]. The software developer enters a web reference to the service into the tool. Then, the WSDL document of the service is automatically looked up, analysed and code for a proxy class is generated. Programmers can invoke web methods on this class just like on a regular class and do not have to take into account that they are actually dealing with remote procedure calls (RPCs). Clearly, the issues mentioned above are not addressed: (1) services are selected and integrated in a static manner at design time, (2) code that deals with managing multi-partner processes has to be written manually, needs to be duplicated for each service and becomes scattered in different modules of the application code, (3) the application has to deal with the potential unavailability of services by manually including code that again results tangled and scattered (4) changes in the environment can only be dealt with by stopping and rewriting the application code.

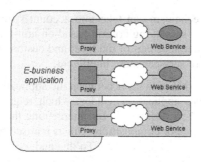

Fig. 1. The Wrapper Approach to integrate services

A more dynamic solution is provided when using a **tModel** [11] instead of a concrete service. In this approach, a service can be invoked to deliver the required functionality if it follows the overall system's tModel specification. However, this only solves some of the identified issues: (1) only services that exactly implement the tModel can be dynamically integrated, while services with other interfaces and service compositions that deliver the same functionality cannot be straightforwardly included, (2) management code still needs to be written manually and remains scattered over the application code. Problem (3) is addressed as the dependency on a certain service is weakened because dynamic switching to other similar services can be achieved in a straightforward manner; however this is only tackled to some degree since that code needs to be written manually. Finally, (4) is addressed as services that match a tModel can be registered at runtime in a UDDI-register [3] and can as such be included in the application without having to make any changes.

We propose an abstraction layer, called **Web Services Management Layer (WSML)**, which is placed between the application and the world of web services and deals with the identified requirements. We introduce the basic architecture and its objectives in the next section.

3   Design of WSML

The WSML allows decoupling web services from the core application. It realises the concept of *just-in-time integration of services*: multiple services or compositions of services can be used to provide the same functionality. The advantages of this approach are:

- The application becomes more flexible as it can continuously adapt to the changing business environment and communicate with new services that were not known or available at design time.

- Extracting all web service related code from the core application facilitates future maintenance of the code.

- By weakening the link between the application and the service, hot swapping functionality can be installed. This mechanism enables switching to other services when they become unreachable due to network conditions or service-related problems.

- The hot-swapping mechanism can take into account specific application requirements. This way, rules specifying criteria based on non-functional requirements of services can be considered as part of the layer and customized for each application, making the selection of services more intelligent.

Figure 2 shows the WSML as a layer between the application and the web services. On the left side the core application resides, which requests service functionality when needed. The WSML is responsible for intercepting these requests and choosing the most appropriate service or composition. This is realised by the **Selection Module** by considering different service properties. To this end, collaboration with the **Monitoring Module** is required as several properties of services might need observation over time. Available services are looked up in a central UDDI-register [3] or discovered using decentralised Web Services Inspection Language (WSIL) documents [12].

Generic functionality, necessary to provide support for multi-partner processes (e.g. to guarantee security, transactions, etc) also resides in the layer, depending on specific application requirements. Examples of this generic management functionality are:

- **Traffic Optimisation:** in order to reduce traffic over the network to avoid slowing response times, losing packages, congesting networks, etc., a caching mechanism can be considered. Instead of invoking the services each time the application requests certain service functionality, the results are retrieved from a cache.

- **Billing:** services can specify their own billing strategies and the application might want to control how billing is applied. Analogously, services might need to be billed for being integrated in the client applications.

- **Accounting:** many industries are required to provide tracing and logging capabilities for accounting as well as regulatory purposes.

- **Security:** web services might have several security mechanisms (e.g. WS-Security [21]) depending on the environment where they are deployed. Data sent over the network can be encrypted and user authentication and authorisation might be required.

- **Transaction:** if the communication with a web service is transaction based and if in the middle of a transaction the layer must switch to another service, some compensation or roll-back mechanism might be used to restore the state of the previous service.

In section 5 an AOP solution for the encapsulation of these concerns as part of the WSML is presented. It is important to note that the WSML is reusable in different applications and is fully configurable to avoid unnecessary overhead. In the following sections we present the technical decisions made for the implementation of the layer.

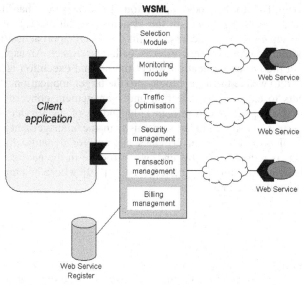

Fig. 2. General Architecture of WSML

4 AOP for WSML

4.1 Motivation for AOP

To achieve high flexibility in the selection of services, hard wiring references to concrete services in the applications must be avoided. Using traditional software engineering methodologies it would be the responsibility of the applications to decide which the most suitable services are for a given request or to explicitly request the layer to do that. In both cases, code for either implementing or triggering the service selection would be written at each point where some service functionality is required. As a consequence selection code would also result scattered in different places in the application and tangled with code that solves other concerns. Thus, we need support for encapsulating this crosscutting code separated from the application and plug it in and out in a non-invasive way. To achieve this we need to intercept the points in the execution of the application where concrete services are invoked and make the layer decide which the most suitable services for those requests are.

Moreover the selection of services also involves other management issues to be considered at the moment the services are selected to be integrated in the applications. For instance, services might need to control security, accounting, billing concerns at the time their functionality is requested. This also results in crosscutting code since the application developer would need to include this management code each time a service is requested.

Thus, to avoid tangling the application code with service related code we believe *Aspect Oriented Programming* (AOP) is needed. AOP argues that some concerns of a system, such as synchronisation and logging, cannot be cleanly modularized using current software engineering methodologies as they are scattered over different modules of the system. Due to this code duplication, it becomes very hard to add, edit and remove such a *crosscutting* aspect in the system. The ultimate goal of AOP is to achieve a better separation of concerns. To this end, AOP approaches introduce a new concept to modularize crosscutting concerns, called an *aspect*. An aspect defines a set of *join points* in the target application where the normal execution is altered. Aspect *weavers* are used to weave the aspect logic into the target application.

Using aspects to express the selection and management concerns as part of the WSML allows the application to remain independent of the service selection infrastructure. Moreover, we also pursue dynamism in the management of services and therefore an AOP technology that provides support for dynamic inclusion and removal of aspects is required. To this end, we introduce in the next section an aspect-oriented implementation language called JAsCo [8,9] whose features are ideal for achieving the identified requirements.

4.2 JAsCo

JAsCo is primarily based upon two existing AOP approaches: *AspectJ* [13] and *Aspectual Components* [14]. AspectJ's main advantage is the expressiveness of its language to describe the join points. However, AspectJ's aspects are not reusable, since the context needed by an aspect to be deployed, is specified directly in the aspect definition. To overcome this problem, Karl Lieberherr et al. introduce the concept of

Aspectual Components. They claim that when using AOP one must be able to express each aspect separately, in terms of its own modular structure. Using this model, an aspect is described as a set of abstract join points which are resolved when an aspect is combined with the base modules of a software system. This way, the aspect behaviour is kept separate from the base components, even at run time.

JAsCo combines the expressive power of AspectJ with the aspect independency idea of Aspectual Components. The advantages of JAsCo are:

- Aspects are described independent of a concrete context, making them highly reusable.

- JAsCo allows easy application and removal of aspects at run time.

- JAsCo has extensive support for specifying aspect combinations.

The JAsCo language itself stays as close as possible to the regular Java syntax and it introduces two new concepts that are highly valuable in the context of this research:

- **Aspect Beans:** an aspect bean is an extension of the Java Bean component that specifies crosscutting behaviour in a reusable manner. It can hold hook definitions, which specify *when* the normal execution of a method should be intercepted and *what* extra behaviour should be executed.

- **Connectors:** a JAsCo connector is responsible for applying the crosscutting behaviour of the aspect beans and for declaring how several of these aspects collaborate. It specifies *where* the crosscutting behaviour should be deployed.

On a technical level a new, backward compatible component model is introduced that enables the run-time application and removal of connectors. This high flexibility and configurability is exactly what is needed in the context of web services. JAsCo's connectors are ideal to achieve the dynamic behaviour of the WSML and to allow the runtime integration and management of services without invasively having to change the core application. Section 5 shows code examples of how JAsCo connectors and aspect beans are used. For more information about JAsCo and the JAsCo component model, we refer to [8,9].

5   Implementation of WSML

5.1   Architecture of WSML

Figure 3 shows the implementation of the WSML using aspect beans for the generic functionality of the layer and dynamic JAsCo connectors to specify when they need to be deployed. The left part of figure 3 illustrates the application requesting web service functionality. The right part shows four semantically equivalent services that are available to answer the request.

To enable the application to make requests without referencing concrete services the concept of *Abstract Service Interfaces* is introduced in section 5.2. The mechanism based on redirection aspects that allow requests redirection and hot-swapping is discussed in section 5.3. Additional management aspects to deal with concerns such as accounting and billing are described in section 5.4. Finally, in section 5.5 the selection and monitoring modules of the WSML responsible for enabling intelligent service selections are discussed.

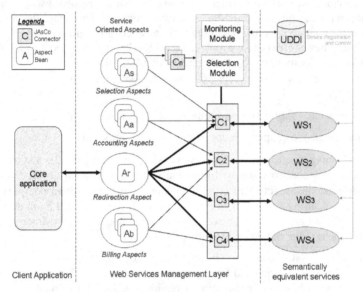

Fig. 3. Detailed Architecture of the WSML

5.2   Abstract Service Interfaces (ASI)

A basic requirement as identified in section 2 is that hard-wiring of services should be avoided. Therefore, service requests must be formulated in an abstract way at the left side of the layer and the WSML will be responsible for making the translation to a concrete service at the right side. The requests of the application are formulated in an abstract way as specified in an **Abstract Service Interface (ASI)**. This can be seen as a contract specified by the application towards the services. This way the syntactical differences between semantically equivalent services can be hidden. After all, if the same functionality is implemented by two different parties, it will be done in a different manner. Two services may offer the same functionality but differ on a number of considerations like:

- Web method names
- Synchronous / Asynchronous methods
- Parameter types & return types
- Semantics of parameters & return values
- Method sequencing order

By introducing the WSML, we can hide the heterogeneity of those services. This approach differs from the concept of tModels [11] where the services must all have identical interfaces. Our solution is complementary because we also support services with different interfaces and even service compositions. In order to enable this we introduce the concept of mapping schemas to unambiguously describe how the service or service composition maps to the ASI. These schemas can be provided by the service owner or can be specified by the application developer. The idea of using sequence diagrams for expressing this mapping is followed here. This solution is also applied in PacoSuite [15], a component based development tool where sequence diagrams are used to determine if composition patterns and components are compatible and to automatically generate glue code to connect the components. In the same way, sequence diagrams can be used to specify the mapping between ASIs and concrete service interfaces.

To illustrate these ideas an example of a travel agency application is introduced. The application offers the functionality to book holidays online which customers can use to make reservations for both flights and hotels. To achieve this functionality this application integrates different web services. Suppose `HotelServiceA` and `Hotel-ServiceB` are services that offer the same functionality for the online booking of hotels. Each hotel service returns exactly the same results.

Assume in the client-application a list of hotels has to be presented to the customer. Thus, to this end a `HotelServiceASI` is defined which specifies the following method: `HotelList giveAvailableHotels (Date,Date,CityCode)`. At deployment or run time the following two services are available:

`HotelServiceA` provides the method: `giveHotels (CityCode,Date,Date)`

`HotelServiceB` provides the method: `listHotels (Date,Date,CityName)`

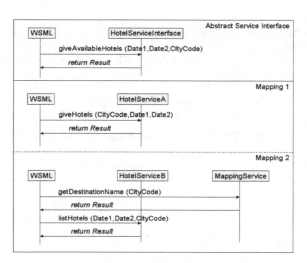

Fig. 4. Example of Sequence diagram for Abstract Service Interface mapping

Figure 4 shows how the `HotelServiceASI` is mapped to the concrete interfaces provided by these services. In the first example, both the name and the order of the arguments of the ASI differ from the ones specified in `HotelServiceA`. In the second example a simple service composition is needed. Because `HotelServiceB` requires city names instead of city codes, a third service is required to perform the translation between city names and codes.

5.3   Redirection Aspect

In the previous section we introduced how ASIs can be used to make the application independent of concrete details about specific services by referring to them in a generic and uniform way. However, to make this abstraction realisable we need to provide means to map this generic description to concrete service invocations. To achieve this, we make use of the aspect power of JAsCo and define an aspect in charge of redirecting the generic requests to the concrete services that will provide the functionality required.

The redirection aspect defines the logic of intercepting the application requests and replacing them by a concrete invocation on a specific web service. Figure 5 shows the implementation of the redirection aspect. Note that this aspect is generic and does not refer to any concrete web service. The mapping to concrete web services is specified in the connectors that deploy the redirection aspect. Several connectors can exist each in charge of deploying the redirection to a concrete web service. Figure 6 illustrates the deployment of the redirection aspect. The connector `getAvailableHotelsOf-ServiceA` specifies the mapping between the ASI `giveAvailableHotels(Date, Date, CityCode)` and the particular way to invoke that functionality on the web service `HotelServiceA`, i.e., invoking the method `giveHotels(CityCode, Date, Date)`.

```
class getAvailableHotelsRedirection {
  hook RedirectionHook {
    RedirectionHook(method(Date d1, Date d2, CityCode cc)){
      call(method);}
    replace(){specificMethod(d1, d2, cc);}
    abstract public List specificMethod(
                       Date d1, Date d2, CityCode cc);}}
```

Fig. 5. The Redirection Aspect Bean for hotel retrieval

```
static connector getAvailableHotelsOfServiceA {
  HotelServiceAStub hotelServiceA = null;
  try {
    hotelServiceA = HotelServiceAHelper.bind();}
  catch(Exception e) {}
  getAvailableHotelsRedirection.RedirectionHook rhook =
    new getAvailableHotelsRedirection.
    RedirectionHook(Application.giveAvailableHotels(
                        Date, Date, CityCode) {
    public List specificMethod(Date d1, Date d2, CityCode cc){
      return hotelServiceA.giveHotels(cc, d1, d2));}}}
```

Fig. 6. Connector that deploys the redirection aspect on HotelServiceA

Each connector encapsulates the mapping between each generic request in the application and the concrete manner to solve that request in a specific service. Thus, there will be one connector for each different request performed by the application. The WSML is responsible for the creation and management of these connectors.

JAsCo allows the creation of connectors to be done dynamically. This characteristic enables the dynamic integration of new services. When the functionality of a new service has to be integrated in the application, a connector realizing the mapping for that service is created at run time. This is achieved transparently for the application. Note that if the description of the services is extended with the specification of the mapping to ASIs as described in Section 5.2, the creation of connectors can be done automatically in the WSML.

This mechanism enables to realise hot swapping of services. If the response time of a service is too slow or the service becomes unavailable the selection module can "hot swap" to another service by activating its connector and deactivating the previous one. Because JAsCo allows the runtime plugging in and out of connectors, this process is achieved in a completely dynamic way. Note that if the communication with the service involves more complex transactions or if the service is state full, a transaction mechanism is required, as mentioned in section 3.

5.4   Client-Side Service Management

As mentioned earlier, the layer can also deal with other management issues that need to be controlled at the application side. For instance, suppose `HotelServiceA` describes a strategy for billing its use and the application wants to locally control this for auditing reasons. Imagine the service specifies that each time the method `giveHotels (CityCode, Date, Date)` is invoked, an amount of 5 euros has to be paid. If this functionality is implemented as part of the application, code for dealing with the billing concern would be needed at each point in the application where a request to that service is done. Thus, this code would crosscut the core application and should then be decoupled and encapsulated in a separate module.

```
class BillingPerUse {
  hook BillingHook {
    private int total, cost = 0;
    public void setCost(int aCost){cost = aCost;}
    private void pay(){total = total + cost;}
    BillingHook(method(Date d1,Date d2,CityCode cc)) {
      call(method);}
      after() {pay();}
  }
}
```

Fig. 7. Billing Aspect

We can achieve this by defining a new aspect that abstracts the logic for a *"pay per use"* billing strategy. Figure 7 shows the implementation of this aspect. Note that this aspect is generic and can be deployed and customised for other services that adopt this billing policy. This deployment is specified as part of the connector shown in Figure 8. In this example, the billing is done when `getAvailableHotels` is invoked in the application. However, as the connector `getAvailableHotelsOfServiceA` implements this method as a call to `HotelServiceA`, the billing is only done when this concrete service is used. Note that the hook can also be initialised with multiple functionalities provided by a web service.

The aspect `BillingPerUse` defines a billing template that can be reused by different services. Other more complex billing aspects can be formulated and implemented in a similar way. This simple example illustrates that a generic library of aspects can be created to achieve high flexibility in the creation and manipulation of aspects that implement several management issues.

```
static connector getAvailableHotelsOfServiceA {
  ...
  BillingPerUse.BillingHook billPerUse =
    new BillingPerUse.BillingHook(List
      Application.giveAvailableHotels(Date, Date, CityCode));
  billPerUse.setCost(5);
  rhook.replace();
  billPerUse.after();
}
```

Fig. 8. Connector extended with Billing

5.5   Service Selection & Monitoring

In section 5.3 we discussed how ASIs can be mapped to concrete services and service compositions. This mechanism enables the layer to decide which semantically equivalent services will be effectively chosen when the application invokes certain functionality. This is achieved by means of dynamically selecting and activating the corresponding service connectors. The selection module is responsible for regulating the activation of connectors. A service will effectively deal with a given request if the selection module of the WSML selected and activated its connector.

In order to control the properties of the web services that influence the decision, monitoring is required. A solution using aspects, similar to the one introduced in section 5.4 can be applied to dynamically install the necessary measurement points. For instance, if the response time of the services is an important criterion, then a monitoring aspect can be plugged in to intercept the web service invocations and provide information on the response time to the selection module.

Note that to be able to specify non-functional properties on web services, an extension of WSDL is required. WSOL, the Web Service Offering Language [16] can be used for this purpose. This is however outside the scope of this paper and is the subject of future research.

6   Related Work

We realize that a lot of research is going on in this context and that a lot of vendors are currently working on web service management platforms. However, most of these products focus on the service side management of web services. They allow developers to build and deploy web services and also provide some management capabilities such as load balancing, concurrency, monitoring, error handling, etc. On the contrary, our approach provides support for the client applications that want to integrate differ-ent third-party web services and manage them. Some of the most relevant approaches are: The Web Service Description Service (WSDF) [17] incorporates ideas from the Semantic Web community [18] suggesting an ontological approach for the side effect free invocations of services. The Web Services Mediator (WSM) [19] also identifies the need for a mediation layer to achieve dynamic integration of services. However, as far as we know there is no implementation available.

The Web Services Invocation Framework (WSIF) [20] supports a Java API for in-voking web services irrespective of how and where the services are provided. WSIF mostly focuses on making the client unaware of service migrations and change of protocols. We are analyzing how we can incorporate WSIF capabilities into the WSML.

A lot of work is being done towards standardization of various web service proto-cols covering security (WS-Security [21]), policy assertions (WS-Policy [22]) or transaction support (WS-Transaction [23]), business process definition languages (BPEL4WS [24]), etc. These protocols all require communicating with web services in a specific manner. The approach presented in this paper can be used to hide these differences from the core application.

The idea of applying AOP ideas to web services is quite innovative and thus not many approaches have been developed focusing on this field. However, Arsanjani et al. [25] have recently identified the suitability of AOSD to modularize the heteroge-neous concerns involved in web services. In particular they refer to technologies like Aspect/J [13] and the Hyper/J [26,27] for Multi-dimension Separation of Concerns (MDSOC). However these approaches only allow static aspect weaving, contrary to JAsCo which supports dynamic pluggability of aspects. They also identify the need for the web services to include the definition of non-functional interfaces that permit control over performance, reliability, availability, metering and level of service to take into account at service selection time.

7   Conclusion

In this paper we propose a new management layer WSML to control the integration and configuration of web services in client application. We identified the need to use AOP as we are dealing with crosscutting concerns. We propose to use a dynamic AOP implementation language JAsCo to enable hot-swapping and runtime manage-ment of services.

This approach has the advantage that applications become more robust as the layer can dynamically deal with potential service failures and hot swap to new functionally equivalent services. Moreover, a high flexibility for the integration of services is achieved by supporting the "on the fly" pluggability of services.

We are currently working on the definition of a library of reusable aspects that would allow the application developer to dynamically instantiate and configure the needed aspects to deal with different service management concerns. These reusable aspects can be seen as generic templates that can be customised and integrated "on demand" to accommodate to service requirements.

We are also working on realising the hot swapping mechanism in a more intelli-gent way by considering service oriented rules. These rules are derived from the application requirements and are based on the non-functional properties of services. They govern the selection of services specifying under which conditions the services have to be selected.

Other direction of research under attention is the automatic generation of the connector code. The idea is that each time a service has to be considered the WSML generates the connector code that will allow the future integration of that service into the application. To achieve this, the mapping between the ASIs and the concrete service functionality has to be dynamically parsed and translated into code. The non-functional properties of services also have to be analysed to instantiate the necessary management aspects. Note that this has to be achieved dynamically, without stopping the client application.

References

[1]   W3C, "Simple Object Access Protocol (SOAP) v1.2", Whitepaper, W3C Technical Publications, http://www.w3.org/TR/SOAP/

[2]   W3C, "Web Service Description Language (WSDL) v1.2", Whitepaper, W3C Technical Publications, http://www.w3.org/TR/wsdl12/

[3]   Uddi.org, "Universal Description, Discovery and Integration," UDDI Executive Whitepaper, November 2001

[4]   J. Malhotra, Ph.D., Co-Founder & CEO interKeel Inc., "Challenges in Developing Web Services-based e-Business Applications", Whitepaper, interKeel Inc., 2001

[5]   C. Szyperski, "Components and Web Services," Beyond Objects column, Software Development. Vol. 9, No. 8, Augustus 2001.

[6]   Aspect-Oriented Software Development. http://www.aosd.net/

[7]   Communications of the ACM. Aspect-Oriented Software Development, October 2001.

[8]   D. Suvée and W. Vanderperren. "JAsCo: an Aspect-Oriented approach tailored for Component Based Software Development." Proc. of 2nd Int. Conf. on AOSD, USA, 2003.

[9]   W. Vanderperren, D. Suvée, B. Wydaeghe and V. Jonckers. "PacoSuite & JAsCo: A visual component composition environment with advanced aspect separation features". Proc. of Int. Conf. on FASE, Warshaw, Poland, April 2003.

[10] Microsoft, "XML Web services," Visual Studio.NET Technical Resources, http://msdn.microsoft.com/vstudio/techinfo/articles/xmlwebservices/default.asp

[11] Microsoft, "Introduction to UDDI Services and tModels", 2002, http://isb.oio.dk/uddi/help/en/intro.whatisuddi.aspx

[12] T. Appnel, "An Introduction to WSIL, the Web Services Inspection Language," O'Reilly on Java.com, 2002, http://www.onjava.com/pub/a/onjava/2002/10/16/wsil.html

[13] G. Kiczales, E. Hilsdale, J. Hugunin, M. Kersen, J. Palm, and W. G. Griswold. "An overview of AspectJ". In Proc. ECOOP 2001, Hungary.

[14] K. Lieberherr, D. Lorenz and M. Mezini, "Programming with Aspectual Components. Technical Report," NU-CCS-99-01, March 1999.

[15] W. Vanderperren, "Applying aspect-oriented programming ideas in a component based context: Composition Adapters," In Proc. NetObjectDays 2001, Germany.

[16] V. Tosic, B. Pagurek, K. Patel, "WSOL – A Language for the Formal Specification of Classes of Service for Web Services". To be published in Proceedings of ICWS'03 (The First International Conference on Web Services), Las Vegas, USA, June 2003.

[17] A. Eberhart, "Towards Universal Web Service Clients," Proc. Euroweb 2002, UK.

[18] "The Semantic Web Community Portal," http://www.semanticweb.org/, November 2002.

[19] S. Chatterjee , "Developing Real World Web Services-based Applications", The Java Boutique, http://javaboutique.internet.com/articles/WSApplications/

[20] Apache, "The Web Services Invocation Framework (WSIF)," http://ws.apache.org/wsif/

[21] IBM, "Web Services Security (WS-Security) version 1.0," http://www-106.ibm.com/developerworks/webservices/library/ws-secure/ , April 2002

[22] Microsoft, "Web Services Policy Framework (WS-Policy) version 1.0," http://msdn.microsoft.com/webservices/, December 2002

[23] IBM, 'Web Services Transaction (WS-Transaction) version 1.0," http://www-106.ibm.com/developerworks/library/ws-transpec/, august 2002

[24] BEA Systems, IBM, Microsoft, SAP AG and Siebel Systems, "Business Process Execution Language for Web Services (BPEP4WS) v 1.1," May 2003

[25] A. Arsanjani, B. Hailpern, J. Martin, P. Tarr, "Web Services Promises and Compromises", ACM Queue, Vol. 1 No. 1, March 2003 http://www.acmqueue.org/

[26] H. Ossher and P. Tarr, "Using multidimensional separation of concerns to (re)shape evolving software," Communications of the ACM, 44(10):43–50, Oct. 2001.

[27] P. Tarr, H. Ossher, W. Harrison, and S. M. Sutton, Jr., "N degrees of separation: Multidimensional separation of concerns," Proc. ICSE, 1999.

An XML-Based Adaptive Multi-agent System for Handling E-commerce Activities

Pasquale De Meo[1], Domenico Rosaci[1], Giuseppe M.L. Sarnè[1], Giorgio Terracina[2], and Domenico Ursino[1]

[1] DIMET
Università Mediterranea di Reggio Calabria
Via Graziella, Località Feo di Vito, 89060 Reggio
Calabria, Italy
[2] Dipartimento di Matematica
Università della Calabria, Via Pietro Bucci
87036 Rende (CS), Italy
{demeo,domenico,sarne}@ing.unirc.it, terracina@mat.unical.it,
ursino@unirc.it

Abstract. In this paper we propose an XML-based adaptive multi-agent system for handling e-commerce activities. More specifically, our system aims at supporting a customer, visiting an e-commerce site, in the search of products and/or services present therein and appearing to be appealing according to her/his past interests and behaviour. The system is adaptive w.r.t. the profile of both the customer and the device she/he is exploiting for visiting the site. Finally, the system is XML-based since XML is exploited for both storing the agent ontologies and handling the agent communication.

1 Introduction

1.1 Motivations

In the last decade e-commerce has emerged as a significant, both social and cultural, phenomenon; indeed, many vendors provide their customers with the possibility to buy their products also by using the Internet; moreover, several trading companies exist carrying out their activity only via Web (e.g., Amazon).

Operations executed by a customer, whenever she/he buys a product or a service from an e-commerce site, can be usually grouped into two main activities, namely: *(i)* the exploitation of a Web search engine (such as Altavista or Google) for finding potentially interesting sites; *(ii)* the use of a Web browser for navigating through the pages of a site she/he judged interesting. While a large variety of tools already exists over the Internet for helping a customer in searching potentially interesting sites, only few applications are available for supporting the navigation through an interesting site.

Some of the most common of these applications are based on *recommender systems* [14,15]. These have been conceived for helping the customer of an e-

M. Jeckle and L.-J. Zhang (Eds.): ICWS-Europe 2003, LNCS 2853, pp. 152–166, 2003.
© Springer-Verlag Berlin Heidelberg 2003

commerce site in her/his purchase activity. In order to perform its tasks, a recommender system must process available data; this can be done by exploiting various computation tools such as cross-sell lists and information filters.

Another important tool available in a large number of e-commerce sites is a (usually rough) manager of customer profiles, exploited for proposing personalized offers. However, the profile construction methodology causes some problems. Indeed, it requires a customer to spend a certain amount of time for constructing and/or updating her/his profile; in addition, it stores only information about the issues which the customer claims to be interested in, without considering other issues somehow related to those just provided, possibly interesting her/him in the future and that she/he disregarded to take into account in the past.

In spite of recommender systems and customer profile managers, generally, when accessing an e-commerce site, a customer must personally search the issues of her/his interest through the site. We argue that, for improving the effectiveness of the e-commerce service, it is necessary to increase the interaction between the site and the customer, on the one hand, and to construct a rich profile of the customer, taking into account her/his desires, interests and behaviour, on the other hand.

In addition to this, it is necessary to take into account a further, important factor. Presently, many of the e-commerce sites, as well as many of the e-service providers, assume the visitor operates with a large color display and fast network connections. However, nowadays, electronic and telecommunications technology is rapidly evolving in such a way to allow cell phones, palmtops and wireless Personal Digital Assistants to navigate on the Web. These mobile devices do not have the same display or bandwidth capabilities as their desktop counterparts; nonetheless present e-service providers deliver the same content to all device typologies [1].

In order to overcome the problems outlined previously, some challenges must be tackled. First, a customer can access *many* e-commerce sites; a faithful and complete profile of her/him can be constructed only taking into account her/his behaviour on accessing all these sites. In other words, it should be possible to construct a *unique structure on the customer side*, storing her/his profile and, therefore, representing her/his behaviour on accessing *all these sites*.

Second, for a given customer and e-commerce site, it should be possible to compare the profile of the customer with the offers of the site for extracting those issues that probably will interest the customer. Existing techniques for satisfying such a requirement are mainly based on the exploitation of either log files [5, 17] or cookies [12]. Techniques based on *log files* are capable to register only some information about the actions carried out by the customer on accessing the site; however, they are not capable of matching customer preferences and site contents. Vice versa, techniques based on *cookies* are able to carry out a certain, even if primitive, matching; however they need to know and exploit some personal information that a customer might consider private.

Third, it should be necessary to overcome the typical "one-size-fits-all" philosophy of present e-service providers by developing systems capable of adapting their behaviour to both the profile of the user and the characteristics of the device she/he is exploiting for accessing them [2]. In the past, various approaches have been proposed for handling e-commerce activities. Some of them are based on traditional recommender systems [1]; other ones (e.g., *Firefly* [16], *Tete-a-Tete* [9], *WEBS* [10], *SETA* [4], *e-CoUSAL* [7]) have been designed in the context of the agent technology. These approaches construct, maintain and exploit a customer profile; therefore, we can consider them adaptive w.r.t. the customer; however, to the best of our knowledge, none of them is adaptive w.r.t. the device.

On the other side, in various computer science research fields, a large variety of approaches adapting their behaviour to the device that the user is exploiting, has been proposed [3,6]. These are particularly general and interesting; however, to the best of our knowledge, none of them has been conceived for handling e-commerce activities.

1.2   General Characteristics of the Approach

This paper aims at providing a contribution in this setting; indeed, it is an attempt to solve all the three problems mentioned previously. More specifically, it presents *ec-XAMAS* (e-commerce oriented XML-based Adaptive Multi-Agent System), a multi-agent system for handling e-commerce activities capable of adapting its behaviour to both user and device profiles. In *ec-XAMAS* an agent is present in each e-commerce site, handling the information stored therein, as well as the interaction with the customers. In addition, an agent is associated with each customer, adapting its behaviour to the profiles of both the customer and the device she/he is exploiting for visiting the sites.

Actually, since a customer can access an e-commerce site by different devices, her/his profile cannot be stored in only one of them; as a matter of fact, it is necessary to have a unique copy of the customer profile which registers her/his behaviour in visiting e-commerce sites during the various sessions, possibly carried out by means of different devices. For this reason the customer profile must be handled and stored in a support different from the devices generally exploited for accessing the sites. As a consequence, on the customer side, it appears compulsory the exploitation of a client-server multi-agent system consisting of: *(i)* a *server agent*, which stores the profiles of both involved customers and devices; *(ii)* a *client agent*, associated with a specific customer operating with a specific device, which supports the customer in her/his activities and is deactivated at the end of the session. We call *XAMAS* such a multi-agent, customer oriented, component of *ec-XAMAS*.

The previous description points out that three typologies of agents operate in *ec-XAMAS* for each navigation session, namely: *(i)* a *Site Agent*, associated with an e-commerce site; *(ii)* a *XAMAS Client* associated with a specific customer and a specific device, supporting the customer activities during a specific e-commerce session; *(iii)* a *XAMAS Server*, storing and handling both customer and device profiles.

Our approach constructs and maintains a profile for each customer; it stores information about the visits she/he carried out on e-commerce sites in the various sessions. Whenever a customer visits an e-commerce site, the *XAMAS*

Client and Server cooperate for updating her/his profile. As a consequence, for each customer, a *unique profile* is maintained, storing information about her/his behaviour in visiting *all e-commerce sites*. In this way, our approach solves the first problem mentioned above.

Whenever a customer accesses an e-commerce site, the corresponding agent sends its ontology to the *XAMAS* Client associated with the customer and the device she/he is exploiting. As it will be clear in the following, the site agent ontology stores information about available products and/or services. The *XAMAS* Client determines similarities between the products/services offered by the site and the interests of the customer. Each of these similarities represents an issue of interest for the customer offered by the e-commerce site. For each similarity, both the site agent and the *XAMAS* Client agent cooperate for presenting to the customer a group of Web pages illustrating the offers of the site appearing of interest for her/him.

We argue that this behaviour provides our model with the capability of supporting the customer in searching interesting products in the e-commerce sites. Moreover, as it will be clear in the following, the technique our approach uses for constructing the Web pages presented to the customer allows to determine not only information probably interesting for the customer but also other issues possibly interesting for her/him in the future and that she/he disregarded to take into account in the past. As previously pointed out, this is a particularly interesting feature for an approach devoted to deal with e-commerce services.

Last, but not the least, it is worth observing that, since *the customer profile management is carried out at the customer side*, no information about the customer profile is sent to the e-commerce site. In this way, *ec-XAMAS* solves privacy problems left open by cookies. All this reasoning allows us to claim that also the second problem introduced previously is solved by our approach.

As previously pointed out, in *ec-XAMAS*, the device profile plays a central role. Indeed, the Web pages of an e-commerce site presented to a customer, as well as their formats, depend on the characteristics of the device she/he is presently exploiting. However, the capability of *ec-XAMAS* of adapting its behaviour to the device the customer is exploiting is not restricted to the Web page visualization; indeed, the exploited device influences also the computation of the interest degree of a customer for the products and/or services available at each site. More specifically, as it will be clear in the following, one of the parameters, which the interest degree associated with a product/service is based on, is the time the customer spends in visiting the corresponding Web pages. This time is not to be considered as an absolute measure, but it must be normalized w.r.t. both the characteristics of the exploited device and the navigation costs. The following example allows to clarify this intuition. Assume that a user visits a Web page for two times and that each visit takes n seconds. Suppose, also, that during the first access she/he exploits a mobile phone having a low processor clock and supporting a connection characterized by a low bandwidth and a high cost. During the second occurrence, she/he uses a personal computer having a high processor clock and supporting a connection characterized by a high bandwidth and a low cost. It is possible to argue that the interest the user exhibited for the page in the former access is greater than that she/he exhibited in the latter one. Also other device parameters influence the behaviour of *ec-XAMAS*; they are illustrated below. All this reasoning allows us to argue that *ec-XAMAS* solves also the third problem mentioned above.

The previous description points out that, in *ec-XAMAS*, many agents are simultaneously active; they strongly interact each other and continuously exchange information. In this scenario, an efficient management of information exchange appears crucial. Actually, the efficiency in the information exchange management has become a challenging issue in most areas of computer science research, particularly for Web-based information systems. In this area, the most promising solution to this problem was the definition of XML, a novel language for representing and exchanging data over the Internet. XML embodies both representation capabilities, typical of HTML, and data management features, typical of DBMS's; it is presently considered as a standard for the Web. XML capabilities make it particularly suited to be exploited in the agent research; as a matter of fact, agents using XML for both representing and handling their own ontology have been already proposed in the literature [8]. In *ec-XAMAS* the role of XML is even more central since it is crucial for guaranteeing the management of an information base (e.g., the agent ontology) in devices characterized by limited bandwidth and processor clock (where traditional, generally resource-expensive, information source handlers cannot operate).

2   The ec-XAMAS Component Managing the Customer Activities

As previously pointed out, in the customer side of *ec-XAMAS* a client-server multi-agent system, called *XAMAS*, operates. In *XAMAS*, a *Client Agent* CA_{ij} is associated with a user U_j exploiting a device D_i; it supports U_j during her/his navigation activities carried out by means of D_i. Observe that more than one Client Agent can be associated with the same user, if she/he exploits different devices; analogously, more than one Client Agent can be associated with the same device, if it is exploited by different users.

A *Server Agent SA* stores and manages information about both user and device profiles; it supplies also a set of services to the clients.

2.1   The XAMAS Client Agent

A *XAMAS* Client Agent CA_{ij} is associated with a device D_i and a user U_j. It is activated at the beginning of a navigation session which U_j carries out by means of D_i; it supports U_j in the activities she/he performs during the session and is deactivated at the end of the session.

After its activation, CA_{ij} requires to the Server Agent SA the current profile UP_j of U_j and retrieves from D_i the device profile DP_i. It stores UP_j and DP_i in its own ontology and exploits them for supporting U_j in her/his navigation activity. In addition, it registers information about the behaviour of U_j during the session.

At the end of the session, CA_{ij} contacts SA and provides it with the collected information about the behaviour of U_j; such an information is exploited by SA for updating the profile of U_j in its own ontology.

Ontology

The ontology of CA_{ij} consists of a tuple $\langle DP_i, UP_j, VisitedC_{ij}, VisitedR_{ij} \rangle$, where DP_i indicates a Device Profile, UP_j is relative to a User Profile, $VisitedC_{ij}$ stores information about the concepts which U_j visited during the current session and $VisitedR_{ij}$ contains information about the relationships existing among concepts belonging to $VisitedC_{ij}$.

The Device Profile DP_i.

DP_i stores the characteristics of the device D_i. More specifically, a tuple $\langle DId_i, B_i, PPB_i, MIS_i, TE_i, AE_i, VE_i, PE_i, SE_i, PC_i \rangle$ is associated with D_i, where: *(i) DId_i* is the *Identifier* of D_i. *(ii) B_i* is the *Bandwidth* of D_i; it denotes the maximum bit rate guaranteed by D_i during the data transmission activities. *(iii) PPB_i* is the *Price Per Byte* of D_i; it indicates the cost for sending or receiving a byte of data by means of D_i. *(iv) MIS_i* is the *Max Item Size* of D_i; it denotes the maximum size that a Web page could have for being accessed by means of D_i. *(v) TE_i* (resp., AE_i, VE_i) is the *Text Enabled* (resp., *Audio Enabled, Video Enabled*) field of D_i; it indicates if D_i can handle a text (resp., an audio, a video). *(vi) PE_i* (resp., SE_i) is the *Printing Enabled* (resp., *Storage Enabled*) field; it denotes if D_i is capable of printing (resp., storing) data. *(vii) PC_i* is the *Processor Clock* of D_i; it denotes the CPU clock of D_i.

The User Profile UP_j.

UP_j can be described by a tuple $\langle UId_j, SCounter_j, CSet_j, RSet_j \rangle$. More specifically:

- UId_j is a code identifying U_j.
- $SCounter_j$ counts the number of sessions carried out by U_j.
- $CSet_j = \{C_1, C_2, \ldots, C_p\}$ is the set of concepts interesting for U_j. A tuple $\langle CId_l, Name_l, FVTS_l, LVTS_l, VC_l, ATI_l, PI_l, SI_l, IDegree_l \rangle$ is associated with each concept $C_l \in CSet_j$. Here:
  - CId_l is the *Identifier* of the concept C_l;
  - $Name_l$ is the *Name* of C_l;
  - $FVTS_l$ is the *First Visit Time Stamp* associated with C_l; it represents the first time instant in which some instance of C_l has been accessed;
  - $LVTS_l$ is the *Last Visit Time Stamp* relative to C_l; it indicates the time instant in which U_j concluded to visit the lastly accessed instance of C_l;
  - VC_l is the *Visit Counter* of C_l; it represents the total number of accesses to instances of C_l carried out by U_j;
  - ATI_l is the *Access Time Indicator* associated with C_l. As pointed out in the Introduction, our model takes into account that the user navigation is highly influenced by both the characteristics of the exploited device and the navigation costs. In particular, the time spent by the user in

accessing a concept is not to be considered as an absolute measure, but it is necessary to "normalize" it w.r.t. both the characteristics of the device she/he is exploiting and the navigation costs; ATI_l has been conceived for handling this aspect. More specifically, ATI_l is defined as: $ATI_l = \sum_{k=1}^{SCounter_j} \left(ATI_l^k\right)$, where ATI_l^k is the Access Time Indicator relative to the concept C_l in Session k. It is defined as $ATI_l^k = \frac{T_l^k \times PPB_i^k}{B_i^k \times PC_i^k}$, where T_l^k represents the time U_j spent for visiting instances of C_l during Session k whereas PPB_i^k, B_i^k and PC_i^k denote, respectively, the Price Per Bite, the Bandwidth and the Processor Clock relative to the device D_i exploited by U_j for visiting C_l during the kth Session.

- PI_l is the *Printing Indicator* associated with C_l. It is an indicator of the interest of U_j for C_l. Indeed, it assumes that if, during a session, U_j has a device capable of printing and does not print any instance of C_l, then U_j shows a low interest for C_l. PI_l can be computed as: $PI_l = \frac{\sum_{k=1}^{SCounter_j} PI_l^k}{SCounter_j}$, where PI_l^k is the Printing Indicator relative to the concept C_l in Session k. If PE_i^k indicates the *Printing Enabled* field of the device D_i exploited by U_j in Session k, PI_l^k can be defined as:

$$PI_l^k = \begin{cases} 0.5 & \text{if } PE_i^k = 0 \\ 1 & \text{if } PE_i^k = 1 \text{ and at least one instance of } C_l \text{ has been printed} \\ & \text{in Session } k \\ 0 & \text{if } PE_i^k = 1 \text{ and no instance of } C_l \text{ has been printed} \\ & \text{in Session } k \end{cases}$$

Observe that, if $PE_i^k = 0$, it is not possible to derive any information about the desire of U_j of printing an instance of C_l during Session k. This uncertainty is expressed by setting PI_l^k to 0.5.

- SI_l is the *Storage Indicator* associated with C_l. It is analogous to the *Printing Indicator* and can be computed as: $SI_l = \frac{\sum_{k=1}^{SCounter_j} SI_l^k}{SCounter_j}$, where:

$$SI_l^k = \begin{cases} 0.5 & \text{if } SE_i^k = 0 \\ 1 & \text{if } SE_i^k = 1 \text{ and at least one instance of } C_l \text{ has been stored} \\ & \text{in Session } k \\ 0 & \text{if } SE_i^k = 1 \text{ and no instance of } C_l \text{ has been stored} \\ & \text{in Session } k \end{cases}$$

Here, SE_i^k is the *Storage Enabled* field of the device D_i exploited by U_j during Session k.

- $IDegree_l$ denotes the *Degree of Interest* of U_j for C_l. In order to define a formula for computing $IDegree_l$ the following observations have been taken into account [6]: *(i)* The interest that a user shows for a concept C_l is strictly related to the time she/he spent for visiting the various instances of C_l. As a consequence, $IDegree_l$ is directly proportional to ATI_l. *(ii)* The interest of a user for a concept C_l grows with the growing of the number of accesses to the instances of C_l. Therefore, $IDegree_l$ is directly proportional to VC_l. *(iii)* The more remote (resp., recent) the First Visit Time Stamp (resp., the Last Visit Time Stamp) is, the higher the Interest Degree is. A good indicator of this intuition is given by the ratio $\frac{LVTS_l - FVTS_l}{TS - FVTS_l}$, where $FVTS_l$ (resp., $LVTS_l$) indicates the First Visit Time Stamp (resp., Last Visit Time Stamp) of C_l and TS denotes the current Time Stamp. *(iv)* The interest that a user shows for a concept C_l is directly proportional to both the Printing Indicator PI_l of C_l and the Storage Indicator SI_l of C_l.

From the considerations outlined above, we deduce that $IDegree_l$ can be computed as:

$$IDegree_l = ATI_l \times VC_l \times \left(\frac{LVTS_l - FVTS_l}{TS - FVTS_l} \right) \times PI_l \times SI_l$$

– $RSet_j$ represents the set of relationships existing among concepts belonging to $CSet_j$. In our model, a relationship R_{st} between two concepts C_s and C_t indicates that, in the past, U_j accessed an instance of C_t (*Target Concept*) via an hyperlink present in an instance of C_s (*Source Concept*). A tuple $\langle RId_{st}, C_s, C_t, TC_{st} \rangle$ is associated with each relationship $R_{st} \in RSet_j$. Here: *(i)* RId_{st} is the *Identifier* of the relationship R_{st}; *(ii)* C_s is the *Source Concept* of R_{st}; *(iii)* C_t is the *Target Concept* of R_{st}; *(iv)* TC_{st} is the *Transition Counter* of R_{st}; it specifies how many times an instance of C_t has been accessed via an instance of C_s.

The Set $VisitedC_{ij}$.

The set $VisitedC_{ij}$ stores information about the concepts which U_j visited during the current session. A tuple $\langle CId_l, Name_l, FVTS'_l, LVTS'_l, VC'_l, ATI'_l, PI'_l, SI'_l \rangle$ is associated with each concept $C_l \in VisitedC_{ij}$. The parameters $CId_l, Name_l$, $FVTS'_l, LVTS'_l$ and VC'_l are the same as those we have seen previously for concepts of $CSet_j$, whereas the parameters ATI'_l, PI'_l and SI'_l are analogous to the corresponding ones we have seen for concepts of $CSet_j$ except that they refer to one single session. In particular $ATI'_l = \frac{T_l \times PPB_i}{B_i \times PC_i}$, and

$$PI'_l = \begin{cases} 0.5 & \text{if } PE_i = 0 \\ 1 & \text{if } PE_i = 1 \text{ and at least one} \\ & \text{instance of } C_l \text{ has been} \\ & \text{printed in the current session} \\ 0 & \text{if } PE_i = 1 \text{ and no instance} \\ & \text{of } C_l \text{ has been printed} \\ & \text{in the current session} \end{cases} \quad SI'_l = \begin{cases} 0.5 & \text{if } SE_i = 0 \\ 1 & \text{if } SE_i = 1 \text{ and at least one} \\ & \text{instance of } C_l \text{ has been} \\ & \text{stored in the current session} \\ 0 & \text{if } SE_i = 1 \text{ and no instance} \\ & \text{of } C_l \text{ has been stored} \\ & \text{in the current session} \end{cases}$$

In the previous formulas, PPB_i, B_i, PC_i, PE_i and SE_i are the characteristics of the device D_i exploited by U_j in the current session, whereas T_l is the total time U_j spent in visiting instances of C_l in the current session.

The Set $VisitedR_{ij}$.

$VisitedR_{ij}$ contains information about the relationships existing among concepts belonging to $VisitedC_{ij}$. For each relationship $R_{st} \in VisitedR_{ij}$, a tuple $\langle RId_{st}, C_s, C_t, TC_{st} \rangle$ is defined; the parameters relative to the tuple are the same as those described previously for relationships of $RSet_j$.

In order to simplify the description of the ontology of CA_{ij}, we have represented it by means of abstract data structures, such as sets; however, as previously pointed out, it is actually stored as an XML document; its XML Schema is shown in Figure 1.

```
<?xml version="1.0" >
<xs:schema xmlns:xs="http://www.w3.org/2001/XMLSchema">
    <xs:simpleType name=''YesNoType''>
        <xs:restriction base=''xs:NMTOKEN''>
            <xs:enumeration value=''YES''/>
            <xs:enumeration value=''NO''/>
        </xs:restriction>
    </xs:simpleType>
    <xs:complexType name=''Device_ProfileType''>
        <xs:attribute name=''DeviceIdentifier''
            type=''xs:ID'' use=''required''/>
        <xs:attribute name=''Bandwidth''
            type=''xs:nonNegativeInteger'' use=''required''/>
        <xs:attribute name=''PricePerByte'' type=''xs:float''
            use=''required''/>
        <xs:attribute name=''MaxItemSize''
            type=''xs:nonNegativeInteger'' use=''required''/>
        <xs:attribute name=''TextEnabled'' type=''YesNoType''
            use=''required''/>
        <xs:attribute name=''AudioEnabled'' type=''YesNoType''
            use=''required''/>
        <xs:attribute name=''VideoEnabled'' type=''YesNoType''
            use=''required''/>
        <xs:attribute name=''PrintingEnabled''
            type=''YesNoType'' use=''required''/>
        <xs:attribute name=''StorageEnabled''
            type=''YesNoType'' use=''required''/>
        <xs:attribute name=''ProcessorClock''
            type=''xs:nonNegativeInteger'' use=''required''/>
    </xs:complexType>
    <xs:complexType name=''ConceptType''>
        <xs:attribute name=''ConceptIdentifier''
            type=''xs:ID'' use=''required''/>
        <xs:attribute name=''Name'' type=''xs:string''
            use=''required''/>
        <xs:attribute name=''FirstVisitTimeStamp''
            type=''xs:dateTime'' use=''required''/>
        <xs:attribute name=''LastVisitTimeStamp''
            type=''xs:dateTime'' use=''required''/>
        <xs:attribute name=''VisitCounter''
            type=''xs:nonNegativeInteger'' use=''required''/>
        <xs:attribute name=''AccessTimeIndicator''
            type=''xs:float'' use=''required''/>
        <xs:attribute name=''PrintingIndicator''
            type=''xs:float'' use=''required''/>
        <xs:attribute name=''StorageIndicator''
            type=''xs:float'' use=''required''/>
        <xs:attribute name=''InterestDegree''
            type=''xs:float''/>
    </xs:complexType>
    <xs:complexType name=''RelationshipType''>
        <xs:simpleContent>

            <xs:extension base=''xs:string''>
                <xs:attribute name=''RelationshipIdentifier''
                    type=''xs:ID'' use=''required''/>
                <xs:attribute name=''Source'' type=''xs:IDREF''
                    use=''required''/>
                <xs:attribute name=''Target'' type=''xs:IDREF''
                    use=''required''/>
                <xs:attribute name=''TransitionCounter''
                    type=''xs:nonNegativeInteger'' use=''required''/>
            </xs:extension>
        </xs:simpleContent>
    </xs:complexType>
    <xs:complexType name=''User_ProfileType''>
        <xs:sequence>
            <xs:element name=''Concept'' type=''ConceptType''
                minOccurs=''0'' maxOccurs=''unbounded''/>
            <xs:element name=''Relationship''
                type=''RelationshipType'' minOccurs=''0''
                maxOccurs=''unbounded''/>
        </xs:sequence>
        <xs:attribute name=''UserIdentifier'' type=''xs:ID''
            use=''required''/>
        <xs:attribute name=''SessionCounter''
            type=''xs:nonNegativeInteger'' use=''required''/>
    </xs:complexType>
    <xs:complexType name=''Visited_CType''>
        <xs:sequence>
            <xs:element name=''Concept'' type=''ConceptType''
                minOccurs=''0'' maxOccurs=''unbounded''/>
        </xs:sequence>
    </xs:complexType>
    <xs:complexType name=''Visited_RType''>
        <xs:sequence>
            <xs:element name=''Relationship''
                type=''RelationshipType'' minOccurs=''0''
                maxOccurs=''unbounded''/>
        </xs:sequence>
    </xs:complexType>
    <xs:element name=''XAMAS-Client-Ontology''>
        <xs:complexType>
            <xs:sequence>
                <xs:element name=''Device_Profile''
                    type=''Device_ProfileType''/>
                <xs:element name=''User_Profile''
                    type=''User_ProfileType''/>
                <xs:element name=''Visited_C''
                    type=''Visited_CType''/>
                <xs:element name=''Visited_R''
                    type=''Visited_RType''/>
            </xs:sequence>
        </xs:complexType>
    </xs:element>
</xs:schema>
```

Fig. 1. The XML Schema of a *XAMAS* Client

Behaviour

The behaviour of CA_{ij} consists of five steps:

Step 1. It derives the profile of D_i from D_i itself and stores it in its ontology.

Step 2. It contacts the Server Agent SA for obtaining the profile of U_j. If U_j is already registered in its current ontology, SA returns the current UP_j. Otherwise, SA registers U_j in its ontology, creates an empty UP_j and returns it to CA_{ij}. CA_{ij} stores in its ontology the profile of U_j, as returned by SA.

Step 3. It exploits information stored in its ontology for supporting U_j in her/his activities; in other words, it must be capable of recommending U_j, acting as a Content Based Recommender System [1]; this task is presented in Section 3. It is worth pointing out again that, differently from most of the Recommender Systems already proposed in the literature, CA_{ij} takes into account the device exploited by the user for the navigation and, therefore, it adapts its suggestions also to the characteristics of the device.

Step 4. It monitors U_j in her/his activities during the whole session and stores in its ontology information about the sets of concepts and relationships she/he visited. In particular, assume that U_j accesses a concept C_t via a concept C_s. Assume, also, that the *First Visit Time Stamp*, the *Last Visit Time Stamp*, the *Access Time Indicator*, the *Printing Indicator* and the *Storage Indicator* associated with C_t are $FVTS_t$, $LVTS_t$, ATI_t, PI_t and SI_t. First CA_{ij} must verify if C_t is already present in $VisitedC_{ij}$. Assume that C_t is already present in $VisitedC_{ij}$ where it is associated with the tuple $\langle CId_t, Name_t, FVTS^*, LVTS^*, VC^*, ATI^*, PI^*, SI^* \rangle$, then, CA_{ij} must set $LVTS^* = LVTS_t$, $VC^* = VC^* + 1$, $ATI^* = ATI^* + ATI_t$, $PI^* = max(PI^*, PI_t)$, $SI^* = max(SI^*, SI_t)$. If C_t is not already present in $VisitedC_{ij}$, CA_{ij} must insert C_t, along with the tuple $\langle CId_t, Name_t, FVTS_t, LVTS_t, 1, ATI_t, PI_t, SI_t \rangle$, into $VisitedC_{ij}$. If a relationship R_{st} connecting C_s to C_t, characterized by the tuple $\langle RId_{st}, C_s, C_t, TC_{st} \rangle$, already exists in $VisitedR_{ij}$, CA_{ij} must increment TC_{st} of one unit. Vice versa, if no relationship from C_s to C_t exists in $VisitedR_{ij}$, then the tuple $\langle RId_{st}, C_s, C_t, 1 \rangle$ must be inserted into $VisitedR_{ij}$.

Step 5. At the end of the session, CA_{ij} contacts SA and provides it with UId_j, DP_i, $VisitedC_{ij}$ and $VisitedR_{ij}$.

2.2   The XAMAS Server Agent

The *XAMAS Server Agent SA* is always active. It stores the profiles of users exploiting the system as well as the profiles of available devices. It is capable of performing the following tasks: *(i)* insertion, deletion and update of a user profile; *(ii)* insertion, deletion and update of a device profile; *(iii)* information exchange with the *XAMAS* Client Agents.

Ontology
The ontology of SA consists of a pair $\langle DPSet, UPSet \rangle$, where $DPSet$ is a set of Device Profiles and $UPSet$ is a set of user profiles. More specifically:

- $DPSet = \{DP_1, DP_2, \ldots, DP_n\}$ where DP_i is the profile of the device D_i. DP_i stores information describing the characteristics of the device D_i. A tuple $\langle DId_i, B_i, PPB_i, MIS_i, TE_i, AE_i, VE_i, PE_i, SE_i, PC_i \rangle$ is associated with a Device Profile DP_i. The components of this tuple have the same semantics as those introduced in Section 2.1.
- $UPSet = \{UP_1, UP_2, \ldots, UP_n\}$, where UP_j is the profile of the user U_j. UP_j can be described by a tuple $\langle UId_j, SCounter_j, CSet_j, RSet_j \rangle$ where UId_j, $SCounter_j$, $CSet_j$ and $RSet_j$ have the same structure and semantics as the corresponding ones described in Section 2.1.

As for the Client Agent ontology, also the Server Agent ontology is stored as an XML document; the corresponding XML Schema is similar to that shown in Figure 1; we do not show it for space limitations.

Behaviour

The Server Agent SA can be contacted by a Client Agent CA_{ij} at the beginning of a navigation session for obtaining the profile of the associated user U_j. If U_j is already registered in the ontology of SA, it returns the current profile of U_j to CA_{ij}. Otherwise, SA first registers U_j in its ontology, associates an identifier UId_j and an empty profile UP_j with her/him, and returns both UId_j and UP_j to CA_{ij}.

SA is contacted also by CA_{ij} at the end of a navigation session; in this case, CA_{ij} provides SA with $DP_i, UId_j, VisitedC_{ij}$ and $VisitedR_{ij}$; SA must update its ontology accordingly. More specifically, first SA examines DP_i. If this profile is already stored in its ontology and some of its parameters have been changed, SA must carry out the suitable updates. Otherwise, if DP_i is not already present in its ontology, SA must insert it into $DPSet$.

After this, SA must update information about UP_j. First it examines all concepts in $VisitedC_{ij}$. Let C_t be one of them and let
$\langle CId_t, Name_t, FVTS_t, LVTS_t, VC_t, ATI_t, PI_t, SI_t \rangle$ be the corresponding tuple. Assume that also C_t belongs to $CSet_j$; let
$\langle CId_t, Name_t, FVTS^*, LVTS^*, VC^*, ATI^*, PI^*, SI^*, IDegree^* \rangle$ be the tuple associated with C_t in $CSet_j$ and let $SCounter_j$ be the current number of sessions carried out by U_j. Then, SA sets $LSVT^* = LSVT_t$, $VC^* = VC^* + VC_t$,
$ATI^* = ATI^* + ATI_t$, $PI^* = \frac{PI^* \times SCounter_j + PI_t}{SCounter_j + 1}$, $SI^* = \frac{SI^* \times SCounter_j + SI_t}{SCounter_j + 1}$,
$IDegree^* = ATI^* \times VC^* \times \left(\frac{LVTS^* - FVTS^*}{TS - FVTS^*} \right) \times PI^* \times SI^*$.

Vice versa, if C_t does not belong to $CSet_j$ then it, and the corresponding tuple in $VisitedC_{ij}$, must be inserted into $CSet_j$.

After all concepts of $VisitedC_{ij}$ have been examined, SA processes $VisitedR_{ij}$. Let R_{st} be a relationship of $VisitedR_{ij}$ and let $\langle RId_{st}, C_s, C_t, TC_{st} \rangle$ be its corresponding tuple. Assume that a relationship R_{st}^* from C_s to C_t exists in $RSet_j$ and let $\langle RId_{st}^*, C_s, C_t, TC_{st}^* \rangle$ be the corresponding tuple. In this case, SA must set $TC_{st}^* = TC_{st}^* + TC_{st}$. Vice versa, if no relationship exists in $RSet_j$ from C_s to C_t then SA inserts R_{st}^*, along with the corresponding tuple, into $RSet_j$. Finally, the *Session Counter* of U_j is incremented of one unit.

After SA has examined both $VisitedC_{ij}$ and $VisitedR_{ij}$, it must carry out a pruning activity in order to avoid UP_j to undefinitely increase. The pruning policy implemented by SA is the following. A concept C_l can be pruned from UP_j if it has been not particularly interesting for U_j in the nearest past and appears to be not particularly interesting for her/him in the future.

A concept C_l is considered not particularly interesting for the user in the nearest past if, in UP_j, $IDegree_l$ is smaller than a certain threshold th_{Int}.

A concept C_l is considered not particularly interesting for the user in the future if the "distance" between C_l and each of the interesting concepts present in UP_j is greater than th_{Int}. The notion of "distance" between two concepts C' and C'' is defined as follows. Consider a graph G_{UP_j} such that: (i) each concept in UP_j is represented by a node in G_{UP_j}; (ii) each relationship R_{st} from C_s to C_t is represented by an arc from the node corresponding to C_s to the node corresponding to C_t in G_{UP_j}. The distance between two concepts C' and C'' is the length of the minimum path in G_{UP_j} from the node corresponding to C' to the node corresponding to C''.

Clearly, if a concept is pruned from UP_j, all relationships involving it are pruned from UP_j too.

3   The ec-XAMAS Component Managing the E-commerce Site Activities

As previously pointed out, in the *ec-XAMAS* platform, an agent is present in each e-commerce site, handling the information stored therein, as well as the interaction with the customers. In the next sub-sections we examine its ontology and behaviour.

3.1   Ontology

The ontology of the site agent stores the content of the corresponding site and can be represented as a set of concepts and a set of relationships among concepts. It is worth pointing out that such a kind of representation is general and valid for each typology of sites (e.g., e-commerce, e-learning, e-government) and representation formats (e.g., relational databases interfaced with HTML, XML). In the e-commerce context we are considering in this paper, a concept can be specialized into "product/service typology" and, therefore, relationships among concepts represent relationships existing among product/service typologies[1]. Analogously to the other agents we have introduced previously, also the ontology of the Site Agent is stored as an XML document. However, due to space constraints we do not show it.

In particular, each concept C_l is associated with a tuple $\langle CId_l, Name_l, MaxS_l, DT_l \rangle$, where CId_l is the identifier of the concept C_l, $Name_l$ is its name, $MaxS_l$ is the maximum size (in bytes) that a Web page describing the product/service typology corresponding to the concept might have, and DT_l indicates the Data Type of C_l, i.e., it denotes whether C_l is represented as a text, an audio or a video in the site. Analogously, each relationship R_{st} is associated with a tuple $\langle RId_{st}, C_s, C_t \rangle$, where RId_{st} is the identifier of R_{st}, C_s is the source concept and C_t is the target concept. There is a relationship from C_s to C_t if, in the Web page describing C_s, there is at least one link to the Web page describing C_t.

The ontology of the Site Agent is created when the corresponding site is made available over the Internet; such a task is carried out by a software module which examines the site and constructs the catalogue of both the available product typologies and their relationships. The same software module is activated also for suitably modifying the ontology whenever a concept is either created or removed or updated in the corresponding site.

---

[1] Clearly, in an e-commerce context, also concepts stored in the customer profile of *XAMAS* Clients and server represent product typologies and, consequently, the consistency of our model is guaranteed.

3.2   Behaviour

We are now able to examine the bahaviour of the Site Agent and, more in general, of the whole *ec-XAMAS* platform.

Let $CustSet = \{c_1, c_2, \ldots, c_n\}$ be a set of customers and let $SiteSet = \{s_1, s_2, \ldots, s_m\}$ be a set of e-commerce sites; assume that each customer of $CustSet$ and each site of $SiteSet$ have an associated agent and let $CustAgSet = \{CustAg_1, \ldots, CustAg_n\}$ and $SiteAgSet = \{SiteAg_1, \ldots, SiteAg_m\}$ be the sets of these agents.

Each $CustAg_p$ is a *XAMAS* Client; in particular, if, during a session, a customer c_j is exploiting a device D_i for carrying out her/his e-commerce activities, $CustAg_p$ is a *XAMAS* Client CA_{ij}. Such an architecture leads to the following consequences: *(i)* if, in different sessions, a customer exploits different devices for navigation, then different *XAMAS* Clients are associated with her/him; *(ii)* all involved customers and devices are registered in a *XAMAS* Server SA.

Let c_p be a customer and let s_q be an e-commerce site. We assume that a Customer Agent $CustAg_p$ (resp., a Site Agent $SiteAg_q$) is associated with c_p (resp., s_q) and that the ontology of $CustAg_p$ (resp., $SiteAg_q$) is stored in the XML document $XOnt_p$ (resp., $XOnt_q$).

For each visit of c_p to s_q, the following four steps are carried out:

Step 1. $SiteAg_q$ sends to $CustAg_p$ a copy of $XOnt_q$. Note that the choice to exploit XML for handling both agent ontologies and agent communications makes sending an ontology from an agent to another one extremely simple and direct.

Step 2. When $CustAg_p$ receives $XOnt_q$, it selects the subset CS of the concepts stored therein appearing to be interesting for c_p, according to her/his profile. More specifically, each concept C_l, such that it, or one of its synonyms, is also in $XOnt_p$, is inserted into CS^2. For each relationship $\langle RId_{st}, C_s, C_t \rangle$ of $XOnt_q$ such that C_s, or one of its synonyms, belongs to $XOnt_p$, C_t is added to CS. In this way, CS captures not only the concepts that could be appealing to c_p, according to her/his past interests, but also related concepts that could interest c_p in the future and whose existence she/he possibly ignored.

After this, each concept C_l in CS is ranked, i.e., a coefficient $Rank_l$ is associated with it. $Rank_l$ indicates how much C_l could be of interest for c_p; it takes into account both the previous interest degree c_p has shown for C_l and the device D she/he is exploiting in the current session. Assume that the tuple $\langle DId, B, PPB, MIS, TE, AE, VE, PE, SE, PC \rangle$ describes D in $XOnt_p$. Assume, moreover, that the tuple $\langle CId_l, C_l, MaxS_l, DT_l \rangle$ is associated with C_l in $XOnt_q$ and that $IDegree_l$ is the Interest Degree of the user for C_l, stored in the profile of c_p (if neither C_l nor one of its synonyms are present in $XOnt_p$, $IDegree_l$ is set to 0). $Rank_l$ is computed as follows:

$$Rank_l = DTCoeff(DT_l, TE, AE, VE) \times (1 + IDegree_l) \times \frac{B \times PC}{MaxS_l \times PPB}$$

where,

---

² In order to obtain concept synonymies $CustAg_p$ exploits existing tools such as *WordNet* [11] or *MindNet* [13].

$$DTCoeff(DT_l, TE, AE, VE) = \begin{cases} 0 \text{ if } DT_l = \texttt{TEXT} \text{ (resp., } \texttt{AUDIO, VIDEO)} \\ \quad \text{and } TE = 0 \text{ (resp., } AE = 0, VE = 0) \\ 1 \text{ otherwise} \end{cases}$$

Here, $DTCoeff$ is a coefficient indicating if the data type associated with the concept C_l can be processed by the device D which c_p is exploiting. The term $\frac{B \times PC}{MaxS_l \times PPB}$ is a coefficient which measures the capability of D in downloading and handling instances of C_l.

After a rank has been associated with each concept of CS, $CustAg_p$ sends the ranked CS to $SiteAg_q$.

Step 3. $SiteAg_q$ selects only the portions of the associated e-commerce site containing instances of the concepts stored in CS and sends them to $CustAg_p$.

Step 4. $CustAg_p$ visualizes them to c_p in order to let her/him to carry out her/his choices; the visualization policy takes into account the ranking of the concepts in CS. Whenever c_p makes a choice, and therefore accesses a concept stored in s_q, her/his profile is updated, according to the technique illustrated in Section 2.1, for registering this event.

4   Conclusions

In this paper we have proposed *ec-XAMAS*, an XML-based and adaptive multi-agent system for supporting a customer, visiting an e-commerce site, in the search of products and/or services present therein and appearing to be appealing according to her/his past interests and behaviour.

We have seen that, in *ec-XAMAS*, three typologies of agents are present, namely: *(i)* a *Client Agent*, associated with a specific customer, operating on a specific device, which supports her/him during a navigation session; *(ii)* a *Server Agent*, which stores the profiles of both the involved customers and devices; *(iii)* a *Site Agent*, associated with an e-commerce site, which handles both the information stored therein and the interaction with the customers.

We have shown that *ec-XAMAS* is adaptive w.r.t. the profile of both the customer and the device she/he is exploiting for visiting the site. Finally, we have seen that it is XML-based since XML is exploited for both storing the agent ontologies and handling the agent communication.

As for future work, we plan to study the possibility to enrich the proposed multi-agent model with other features capable of improving its effectiveness and completeness in supporting the various activities related to e-commerce. As an example, it may be interesting to categorize involved customers on the basis of their profiles, as well as involved e-commerce sites on the basis of their contents.

We plan also to make the proposed model even more adaptive by considering the possibility to adapt its behaviour on the basis not only of the device a customer is exploiting during a navigation session but also of the context (e.g., job, holidays) in which she/he is operating.

Acknowledgment. This work was partially funded by the Information Society Technologies programme of the European Commission, Future and Emerging Technologies under the IST-2001-33570 INFOMIX project and the IST-2001-37004 WASP project.

References

1. Communications of ACM, "Recommender Systems". volume 40(3). ACM, 1997.
2. Communications of ACM, "Adaptive Web". volume 45(5). ACM, 2002.
3. C. R. Anderson, P. Domingos, and D. S. Weld. Adaptive web navigation for wireless devices. In *Proc. of the Seventeenth International Joint Conference on Artificial Intelligence (IJCAI 2001)*, pages 879–884, Seattle, Washington, USA, 2001. Morgan Kaufmann.
4. L. Ardissono, A. Goy, G. Petrone, M. Segnan, L. Console, L. Lesmo, C. Simone, and P. Torasso. Agent technologies for the development of adaptive web stores. In *Agent Mediated Electronic Commerce, The European AgentLink Perspective*, pages 194–213. Lecture Notes in Computer Science, Springer-Verlag, 2001.
5. A.G. Buchner and M.D. Mulvenna. Discovering internet marketing intelligence through online analytical web usage mining. *SIGMOD Record*, 27(4): 54–61, 1998.
6. P.K. Chan. A non-invasive learning approach to building web user profiles. In *Proc. of KDD-99 Workshop on Web Usage Analysis and User Profiling (WebKDD'99)*, pages 7–12, San Diego, California, USA, 1999. Lecture Notes in Computer Science, Springer.
7. F.J. Garcia, F. Paternò, and A.B. Gil. An adaptive e-commerce system definition. In *Proc. of International Conference on Adaptive Hypermedia and Adaptive Web-Based Systems (AH'02)*, pages 505–509, Malaga, Spain, 2002. Lecture Notes in Computer Science, Springer-Verlag.
8. R.J. Glushko, J.M. Tenenbaum, and B. Meltzer. An xml framework for agent-based e-commerce. *Communications of the ACM*, 42(3): 106–114, 1999.
9. R.H. Guttman, A.G. Moukas, and P.Maes. Agent-mediated electronic commerce: A survey. *Knowledge Engineering Review*, 13(2): 147–159, 1998.
10. R. Lau, A. Hofstede, and P. Bruza. Adaptive profiling agents for electronic commerce. In *Proc. of the CollECTeR Conference on Electronic Commerce (CollECTeR 2000)*, Breckenridge, Colorado, USA, 2000.
11. A.G. Miller. WordNet: A lexical database for English. *Communications of the ACM*, 38(11): 39–41, 1995.
12. J.S. Park and R.S. Sandhu. Secure cookies on the web. *IEEE Internet Computing*, 4(4): 36–44, 2000.
13. S.D. Richardson, W.B. Dolan, and L. Vanderwende. MindNet: acquiring and structuring semantic information from text. In *Proc. of International Conference on Computational Linguistics (COLING-ACL'98)*, pages 1098–1102, Montreal, Quebec, Canada, 1998. Morgan Kaufmann.
14. B.M. Sarwar, G. Karypis, J.A. Konstan, and J. Riedl. Analysis of recommendation algorithms for e-commerce. In *Proc. of ACM Conference on Electronic Commerce (EC-00)*, pages 158–167, Minneapolis, Minnesota, USA, 2000. ACM Press.
15. J.B. Schafer, J.A. Konstan, and J. Riedl. E-commerce recommendation applications. *Data Mining and Knowledge Discovery*, 5(1-2): 115–153, 2001.
16. U. Shardanand and P. Maes. Social information filtering: Algorithms for automating "word of mouth". In *Proc. of the Computer-Human Interaction Conference (CHI'95)*, pages 210–217, Denver, Colorado, 1995. Addison-Wesley.
17. O.R. Zaiane, M. Xin, and J. Han. Discovering web access patterns and trends by applying OLAP and data mining technology on web logs. In *Proc. of the IEEE Forum on Reasearch and Technology Advances in Digital Libraries (ADL'98)*, pages 19–29, Santa Barbara, California, USA, 1998. IEEE Computer Society.

Towards Agent-Based Rational Service Composition – RACING Approach

Vadim Ermolayev, Natalya Keberle, and Sergey Plaksin

Dept. of Mathematical Modeling and IT, Zaporozhye State Univ.,
66, Zhukovskogo st., 69063, Zaporozhye, Ukraine
{eva,kenga,psl}@zsu.zp.ua

Abstract. Presented is the vision of the authors on how diverse web services may be composed, mediated by dynamic task coalitions of agents performing tasks for service requestors. The focus and the contribution of the paper is the proposal of the layered web service mediation architecture. Middle Agent Layer is introduced to conduct service request to task transformation, agent-enabled cooperative task decomposition and performance. Presented are the formal means to arrange agents' negotiation, to represent the semantic structure of task-activity-service hierarchy and to assess fellow-agents' capabilities and credibility factors. Finally, it is argued that the presented formal technique is applicable to various application domains. Presented is the ongoing work on building agent-based layered architecture for intelligent rational information and document retrieval mediation in frame of the RACING[1] project.

1 Introduction

Web services are the emerging technology promising to become one of the future key enablers of the Semantic Web. There are strong prerequisites that, being self-described and self-contained modular active components, web services will appear to be the key elements in assembling intelligent infrastructures for e-Business in the near future.

There is the emerging consensus that the ultimate challenge is to make web services automatically tradable and usable by artificial agents in their rational, pro-active interoperation on the next generation of the Web. It may be solved by creating effective frameworks, standards and software for automatic web service discovery, execution, composition, interoperation and monitoring [1]. Personal opinion of the authors is that the list should be extended by the means for making services the subject of automated negotiation and trade. It is also important for future service enabled web infrastructures to cope with business rules[2], notions and mechanisms of reputation and

---

[1]RACING: Rational Agent Coalitions for Intelligent Mediation of Information Retrieval on the Net. Project funded by Ukrainian Ministry of Education and Science. http://www.zsu.zp.ua/racing/
[2]International Workshop on Rule Markup Languages for Business Rules on the Semantic Web, 14 June 2002, Sardinia (Italy) http://tmitwww.tm.tue.nl/staff/gwagner/RuleML-BR-SW.html
Diffuse: Guide to Web Services http://www.diffuse.org/WebServices.html

M. Jeckle and L.-J. Zhang (Eds.): ICWS-Europe 2003, LNCS 2853, pp. 167–182, 2003.
© Springer-Verlag Berlin Heidelberg 2003

trust with respect to services and service providing agents, dynamic character, flexi-bility, reconfigurability of partial plans [2], workflows, modeled business processes.

Current industry landscape provides only initial and very partial solutions of the ultimate problem. Existing de-facto standards for web service description (WSDL [3]), publication, registration and discovery (UDDI [4]), binding, invocation, commu-nication (SOAP [5]) provide merely syntactical capabilities and unfortunately do not really cope with service semantics. Known industrial implementations such as HP E-speak [6] base on these standards and do not completely solve the challenge of se-mantic service interoperability. It should be mentioned that major industrial players realize the necessity of further targeted joint research and development in the field [7].

More recent research and standardization activities of DARPA DAML community resulted in offering semantic service markup language DAML-S [8] based on RDF platform. The constellation of XML based languages/ontologies for business process, logistics description is also expanding: WSFL, ebXML, BPML, RuleML, ...

The goal of the paper is to determine what should be still done on the top of recent research accomplishments in order to achieve the ultimate goal: to make web services automatically tradable and usable by artificial agents in their rational, pro-active in-teroperation on the next generation of the Web. Conceptual frames for this develop-ment are under intensive discussion and some proposals already appear (e.g., WSMF [9]).

The paper offers a new understanding of a service as an agent capability imple-mented as a self-contained software component. From the other hand, provided that agents negotiate and trade exchanging services in the process of their cooperative activities in open organizations, a service may be considered (as, say, in E-speak) a kind of a generalized resource. This approach evidently implies the appearance of the rational service providing agent demanding certain incentive and aiming to increase its utility. If, for example, a service requested from a travel agency is 'BookRound-trip('Kiev', 'Erfurt', 22/09/2003, 25/09/2003, ...)', the price paid by the requestor will com-prise the prices of consumable [10] resources (air fare, hotel room, ...) plus the in-centive paid to the service holder for 'BookRoundtrip' service component usage. This remark seems to be rational as far we are paying either salary to a secretary or a fee to a travel agent, who makes travel arrangements for us in human-business environment. Moreover, it is not in the eye of the service requestor, but the agent performing 'Book-Roundtrip' service will realize according to the service markup (or the Partial Local Plan (PLP) in our terminology [11]) that the requested process [10] (or the task in our terminology [11]) is composite and will require cooperation with at least Air Compa-nies' service providing agents and hotel booking service providing agents. These independent actors will evidently also intend to increase their own utilities by re-questing fees for service usage.

Detailed discussion of this popular travel planning scenario in Section 2 helps to claim that full-scale web service exploitation in e-Business environment needs solu-tions beyond the facilities of today's semantic service markup. The paper focuses on one of the major open problems – dynamic composition of a desired complex service by a coalition of rational cooperative independent agents.

The authors consider that it is a reasonable architectural solution to introduce an Agent Middle Layer (e.g., [12]) between services and service consumers. Negotiation on web service allocation based on the authors' approach [2] is proposed as the mechanism for dynamic composite service formation. DAML-S[10], our Task and Negotiation ontologies [11] are used for service dynamic composition and to facilitate to inter-agent-operability.

Finally, it is described how the approach to dynamic agent-based service composition is applied to intelligent rational information retrieval from distributed autonomous resources – our RACING project.

2 Travel Planning Scenario

Let's consider the mentioned travel planning scenario having in mind that our intentions have become true and web services are available at the desired level of semantic interoperation. The authors have played the following exercise assuming themselves as "intelligent software agents" participating in cooperative execution of a conference trip planning task (Fig. 1.). Each agent possessed his/her beliefs about the environment and capabilities in performing one or another activity related to the overall high-level goal achievement – 'BookRoundtrip("Kiev, Ukraine", "Erfurt, Germany", 22/09/2003, 25/09/2003, "ICWS'03-Europe", ...)'. Agents' capabilities were: their knowledge of relevant websites providing human-oriented services and their ability to operate these services via web interfaces. Agent roles were:

- AUTHOR (A) – an agent representing one of the paper authors intending to attend ICWS'03-Europe and requesting 'BookRoundtrip' service
- TRAVEL AGENT (T) – an agent actually providing 'BookRoundtrip' service by generating and conducting corresponding task execution
- FARE AGENT (F) – agents providing various air fare information and booking services
- ICWS INFO (I) – an agent providing information services on ICWS'03-Europe local arrangements, infrastructure, accommodation, etc in Erfurt
- HOTEL AGENT (H) – agents providing hotel room reservation services
- BUSINESS PARTNER (P) – an agent representing A's business partner in Austria with whom A intends to meet in Germany in time of the conference to discuss a joint proposal

As usual in travel planning an A is capable just to invoke a T with 'BookRoundtrip' task, to formulate his constraints, preferences and needs for special arrangements, to approve solutions proposed by the T. According to 'BookRoundtrip' description in terms of *Task Ontology* [11] known both to A and T (but with different granularity) service inputs are[3]:

```
Starting_Point= "Kiev, Ukraine"
Destination="Erfurt, Germany"
Beg_Date =22/09/2003
End_Date=25/09/2003
```

---

[3] Service inputs are given semi-formally in order to avoid unnecessary details and save the paper space.

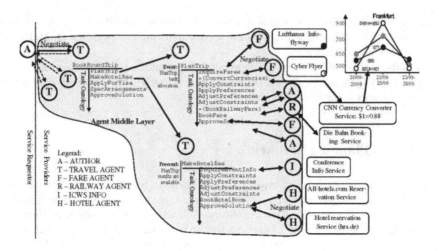

Fig. 1. "BookRoundTrip" task execution and service composition

```
Event="ICWS'03-Europe"
Preferences=("low fare, fast connections", "4-star ho-
tel, continental breakfast, conference discounts")
Constraints=(Budget = €1500,Payment=(VISA, USD),
Hotel >= 3-star, Room-per-night <= €110, Ho-
tel_Location="in Max 20 min walk from the Conference
venue")
Special_Arrangements=((Event="business dinner",
Agent = ("Prof. Heinrich C. Mayr", http://www.ifi.uni-
klu.ac.at/IWAS/HM/Staff/Heinrich.Mayr/),
Date=(23/09/2003-24/09/2003), Location=(Erfurt, Mu-
nich)),…)
```

The process starts with the arrangement [2] A undertakes to hire one of T-s as the contractor for the job. The flow of round trip booking, T performs for A, is presented on Fig. 1. At first T accepts the task from A by means of agents' communication inter-face. This interface may be built upon ACL [13] for FIPA[4]-compliant agents (Appendix A-1[5]). T than uses its beliefs on how to 'BookRoundtrip'(Appendix A-2), formalized according to the *Task Ontology* (Appendix A-6), to derive that the accepted task is complex and involves at least 'PlanTrip', 'MakeHotelRes', 'ApplyForVisa', 'SpecArrange-ments' and 'ApproveSolution' activities. 'PlanTrip' activity is chosen (PLP of Task Ontol-ogy [11]) the first to be performed and appears to be also a complex task: 'Inquire-Fares', 'ApplyConstraints', ..., 'BookFare', 'ApproveSolution'. Before allocating Fare In-quiry to F-s T 'notices' that a slight change in the starting or ending date of the trip

---

[4] Foundation for Intelligent Physical Agents, http://www.fipa.org/, last accessed on Apr. 24, 2003.

[5] Appendixes A-1 – A-7 may be downloaded from http://eva.zsu.zp.ua/services/app.htm.

may result in a substantial decrease in the airfare expenses because of the Sunday Rule discounts[6] commonly offered by Air Companies.

For our example this means to T that the dates 20/09-25/09 and 22/09-28/09 should be also rationally considered for the trip. T negotiates these input changes with A asking A to provide desirability values for these dates (Fig. 2 – gray dots) indicating max price A is ready to pay for the fare within the specified dates. Requirements, T specifies for 'InquireFares' service, are thus slightly changed by introducing the list of date pairs for which the service should be performed. Contract Net negotiation is than initiated by T having F-s as participants.

F-s propositions,[7] resulting from 'InquireFares' service execution, are also given on Fig. 2. These results cause the necessity to use one more service, which was not initially planned by T's PLP for the task. As far as the offers are provided in different currencies T needs to change the task and require the service for currency conversion[8] (+('ConvertCurrencies', Appendix A-3), Fig. 1). Conversion results are presented on Fig. 2. It is now easy for T to derive that the acceptable proposition is still for the dates 22/09-25/09, but with the destination at Frankfurt (not at Erfurt), which were not initial 'BookRoundtrip' task inputs from A. However, this result comply with A's preferences as far as there are non-stop flights available from Kiev to Frankfurt (but not to Erfurt and Munich). This implies the necessity for T to 'AdjustPreferences' by inquiring A's service. The mechanism may be similar to inputs negotiation discussed above and the outcomes may cause the invocation of some new activities, e.g., change to a train at Frankfurt-Main Airport – inquire the 'BookRailwayFare' service from Die Bahn[9] Agent. Discussion of these emerging task branches is omitted, as far it is conceptually similar to that already given before. It is however important to notice that activities which were not initially planned often emerge and appear to be critical to the overall goal achievement not only in the discussed scenario.

It is not informative to discuss subsequent activities of T. Hotel booking and visa application services are performed merely in the same manner and agents use similar mechanisms of *task (de-)composition* and *negotiation* for that. Special arrangements list is also considered as the list of trip planning tasks. However, it should be mentioned that the execution of these activities should be properly *coordinated:* note for instance that hotel reservation requires that the fare has been already booked as precondition (check-in and check-out dates, money left) and German Consular Service may require that the fare and the hotel room have been booked before issuing the visa.

---

[6] "One of the most common low fare restrictions is the requirement for your stay to incorporate at least one Sunday. For example, for a round-trip New York to Miami a passenger flying Tuesday to Thursday might pay £328, but a passenger whose stay includes a Sunday would pay much less - £188." –
http://www.flightcatchers.com/helpmenu/Howtofindcheapestfare.htm
last accessed on Apr. 24, 2003.

[7] Lufthansa Infoflyway Booking Service http://lufthansa.com/ (last accessed on Jul. 15, 2003) and Cyber Flyer Booking Service http://cyberflyer.galileo.com/ (last accessed on Jul. 15, 2003) were used in the described exercise to obtain the offers from F-s.

[8] CNN Currency Converter: http://qs.money.cnn.com/tq/currconv/, last accessed on Jul. 16, 2003.

[9] http://www.bahn.de/, last accessed on Jul. 16, 2003.

Other important aspects, not mentioned before, are the ones of *credibility, trust* and *meaning negotiation* among agents participating in cooperative task performance and service composition. Recall Special Arrangements input for the illustration. T will negotiate with P on various aspects while arranging the Business Dinner. The dilemma for P in this environment is if to trust T (as the contractor of A which is the trusted one because of the long record of partnership) and allow him to make the arrangements for P, or to reason that A may be not really experienced in arranging business dinners in Germany and to decide to better rely on his credible (Sect. 3.4) partners from Germany. In the latter case P will inform T that it will better arrange the event on its own. This in turn may effect in the necessity of the approval from A.

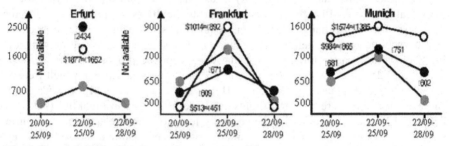

Fig. 2. Fare desirability function and service propositions:
●- for how much (max) A desires the fare, ◐- the propositions of F - Service Providers

3   Cooperative Dynamic Service Composition

Let's enumerate the features needed to rationally provide composite flexible services for the automation of the scenarios like that of travel planning in e-business environment. Intelligent service provider needs to be capable of:

- Understanding the semantics of the activity it is supposed to perform, reasoning on if the activity is atomic or complex, decomposing complex activities according to its knowledge and the experience of the environment

- Adjusting activity inputs, requestor preferences and constraints in order to proactively reach the high level goal

- Negotiating with the requestor, the other service providers in a rational way on optimal service performance, allocation in order to increase its own utility or to obtain common meaning of the service inputs, outputs, pre-conditions and effects

- Monitoring and assessing credibility and trustworthiness of other service providers to minimize risks

- Coordinating services performance flow according to the inputs and pre-conditions

It seems to be obvious that service providing distributed open software systems possessing these capabilities may be most naturally designed and assembled of soft-

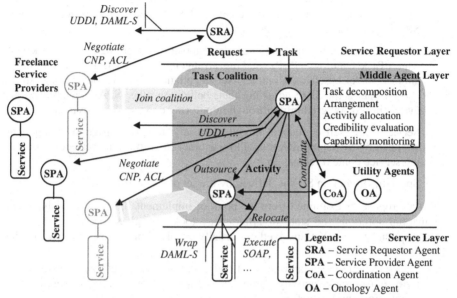

Fig. 3. The proposal of Agent-Based Service Provision Mediation Architecture.

ware agents. Agent platforms and agent-based systems are already used for service brokerage [1], matchmaking [12], coordination [14]. The reminder of this section will shortly present the formal approach to dynamic task decomposition and performance by coalitions of rational agents [2,11].

3.1 Middle Agents for Service Composition

Conceptual idea of service mediation is not originally new and has been argued by many authors. Strong mediation has been for instance claimed as one of the basic principles for WSMF [9]. What seems to be not really explicitly worked out before is the framework for intelligent dynamic service composition and decomposition according to the changes in the environment affected by the service execution flow.

The proposal of the Mediation Framework for Agent-enabled Service Provision targeted to dynamic service composition is presented on Fig. 3. Control flows are labeled with legends in *italic*, data flows are marked by **bold** legends. The principles around which the proposal is centered are:

- Agent-based Middle Layer is required for scalable, intelligent, dynamic service composition
- Composite services are interpreted as tasks comprising activities of varying granularity by the Agent Middle Layer
- Service Mediator is formed dynamically as the coalition of service providing agents (SPAs) participating in the task execution
- SPAs join task coalitions only for the time their service is required for the respective task

– SPAs are economically rational [15], autonomous and independent in taking their decisions – the only fact one SPA believes about the behavior of another SPA is: it will try to increase its utility.

– SPAs are capable of: incoming task decomposition according to its local knowledge (Task Ontology, PLP); making arrangements for activity outsourcing to another SPAs based on Contract Net negotiation; activity outsourcing to the chosen contractor SPA; adjusting their beliefs on other SPAs' capabilities and evaluating SPAs' credibility through monitoring cooperative activities

– Services are self-contained modular loosely coupled program components wrapped by SPAs; an SPA may allow another SPA to use its service by providing service context relocation

– Specialization of an SPA is defined by the set of services it wraps

If the proposal is examined from the point of implementability with existing service markup solutions the state of affairs may look like given on Fig. 3 from the authors' point of view. Yet unsolved or partially unsolved problems of service mediation are:

– Lack of common semantic ground and commonly accepted mechanism for activity outsourcing, activity parameters adjustment and meaning negotiation – negotiation ontologies family

– Insufficient representation of task/activity/service dynamic structure and granularity – task/process ontologies family

– Lack of common specifications/criteria for capability monitoring, credibility and trustworthiness assessment

The proposed architectural layering is likely to remain valid for request-task-activity-service ontology hierarchy: a service request is translated to the task at the requestor layer; these tasks are decomposed into activities at the middle layer; activity descriptions actually wrap service markups. The reminder of the section provides some outlines to approach the solutions of the open issues.

3.2   Negotiation Patterns, Ontology, and Social Norms

In frame of the reported research some work in specifying and designing negotiation patterns for dynamic activity composition and performance has been done already. Negotiation ontology [11] and negotiation mechanism [2] for dynamic task coalition formation were designed to facilitate inter-agent cooperation in open organizations like B2B mediation e-marketplaces [11] or virtual organizations [16]. Mechanism for activity allocation negotiations is based on the metaphor of parametric feedbacks [2] provided as Contract Net participants' proposals in response to activity results' desirability function advertised by the negotiation initiator.

Let's recall 'InquireFares' service negotiation mentioned in Section 2 for illustration and discuss it in more details. First step T needs to perform is to choose contractors providing required service according to its desirability function derived from given

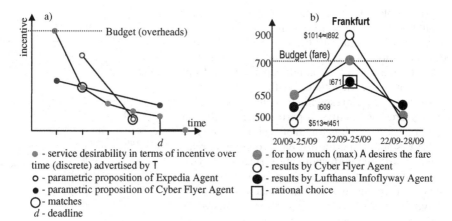

Fig. 4. 'InquireFares' negotiations: a) on service allocation – chosen are the agents proposing the conditions of service provision which match to T desires; b) on service results – see also Fig. 2.

budget and given deadline for service provision[10]. Advertised desirability and two-point parametric responses [2] of negotiation participants are given on Fig. 4a. After the contractors (Lufthansa Infoflyway Agent and Cyber Flyer Agent) are chosen, T allocates 'InquireFares' activity execution to both of them by providing activity description containing inputs and patterns for the results (Appendix A-4). Contractors' feedbacks after applying currency conversion service are shown on Fig. 4b. Negotiations are, thus, used by T to: optimally choose the contractors; get optimal fare information from the chosen contractors.

Contracting negotiation takes place in frame of the Arrangement Phase [2,11] each time there is the need to allocate an activity to SPAs. A kind of FIPA Contract Net Protocol is used for these arrangements. *Negotiation ontology* [11] is used as the namespace and the formal semantic frame for the contents of the messages agents communicate with while negotiating on activity allocation. It is considered that the contractors join the Task Coalition for the time necessary to play their part. Task Coalitions are considered to be a kind of social structures. Coalition members are thus bounded with coalition commitments and convention regulating their ratios of self-interest and benevolence [11].

3.3   Request-Task-Activity-Service Hierarchy

As it was mentioned before service request-task-activity-service semantic hierarchy reflects the principles of the proposed architectural layering. A request belongs to the sphere of Service Requestor Layer and is specified in terms of Task Ontology [11]. The function of the SPA chosen as the contractor for the specified request is to determine if the incoming task is the atomic activity according to its local specifications

---

[10] It is a bit artificially supposed here that F-agents provide their services for an incentive. It is, well, not very realistic for the case, because respective web sites provide their services for free at the moment – i.e. are paid by their holders in some ways.

(Task Ontology). In case the task is complex and should be decomposed into atomic activities at the local level of granularity the next round of activities allocation negotiations is initiated. Only the activities the given SPA is not capable to perform on its own are negotiated with another SPAs, while the ones corresponding to initiator's capabilities are rooted to self-performance. Only an activity, for which it is true that: a) it is atomic and b) SPA is able to perform it on its own, is in relationship with the corresponding service or service loop. Atomic activity execution is performed by SPA by invoking its capability macro-model [2]: activity context is translated into DAML-S markup corresponding to Service Profile; the service is than invoked via the interface specified by its binding (or grounding in terms of DAML-S) description. Service invocation loop may actually

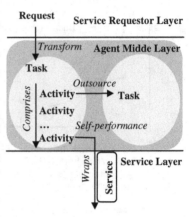

Fig. 5. Semantic layering.

result in one or several service runs depending on the wrapping activity inputs. For example, 'InquireFares' service will be performed three times as far as 3 different date intervals are to be processed (Fig. 4).

Semantic facet of request-task-activity-service layering is presented on Fig. 5. Specifications for 'InquireFares' activity and service are given in Appendix A-5.

3.4 Capability and Credibility Assessment

SRA and SPAs are to be able to determine which of the SPAs are capable to perform the task to be allocated. Possible mechanism to define the perspective contractors is capability matchmaking (e.g., based on LARKS [17]), or service discovery technique based on UDDI, or another service matching facilities (e.g., semantic matching based on DAML-S profiles [18]). However, in case there is some capability beliefs record maintained autonomously by an SPA in the course of cooperative task execution, the use of this knowledge may substantially facilitate to lowering computation costs by eliminating unnecessary directory/matching service usage. Evidently, if A believes that B, C and D are capable of performing desired activity because they did it before, it will rather proceed to contracting negotiation with B, C and D directly instead of trying to find some other SPAs[11] with matching capabilities.

A model and a mechanism of agents' capability assessment based on SPA beliefs representation in the form of Fellows' Capability Expectations Matrix (FCEM) has been elaborated in frame of the reported research [2]. SPAs accumulate and adjust their local beliefs on the capabilities of their collaborators in the course of cooperative performance. New portions of this knowledge appear each time an activity is allocated to the chosen contractor SPA. Subjective beliefs of the SPA requesting the activity on the probability of its fellows' capability to perform the given activity are thus

---

[11] Applying to a capability registry may still appear to be necessary in case B, C and D fail to provide constructive proposals.

updated. FCEM for capability beliefs representation is maintained in the following form:

$$
\mathbf{C} = \begin{array}{c}
\quad\quad a^1 \;\ldots \quad\quad\quad a^j \quad\quad \ldots\; a^m \\
\begin{array}{c} SPA_1 \\ \\ \ldots \\ \\ SPA_n \end{array}
\left[\begin{array}{ccc}
c_1^1 & c_1^j & c_1^k \\
& \ldots & \\
\ldots\; c_i^j = (q_i^j, p_i^j) \;\ldots & & \\
& \ldots & \\
c_n^1 & c_n^j & c_n^m
\end{array} \right]
\end{array}
\tag{1}
$$

where dimensions m and n change reflecting the appearance of new incoming activities and newly discovered or perishing activity providers.

Capability estimations c_i^j change each time an agent negotiates with its fellows to allocate an activity. Element q_i^j in tuple c_i^j stands for the quantity of recorded negotiations with fellow agent SPA_i concerning activity a^j. Element p_i^j stands for the capability expectation. The rule for c_i^j updates is as follows:

$$
\begin{array}{ll}
1. & p_i^j \leftarrow p_i^j + \dfrac{r}{q_i^j}, \\[2ex]
2. & q_i^j \leftarrow q_i^j + 1
\end{array}
\tag{2}
$$

where r is equal to: 0 – if the fellow rejected the activity, 0.5 – if the fellow replied that it can accept the activity and 1 – if the activity was finally allocated to the fellow.

One more aspect providing influence on a task requestor's decision to allocate an activity to one or another negotiation participant is its assessment of the participant's *credibility*. A self-interested SPA, due to the appearance of the new highly attractive activity offers in the competitive environment or due to the peculiarity of its behavior, may lower previously declared capacity [2,11] it is spending for the bulk of the activities under execution. This will lead to the increase of the performance duration and may seriously decrease the requestor's desirability of these results and, thus, lower the credibility value for the SPA selling its' fellows short.

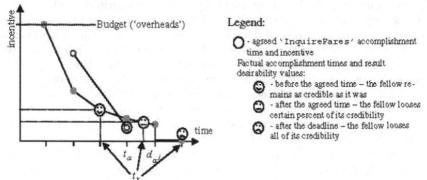

Fig. 6. 'InquireFares' accomplishment times and corresponding credibility changes.

The mechanism of accounting fellows' credibility values is merely the same as that of adjusting the beliefs on changing fellow capabilities (1-2). Credibility assessment values change over time as the requestor agent adjusts its subjective beliefs by comparing the desirability values (Fig. 6) derived from:

1-st – activity duration the executive committed to within the activity allocation arrangement negotiation and

2-nd – actual results delivery time. Corresponding credibility matrix elements are than recomputed due to the following:

$$Cr_{i,j} := Cr_{i,j} \times \begin{cases} 1, t_r \leq t_a \\ p_{a^j}(t_a / t_r), t_a < t_r \leq d_{a^j} \\ 0, t_r > d_{a^j} \end{cases},$$ (3)

where t_a is the time the parties have agreed to accomplish the activity a^j, t_r is the actual time of a^j results delivery, d_{a^j} is the deadline and p_{a^j} is the weight coefficient characterizing the current priority of a^j for the activity requestor agent.

Credibility threshold values associated with respective activities and stored in agents' PLPs are used by task requesting agents to assess possible risks and alter their strategies.

4   RACING Functionalities, Agents, and Services

A reader might argue that, fairly, travel planning is not the task that really requires sophisticated agent-enabled automation technique: negotiations, coalitions, service wrapping and composition – at least from the customer's side. Travel planning is not that time consuming to make its performance impossible without automation. Moreover, a human will sometimes still be better in arranging loosely formalized things that require intuition and context dependent understanding with complexity beyond the capacity of, say, the first order logic based languages. However, the presented technique is applicable not only in case you plan your conference trip [11, 16].

Let's project the above discussion to distributed information and document retrieval domain. In the terms of document retrieval a service request is commonly formulated as a search phrase – a first order logic expression over the list of keywords or phrases. Documents (web pages, scientific papers, magazines, books) are stored at disparately structured distributed autonomously maintained databases or text collections in a digital form, are marked-up according to different standards and *often cost money*. A task for document retrieval may thus be presented as the set of interrelated activities distributed over the document providers. These activities wrap the (partial) queries derived from the initial user's request.

The goal of our RACING project is to provide mediation facilities for user query processing by the means of the query semantic decomposition, the rational distribution among independent, autonomous, rational document retrieval service providers wrapping respective document resources, and the fusion of the obtained results (Fig. 7.). User agents acting on behalf of the human users or real organizations (e.g., libraries) and service providing agents are considered as business representatives or

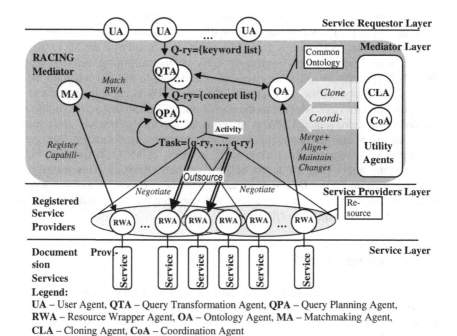

Fig. 7. RACING reference architecture.

Legend:
UA – User Agent, **QTA** – Query Transformation Agent, **QPA** – Query Planning Agent,
RWA – Resource Wrapper Agent, **OA** – Ontology Agent, **MA** – Matchmaking Agent,
CLA – Cloning Agent, **CoA** – Coordination Agent

business models in frame of the project. RACING mediation may thus be classified as B2B mediation. It is evident that such a kind of intelligent activities really needs sophisticated automation to be scalable and gracefully downgradable.

User query processing, resource wrappers registration by the capability matchmaker and common ontology maintenance are the basic functionalities of the RACING mediator (Fig. 7.). Though only query processing may be considered as a real business process involving third-party service providers for money, the other two ones are also performed as tasks and require various types of negotiation and semantic interoperation.

For example, the outline for the User Query Processing scenario is as follows. The process starts at UA with the formulation of the query in terms of the key phrases familiar to the given user. UAs are cloned by CLA utility agent each time a new user comes to the mediator and perish when the user leaves. User profiles (mappings of their most frequently used key words or phrases to the Mediator Common Ontology (MCO) concepts) is incrementally collected, stored at OA [19] in the form of the reference ontology and is used by QTAs. UA actually generates and conducts the task of query processing and acts as the proxy between the user and mediator. Query processing task generated by UA contains 'CloneQTA', 'TransformQry', 'CloneQPA', 'Execute-Qry' activities. The cloning activities are outsourced to CLA which clones QTA and QPA for query processing. 'TransformQry' activity is outsourced to QTA which performs the transformation of the query in terms of keywords to semantically matching query in terms of the concepts of the MCO. The last activity is outsourced to QPA which generates the following set of activities for 'ExecuteQry' task: 'DecomposeQry',

'PerformQryset'. Query decomposition is performed by QPA in order to extract the parts of the incoming query, which may require different capabilities from document service providers. This extraction is guided by topic classification of the MCO. Resulting set of partial queries is performed by QPA as the following activity sequence: 'MatchRWA', 'PerformQry'. Matching activity is allocated to MA for a certain incentive over accomplishment time. MA returns[12] the list of RWAs capable to perform document providing services relevant to the partial query. 'PerformQry' activity allocation is negotiated with pre-selected RWAs in terms of service 'overheads' over time and document price and the contractor is chosen for query performance (Section 3.2). Contractor RWA receives the partial query in terms of MCO. It therefore needs to transform the query into the terms of its Resource Ontology. This transformation activity is outsourced to OA which actually holds the necessary mappings. RWA than invokes document service it wraps with the transformed query and provides documents relevant to the query to QPA.

5   Concluding Remarks

The paper presented the vision of the authors on how diverse web services may be composed, mediated by means of middle agents and their coalitions performing tasks for service requestors. It is also claimed that such a mediation facility may substantially enhance today's solutions available in web service provision. This vision is grounded on the results obtained in agent-enabled business process modeling and management.

It is stated that though the concept of service mediation is not totally new there is still some work to be done before it becomes real engineering technology. For example, from the authors' point of view what seem to be not really explicitly worked out before is the framework for intelligent dynamic service composition and decomposition according to the changes in the environment affected by the service execution flow. The rationale to cope with such kind of dynamic composite service execution representation is argued by the discussion of a popular travel planning scenario. The main focus and the contribution of the paper is the proposal of the layered service mediation architecture. Agent Middle Layer is introduced to conduct service request to task transformation, agent-enabled cooperative task decomposition and performance. Outlined are the formal means to arrange agents' negotiation, to represent the semantic structure of task-activity-service hierarchy and to assess fellow-agents' capabilities and credibility factors. Other important aspects of cooperative agent-enabled service mediation, just mentioned in the paper because of space limits, are the questions of *meaning negotiation* and *activity coordination* among agents participating in cooperative task performance and service composition. Finally, it is argued that the presented formal technique is applicable not only to the tasks like travel planning. Presented is the reference architecture of the rational multi-agent mediator for intelligent information and document retrieval. Further development and deployment of the mediator is in progress in frame of the RACING project.

---

[12] As QPAs in RACING have limited life time, RWAs' credibility and capability assessment (Section 3.4.) is performed by MA for registered resource wrappers. QPAs supply MA with necessary data obtained from cooperation with RWAs.

Though thorough standardization and harmonization work should be performed before the presented approach becomes an engine for web service provision, the authors are certain, that agent-enabled rational web service composition and mediation may provide a substantial contribution bringing closer the day, when the brave new world of machine-processable automated web services comes true at least in e-business domain.

References

1. McIlraith, S. A., Son, T. C. and Zeng, H.: Semantic Web Services, IEEE Intelligent Systems. Sp. Issue on The Semantic Web 16 (2002) 46–53
2. Ermolayev, V. A., Plaksin, S. L.: Cooperation Layers in Agent-Enabled Business Process Management. Problems of Programming 1-2 (2002) 354–368
3. Web Services Description Language (WSDL) 1.1. W3C Note 15 March 2001 http://www.w3.org/TR/2001/NOTE-wsdl-20010315/ Last accessed June 3, 2003
4. UDDI Technical White Paper http://uddi.org/pubs/Iru_UDDI_Technical_White_Paper.PDF Last accessed June 3, 2003
5. Simple Object Access Protocol (SOAP) 1.1. W3C Note 08 May 2000 http://www.w3.org/TR/2000/NOTE-SOAP-20000508/ Last accessed June 3, 2003
6. Karp, A.: E-speak E-xplained HPL-2000-101 20000807 External Technical Report http://www.hpl.hp.com/techreports/2000/HPL-2000-101.pdf Last accessed June 3, 2003
7. Layman, A.: Web Services Framework. In: Proc of W3C Workshop on Web Services 11-12 April 2001, San Jose, CA USA http://www.w3.org/2001/03/wsws-program/ Last accessed June 3, 2003
8. Ankolekar, A., Burstein, M, Hobbs, J. R., Lassila, O., Martin, D., McDermott, D., McIlraith, S. A., Narayanan, S., Paolucci, M., Payne, T., Sycara, K.: DAML-S: Web Service Description for the Semantic Web In: Proc,. of Int. Semantic Web Conference, June 9-12th, 2002 Sardinia, Italy
9. Fensel, D., Bussler, C.: The Web Service Modeling Framework WSMF. White Paper http://www.cs.vu.nl/~dieter/wese/wsmf.paper.pdf. Last accessed June 3, 2002
10. The DAML Services Coalition. DAML-S: Semantic Markup for Web Services. http://www.daml.org/services/daml-s/2001/10/daml-s.pdf Last accessed June 3, 2003
11. Ermolayev, V. Keberle, N., Tolok, V.: OIL Ontologies for Collaborative Task Performance in Coalitions of Self-Interested Actors. In: H. Arisawa, Y. Kambayashi, V. Kumar, H.C. Mayr, I. Hunt (eds.): Conceptual Modeling for New Information Systems Technologies ER 2001 Workshops, HUMACS, DASWIS, ECOMO, and DAMA, Yokohama Japan, November 27–30, 2001. Revised Papers, LNCS, Vol. 2465. Springer-Verlag, Berlin Heidelberg new York (2001) 390–402
12. Sycara, K. P., Klusch, M., Widoff, S., Lu, J.: Dynamic Service Matchmaking Among Agents in Open Information Environments. SIGMOD Record 28(1) (1999) 47–53
13. FIPA Communicative Act Library Specification. Doc. No: XC00037H, Doc. Status: Experimental, http://www.fipa.org/specs/fipa00037/XC00037H.pdf last accessed June 14, 2003.
14. Papadopoulos, G. A.: (2001) Models and Technologies for the Coordination of Internet Agents: A Survey. In: A.Omicini, F.Zambonelli, M.Klusch, R.Tolksdorf (eds.): Coordination for Internet Agents - Models, Technologies, and Applications, Springer-Verlag, Berlin Heidelberg New York (2001)
15. Nwana, H. S.: Software Agents: an Overview. Knowledge Engineering Review, 3(11) (1996) 205–244
16. Ermolayev, V. A., Tolok, V. A.: Modelling Distant Learning Activities by Agent Task Coalitions. In: Q. Jin, J. Li, J. Cheng, C. Yu and S. Noguchi (eds.): Enabling Society with Information Technology, Springer-Verlag, Tokyo (2002)

17. Sycara, K., Widoff, S., Klusch, M., Lu, J.: LARKS: Dynamic Matchmaking Among Heterogeneous Software Agents in Cyberspace. Autonomous Agents and Multi-Agent Systems 5 (2002) 173–203
18. Paolucci, M., Kawamura, T., Payne, T., Sycara, K.: Semantic Matching of Web Services Capabilities In: Proc. of Int. Semantic Web Conference (ISWC'2002), June 9–12, 2002, Sardinia, Italy
19. Ermolayev, V., Keberle, N., Plaksin, S., Vladimirov, V.: Capturing Semantics from Search Phrases: Incremental User Personification and Ontology-Driven Query Transformation. In: Godlevsky, M., Liddle, S., Mayr, H. (eds.): Information Systems Technology and its Applications. Proc. of the 2-nd Int. Conf. ISTA'2003 Lecture Notes in Informatics (LNI) - Proceedings, Vol. P-30, GI-Edition, Bonn (2003) 9–20.

Semantic Web Enabled Web Services: State-of-Art and Industrial Challenges

Vagan Terziyan and Oleksandr Kononenko

Industrial Ontologies Group, MIT Department, University of Jyvaskyla
P.O. Box 35 (Agora), FIN-40014 Jyvaskyla, Finland
vagan@it.jyu.fi, olkonone@cc.jyu.fi

Abstract. Semantic Web technology has a vision to define and link Web data in a way that it can be understood and used by machines for automation, integration and reuse of data across various applications. Ontological definition of every resource as it is assumed in Semantic Web, along with new techniques for semantics processing and new vision Intelligent Web Services is expected to bring Web on its new level. At present, Web Services technology is stressed by the search of a right way for further development. Combination of Semantic Web and Web Services concepts may address many of difficulties of existing technology. It is not a question of whether Semantic Web is coming or not, but a question of when it will come. However without mature standards, proof and actually working industrial cases Semantic Web has small chances to be adopted by industry. In this paper a survey of Web Services recent needs is made, state of the art of Semantic Web technology is discussed in the context of industrial applications. Some new challenges brought by Semantic Web were observed and the industrial maintenance case related to some of these challenges was considered.

1 Introduction

Serious problems emerge in information search, extraction, representation, interpretation and maintenance because no efficient support in processing this information is provided. The possible impact of resolving problems in Knowledge Management, Enterprise Application Integration and e-commerce draws the best minds and research groups to active efforts, which will bring Web to qualitatively new level of service [Fensel & Musen, 2001].

Appearance of Web Services as a technology is tightly connected with initiatives to create e-commerce systems based on Internet and Enterprise Application Integration problem. "Web Services" term refers to available programmatic interfaces that are used in the World Wide Web for application-to-application communication.

The W3C's Metadata Activity was tightly connected with Knowledge Management problems and has grown from idea of having machine-understandable information in the Web. Metadata Activity has provided approach for metadata labeling of web content. Further, the idea has developed into the Semantic Web vision of having data-oriented web with metadata and links between resources to provide effective discovery, integration, automation and interoperability across various semantic-aware

M. Jeckle and L.-J. Zhang (Eds.): ICWS-Europe 2003, LNCS 2853, pp. 183–197, 2003.
© Springer-Verlag Berlin Heidelberg 2003

applications. The primer goal of Semantic Web Activity is development of mature comprehensive standards and technologies for future Web, provision with building blocks that will assist in addressing of critical issues concerning interoperability in the Web, and thus, Web Service technology.

Since Web Service Technology built upon Semantic Web Technology makes strong promises ("Intelligent Web Services", [Fensel et al., 2002(c)]) a series of questions arise [Bussler et al., 2003]. To what extent have these different technologies already been integrated today? How does the combination of those technologies look like? How does this combination make problems like Enterprise Application Integration, Distributed Knowledge Management systems development, easier to solve and the solution more reliable?

The objectives of this work are divided into groups:

1. Analysis of current state of Web Service and Semantic Web technology;

2. Problems of Web Services and Semantic Web as an approach; Intelligent Web Services concept.

3. Challenges and technical issues regarding semantic-aware services. What kind of work has to be done and which tools are required? What are the first steps towards Semantic Web enabled systems in industry?

The rest of the paper is organized as follows. Chapter 2 contains survey of existing technologies and standards around Web Services and Semantic Web. Chapter 3 covers questions about problems of Web Services and about Semantic Web enabled solutions. Analysis of introduced by Semantic Web benefits and challenges are presented and comparison between traditional and semantic-enabled (via Semantic Web) technologies is given. Chapter 4 contains brief description of *OntoServ.Net* framework being developed for the network of industrial maintenance services as a case study of the Sematic Web services concept. Conclusions are in chapter 5.

2 Web Services and Semantic Web

In a broad meaning, *web services* belong to a model in which tasks within e-business processes are distributed and accessible throughout a global network. From another point of view, web services are a stack of emerging standards that describe service-oriented, component-based application architecture. Web Services connect computers and devices with each other using the Internet to exchange data and combine it in new ways. Web Services can be defined as software objects that can be assembled over the Internet using standard protocols to perform functions or execute business processes. The key to Web Services is dynamic service composition using independent, reusable software components. [Fensel & Bussler, 2002].

Main Layers of the Web Services Computing Stack ([Sycara, 2003]) are as follows:

SOAP (Simple Object Access Protocol). SOAP [Mitra, 2003] is an XML based lightweight messaging protocol intended for exchanging structured information between applications in a decentralized, distributed environment.

WSDL (Web Services Description Language). WSDL provides description of connection and communication with a particular web service [Sankar et al., 2003].

UDDI. It [UDDI] stands for Universal Description, Discovery and Integration and represents a set of protocols and was directed to providing of public directory for the registration and real-time lookup of web services and other business processes.

E-Speak is an example of service architecture developed by Hewlett-Packard. The goal of e-Speak is to perform transaction between e-services. E-speak engines run on participating client machines and e-speak service platforms that can exchange XML based information to solve problem of integration of simple services into more complex ones [Sliwa, 2002].

ebXML (http://www.ebxml.org/) stands for Electronic Business XML. It is a project to standardize the exchange of business data. The core infrastructure specifications of ebXML are the messaging service (ebMS specification), the registry and repository (ebRS specification), and the collaborative partner protocol (ebCPP specification). The ebXML Framework allows a Trading Party to express via CPP supported Business Processes and Business Service Interface to other ebXML compliant Trading Parties.

RosettaNet (http://www.rosettanet.org) is a consortium of the world's leading companies in the fields of electronics, IT-sector, semiconductor manufacturing and solution providers. RosettaNet is dedicated to creation, implementation and promotion of open e-business standards. The ultimate goal of RosettaNet is development of standards for common e-business language and open e-business processes, aligning processes between trading partners, which will provide measurable benefits to the evolution of the global, high-technology trading network.

Semantic Web [Berners-Lee et al., 2001] is the presentation of machine-processable semantics of *data* on the Web. It is a collaborative effort led by W3C Consortium with participation from a large number of researchers and industrial partners. It is based on the Resource Description Framework (RDF) and new web languages such as Web Ontology Language (OWL), DARPA Agent Markup Language (DAML), which integrate a variety of applications using XML for syntax and URIs for naming. RDF and RDF Schema provide basic features for information modeling and a simple knowledge representation mechanism for Web resources. DAML+OIL is an ontology description language manifested as RDF Schema extension for expressing far more sophisticated classifications and properties of resources than RDFS [Connolly et al., 2001]. The newest part of the growing stack of W3C recommendations related to the Semantic Web is Web Ontology Language (OWL), which been designed to meet needs for a Web Ontology Language and incorporates lessons learned from the design and application of DAML+OIL [Dean et al., 2002].

3 Semantic Web Enabled Web Services

The next-generation Web Services will transform the web from static content, human-oriented and dependent e-services to a distributed computational system in which intelligent web services complemented by scalable mediation infrastructure to bring on top the performance of the Web. To facilitate full potential of Web Services, appropriate framework is about to be developed [Fensel & Bussler, 2002]. The emerging concept of Intelligent Web Services is shown in Fig. 1.

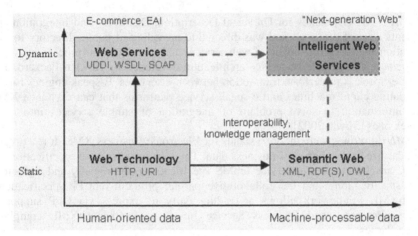

Fig.1. Bringing Web on top of performance with Intelligent Web Services (adopted from [Fensel et al., 2002(c)])

The main objectives of Semantic Web enabled Web Services development:
- Provide a comprehensive Web Service *description* framework.
- Define a Web Service *discovery* framework.
- Provide a scalable Web Service *mediation* platform.

3.1 Requirements to Web Services

Web Services technology nowadays is based on UDDI and WSDL which do not make any use of semantic information, hence, failing to meet the problem of matchmaking between provided capabilities of services and service requestors' needs [Sycara, 2003]. This sought functionality cannot be achieved just on a basis of keyword searches and vocabularies of service types.

But still, though they only partially address requirements sought by the Web Services vision, some lessons have been learnt from UDDI-WSDL-SOAP design. In [Fensel & Bussler, 2002] necessary to scalable web service discovery, mediation and composition elements were identified as:

- *Document Types,* which describe the content of business documents.
- *Semantics,* which is introduced as semantic descriptions to be interpreted correctly by the service requesters and providers.
- *Transport Binding,* which is an agreement between service requestor and service provider on the transport mechanism to be used for service requests.
- *Exchange Sequence Definition,* which is transport-level communication protocol to follow in inherently unreliable data communication networks.
- *Communication Process Definition,* a manifestation of business logic in terms of the business messages exchange sequence.
- *Security.* Data contained in the messages between service requester and service provider should be private and unmodified as well as non-reputable.
- *Syntax.* Documents can be represented in one of syntaxes available.

In UDDI only Transport binding, Exchange Sequence Definition and Communication Process Definition elements' requirements are partially fulfilled via general UDDI architecture, SOAP and WSDL, and provide limited support in automated service recognition and comparison, configuration, combination and automated negotiation. In addition to UDDI, WSDL and SOAP, there are standards such as WSFL, BPSS, XLANG, ebXML, BPML, WSCL and BPEL4WS, WS-Security and WS-Routing, which are intended to fill up other parts of the stack. But they are numerous, overlap each other in addressed problems and have been developed by individual web-services industry players (like IBM, Microsoft, HP, etc.) often for own innovations. It is evident that consistent solution cannot be achieved without combined efforts of industrial leaders and research communities.

3.2   Service Description Framework

Management of resources in Semantic Web is impossible without use of ontologies, which can be considered as high-level metadata about semantics of Web resources [Fensel et al., 2002(d)]. DAML-S is an upper ontology for describing properties and capabilities of Web Services. DAML-S provides an unambiguous, computer interpretable markup language, which enables automation of service use by agents and reasoning about service properties and capabilities [Ankolenkar et al., 2001].

Approaches to defining things followed in RosettaNet and ebXML frameworks are very alike to that in DAML-S. The differences are in the extent and specific of described process. DAML-S follows Semantic Web's line and uses ontology as a foundation for every description. RosettaNet and ebXML are e-business oriented frameworks whereas DAML-S stays aside of any specific service domain. The strength of DAML-S based service description is in adopted from Semantic Web ontology as the schema for metadata provided. ebXML's meta-models are similar to ontology used in DAML-S, though in less general sense and they are dedicated mostly to business process description; tModel, vocabularies and dictionaries in UDDI, e-Speak and RosettaNet are more schemas for description rather then basis for semantic annotation of web services. ebXML and RosettaNet e-commerce frameworks are given here to admit that proposed by DAML-S expressiveness is potential enough to become an important part of semantic-enabled Web Services that will be essential part in EAI and e-business. Fig. 2 depicts the relations between DAML-S, WSDL, UDDI, RosettaNet, ebXML and related frameworks/languages.

UDDI doesn't provide facilities for service descriptions except keyword and industrial service type categorization. Without sharing common definitions and understanding of the concepts, without shared metadata and semantics associated with particular web service, an interaction between UDDI client and web service cannot be performed in the correct manner. Because DAML-S provides no framework for discovery (just syntax for descriptions) and UDDI has a lack of description potential, that make some minds thinking over extension of possibilities proposed by UDDI with DAML-S [Paolucci et al., 2001] to get the best of the two worlds: support from the popular industry standard framework and expressiveness from the Semantic Web.

Will DAML-S become a substantive for WSDL in UDDI framework or new mediation framework initially designed to be semantic-aware will be developed, depends on market, solution providers and adoption of Semantic Web approach.

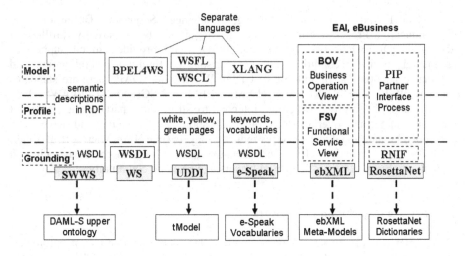

Fig. 2. Technologies and description languages concerning Web Services. Correspondence to *ServiceModel, ServiceProfile* and *ServiceGrounding* parts of DAML-S service description

3.3   Requirements to Service Description

Each of popular frameworks (e-Speak, UDDI, ebXML, RosettaNet) uses own mechanism to make descriptive advertisements about services. The basic requirements to service description language in [Trastour et al., 2001], formulated as:

Requirement 1:	High degree of flexibility and expressiveness;
Requirement 2:	Ability to express semi-structured data;
Requirement 3:	Support for types and subsumption (categorization);
Requirement 4:	Ability to express constraints.

Considering these requirements and comparing proposed by Semantic Web ontological descriptions (written in DAML-S) with other mentioned frameworks, the following conclusions are derived:

- in DAML-S: RDF layer as a representation basis covers requirements 1 and 2, RDFS layer covers 3rd and refines 1st , whereas DAML layer meets 4th requirement;
- in UDDI:
  - tModels have no classification or data structures organization as demanded by requirement 3);
  - tModels only provide a labeling mechanism and only a first level filtering is provided. Further selection is done in communication with service provider (see requirement 2);
  - searching is only done by string equality matching on some fields such as name, location or URL (see requirements 3 and 4);
  - there is no possibility to extend the description schema (requirements 1, 2);
- ebXML framework is too focused on defining business processes and business documents payload; the Core Component vocabulary meta-model does not look

very rich and do not provide support for semi-structured data (requirement 1), inheritance (requirement 3) and constraints (requirement 4);

- neither e-Speak, nor RosettaNet seem to provide anything beyond a basic ontology definition (vocabularies and dictionaries can be seen as primitive ontologies with limited capabilities).

ProcessModel in DAML-S description of service provide description of workflow within service. There are at least two reasons for that. The first reason is to enable monitoring of service execution stages; this can be used for complex transactions management with many services involved, where execution of services can be stopped due to some conditions. The second reason is to provide additional service semantic that will be used for better service matching.

Hence, DAML-S provides better the means for a web service to advertise its functionality to potential users of the service. The detailed process description of the service enriched with ontology features, thus leads to more accurate matchmaking.

RDF-Based Serialization (RDF vs. SOAP). SOAP message consists of the SOAP envelope for expressing *what* is in a message; *who* should deal with it, and *whether* it is optional or mandatory. The SOAP encoding rules define a serialization mechanism and a convention that can be used to represent remote procedure calls and responses.

SOAP standard matches perfectly initial idea of exchange instances of application-defined data types in heterogeneous distributed environment, but there are some limitations of SOAP to be a base standard of universal messaging framework for Web Service technology:

- SOAP message formats are provided as a part of higher level standards, e.g. WSDL, hence communication requires a-priori agreement between Web Services on message format and protocol;
- SOAP standard has no communicative speech acts: there is no way to determine intention of the message sender or what the message trying to achieve (semantic of message is not introduced explicitly).

From the point of view of Semantic Web enabled Web Services approach, SOAP is not suitable as container language for semantic-aware mediation since it, first, has no semantic and, second, scores low on possibility to be used in situation when there is no a priori message format are defined.

It is possible to use RDF payload in SOAP (as a first step from SOAP to RDF messaging) or even SOAP-less pure-RDF messaging system. Corresponding ontology support and mediation framework are required. RDF can be chosen as a messaging language for Web Services because:

- it is not *structure-oriented* as SOAP, but *semantic-oriented*; there is a resource description model behind the RDF which binds assertions (RDF statements) in the message to ontology and there is XML Schema behind SOAP which only restricts XML serialization structure of the message;
- it is easy to parse (as easy as SOAP since both are XML based), less strict, since statements' order in RDF is not important, and more flexible, since parts of RDF can represent virtually any kind of message;
- it supports knowledge representation for service description and any other asserts (e.g. about preferences, security etc.), allowing inference on such information;
- it will be widely used for resources description and developed tools will be reused for web service if appropriate web service ontology exist;

- RDF and ontologies in Semantic Web are going to be universal semantic description framework and their adoption will be a crucial point in the future knowledge management technologies, so accepting it in advance is reasonable.

From above statements two conclusions become obvious:

1) SOAP needs semantics "injected" in it or to be superseded by another semantic-enabled standard;
2) RDF and "mediation" ontology for Web Services are possible substitutes proposed by Semantic Web.

Semantic Web Services are harder to build comparatively to SOAP services. Especially because there are already powerful tools developed for traditional services technology that supports SOAP (like Microsoft .NET, for instance), but there is no more than advanced pilot implementation of tools for Semantic Web in some projects. And it's clear, why it is so; Semantic Web-based technologies are being just developed. There is a gap between ideas and reality, but it will be filled soon [Ohlms, 2002]. Semantic Web Services require efforts at the outset, but make it more likely that services will stay longer and play well with others.

3.4   Service Composition

Composition of web services that have been previously annotated with semantics and discovered by a mediation platform is another benefit proposed by Semantic Web for Web Services. Composition of services can be quite simple sequence of service calls passing outputs of one service to the next and much more complex, where *execution path* (service workflow) is not a sequence but more sophisticated structure, or intermediate data transformation is required to join outputs of one service with inputs of another. Within traditional approach such service composition can be created but with limitations: since semantics of inputs/outputs is not introduced explicitly, the only way to find matching service is to follow data types of its inputs and/or know exactly what service is required. This approach works for simple composition problem but fails for problems required for the future Web Services for e-commerce.

As an example of composition, let's consider combination of two web services, an on-line language translator and a dictionary service, where the first one translates text between several language pairs and the second returns the meaning of English words. Together they can perform, what otherwise cannot be done, e.g. a *FinnishDictionary* service (the input can be translated from Finnish to English, processed through the English Dictionary, and then translated back to Finnish). The dynamic composition of such services is difficult using just the WSDL descriptions, since each description would designate strings as input and output, rather than the necessary concept for combining them (that is, some of these input strings must be the name of languages, others must be the strings representing user inputs and the translator's outputs). In order to provide the semantic concepts like *language* or *Finnish*, we have to use the ontologies.

Service composition can also be used in linking Web (and Semantic Web) concepts to services provided in other network-based environments [Sirin et al., 2002]. One example is the sensor network environment, which includes two types of services; basic sensor services and sensor processing services. Each sensor is related to one web service, which returns the sensor data as the output. Sensor processing services combine the data coming from different sensors in some way and produce a new output. These sensors have properties that describe their capabilities, such as sensitivity, range, etc., as well as some non-functional attributes, such as name, location, etc. These attributes, taken together tell whether the sensor's service is relevant for some specific task.

In DAML-S *ServiceGrounding* part of service description provides knowledge required to access service (where, what data, in what sequence communication goes) and *ServiceProfile* part provides references to the *meaning* what service is used for. Both these pieces of information are enough (as it supposed by Semantic Web vision) to be used by intelligent mediator (intelligent agent, mediation platform, transaction manager etc.) for using this service directly or as a part of compound service.

The implementation of service composer [Sirin et al., 2002] shows how to use semantic descriptions to aid in the composition of web services-- it directly combines the DAML-S semantic service descriptions with actual invocations of the WSDL descriptions allowing us to execute the composed services on the Web. The prototype system can compose the actual web services deployed on the Internet as well as providing filtering capabilities where a large number of similar services may be available.

4 Industrial Case of Semantic Web Enabled Web Services Application

We are developing a framework for industrial semantics-enabled maintenance services organized in peer-to-peer network of services platforms embedded into maintained devices and specific maintenance centre nodes. *OntoServ.Net* (see Fig. 3) is based on Web Services and Semantic Web technologies and meant to provide solution for building large-scale industrial maintenance networks. Semantic Web provide interoperability and Web Services allow integration in such environment.

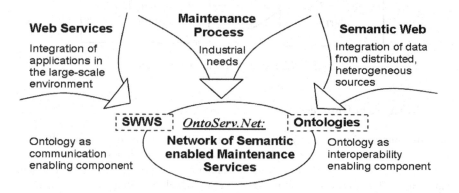

Fig. 3. OntoServ.Net concept

4.1   Industrial Maintenance

Maintenance of complex industrial machines such as paper-machines, mills, turbines, etc. is a complicated and important task. Maintenance activities include condition monitoring, predictive maintenance, tuning, repair works. Unlike condition monitoring systems, predictive maintenance is directed to analysis of current device state with the object to reveal some *possible* (not detected post facto) emerging problems, thus preventing failures via adjustment of parameters, change of parts, tuning, etc. beforehand, and it leads to lower expenses for device maintenance (because failures can damage devices very hard sometimes). Advanced data mining and machine learning techniques are used for prediction of faults. In order to recognize some dimensions of the device state and derive useful patterns from this information, which can be considered as "symptoms" of the device "health", both batch learning and online learning techniques use historical data within predictive maintenance activities.

Since maintenance-related processes rely on relevant information, comprehensive and timely information delivery to the individuals involved in the maintenance can significantly benefit the process. This makes automated maintenance system, which can integrate maintenance-related information from many sources, highly desired in order to give appropriate maintenance support. The typical lifecycle of maintenance activities is shown in Fig. 4.

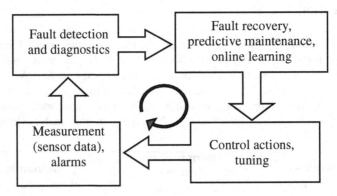

Fig. 4. Lifecycle of maintenance activities

4.2   Principles of OntoServ.*Net*

Growing interest to machines with embedded intelligent maintenance capabilities lead to a special kind of industrial products – smart-devices (machines). The expectations from smart devices include advanced diagnostics and predictive maintenance capabilities. The concerns in this area are to develop a diagnostics system that automatically follows up the performance and maintenance needs of field devices offering also easy access to this information.

Field Agent concept is used for a software component that automatically follows the "health" of field devices. Field Agent component is autonomous and communicates with its environment and other Field Agents; it is capable of learning new things and delivering new information to other Field Agents. It delivers reports and alarms to the user by means of existing and well-known technologies such as intranet and e-mail messages.

Easy on-line access to the knowledge describing field device performance and maintenance needs is crucial. There is also growing need to provide automatic access to this knowledge not only to humans but also to other devices, applications, expert systems, agents etc., which can use this knowledge for different purposes of further device diagnostics and maintenance. Also the reuse of collected and shared knowledge is important for other field agents to manage maintenance in similar cases.

In any case history data, derived patterns and diagnoses can be stored and used locally however there should be a possibility to easy access this information and also to share it with other maintenance platforms for reuse purposes.

Appropriate field agents should communicate with each other (e.g. in peer-to-peer manner) to share locally stored online and historical information, thus, improving the performance of the diagnostic algorithms, allowing even the co-operative use of heterogeneous field devices produced by different companies, which share common communication standards and ontologies. Maintenance centres supported by machine manufacturers or by some other parties will provide entry points to a maintenance network and play role of mediator of the maintenance networking (see Fig. 5). Communication between nodes in the maintenance network is to be built as web services communication. Maintenance centers mediate such communication providing service discovery capabilities and provide own services that can compose web services to deliver complex ones to embedded maintenance platform of smart-devices.

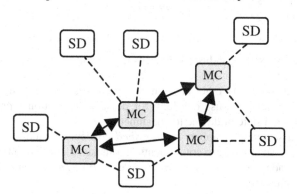

Fig. 5. Smart-devices and maintenance centers in OntoServ.Net

Ontological descriptions in OntoServ.*Net* play role of enabling technology that will provide efficient service discovery and automated services use in such environment. DAML-S is used for web services descriptions. RDF serialization of data is assumed. Most of interactions is done in form of *semantic queries*, so appropriate communication ontology is required for exchanging such queries and other communication messages.

In order to provide interoperability in information exchange between nodes in OntoServ.*Net*, passed data has to be annotated using some common ontology for all nodes this data will be delivered. Since virtually any part of embedded maintenance platform can use network resources (access maintenance web services and provide own services), it is required to have data annotated immediately after its creation and process it with semantic-aware applications in the embedded platform. General maintenance process follows structure and data flows as it is shown in Fig. 6.

Major ontology providers of the network (groups of manufactures) organize ontology management in OntoServ.Net. If there are several groups (as it is naturally so) ontology mapping between different *"maintenance contexts"* have to be supported by them when appropriate.

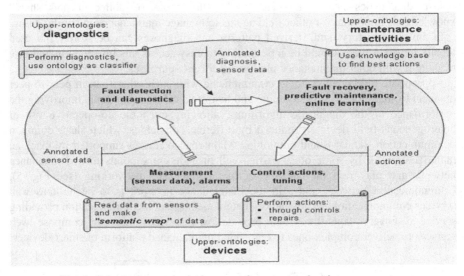

Fig. 6. Schema for ontological support for automated maintenance system

In order to adapt existing industrial devices to semantic-enabled environment, such as OntoServ.*Net,* we use concept of *semantic wrapper,* which is device-specific software that presents device to other environment members (services, monitoring tools, etc.). Standardized adapters use ontology for devices description representation and delivering monitored state of device to consumers.

Similarly to a semantic wrapper, *service shell* concept provides possibility to develop services as usual software components and makes them Semantic Web enabled via service shell adapter. *Services ontology* here (also as *Device ontology*) plays role of an industrial standard.

5 Conclusions

One of Semantic Web promises is to provide intelligent access to the distributed and heterogeneous information and enable mediation via software products between user needs and the available information sources.

Web Services technology resides on the edge of limitation of the current web and desperately needs advanced semantic provision oriented approach. Also the promising Web services idea to allow services to be automatically accessed and executed has no yet facilities to efficiently discover web services by those who need them. All service descriptions are based on semi-formal natural language descriptions and put limits to find them easily. Bringing Web services to their full potential requires their combination with approach proposed by Semantic Web technology. It will provide automation in service discovery, configuration, matching client's needs and composition. Today there are much less doubts both in research and development world, than few months ago, whether Semantic Web approach is feasible within at least 5-10 years.

The importance of Web services has been recognized and widely accepted by industry and academic research. However, the two worlds have proposed solutions that progress along different dimensions. Academic research has been mostly concerned with expressiveness of service descriptions, while industry has focused on modularization of service layers for usability in the short term [Sollazzo et al., 2002].

Web services technologies are rapidly changing, and a long list of additional features and functionality is required to complete the vision. The basic Web services standards (SOAP, WSDL, and UDDI) are immediately useful for many applications, such as publishing interfaces to automated business processes, bridging disparate software domains, and connecting wireless clients to Web functions [Newcomer, 2002]. With UDDI, SOAP, WSDL, industry has made a bold move forward and started initiatives that target the potential benefits of Web services. In contrast to the industry academic research has investigated languages that offer extensible ontology frameworks for the Semantic Web services. The benefits of the integration include increased visibility of Web services, because open ontology frameworks allow for semantically expressive advertising on the Web that may be found by Web crawlers.

After looking at the industry standards, it is obvious that further work is required in following areas:

- Providing a comprehensive Web Service description framework that includes service modeling (it seems to be a weakness in DAML-S).

- Establishing a tight connection to industrial efforts like XML, RDF, WSDL, WSFL and research efforts like, DAML+OIL, OWL, DAML-S etc., popularization of Semantic Web approach in the industry and, finally, pointing to industry needs for new technologies and that they are available soon.

- Defining a Web Service discovery framework that goes beyond simple registration means (like UDDI) and provides advanced ontology-based and metadata driven service discovery (DAML-S currently provides means but doesn't specify how to do it).

- Providing a scalable Web Service mediation framework that is fundamentally based on the P2P approach in order to provide direct connectivity between requestors and providers of service (only centralized architectures are in use now). This framework also includes means for configuration, composition and negotiation.

- Investigate recent trends around the Semantic Web and Web Services and their potential in scientific terms (more researches in ontology management and services composition, also, policing issues of the *Web Of Trust*)

- Building a large core consortium for Semantic Web and Web Services related challenges to provide stable standardization process.

A large amount of work exists around this problem that has not found yet its way into real applications and industry. Further efforts have to be concentrated in:

- exploring and extending Semantic Web technology;
- resolving the bottlenecks of Semantic Web technology;
- bring the latest Semantic Web technology to industry;
- applying and improving the existing Semantic Web technology in the real-life cases.

Acknowledgements. Authors are grateful to Dr. Jouni Pyotsia and his colleagues from Metso Corporation and Metso business units for useful consultations and materials. Also we would like to thank our colleagues from Industrial Ontologies Group (Oleksiy Khriyenko and Andriy Zharko) for useful discussions within the scope of this paper. Support from the InBCT Tekes Project (Innovations of Business, Communications and Technology) led by Agora Center, University of Jyvaskyla, is also highly appreciated.

References

[Ankolenkar et al., 2001] A. Ankolekar, M. Burstein, J.R. Hobbs, O. Lassila, D.L. Martin, D. McDermott, S.A. McIlraith, S. Narayanan, M. Paolucci, T.R. Payne, K. Sycara, DAML-S: Web Service Description for the Semantic Web.

[Berners-Lee et al., 2001] T. Berners-Lee, J. Hendler, O. Lassila, The Semantic Web, Scientific American, May 2001.

[Bussler et al., 2003] C. Bussler, D. Fensel, L. Franzens, Semantic Web Services and Their Role in Enterprise Application Integration and E-Commerce, Special Issue of the International Journal of Electronic Commerce (IJEC), 2003.

[Connolly et al., 2001] D. Connolly, F. van Harmelen, I. Horrocks, D.L. McGuinness, P.F. Patel-Schneider, L.A. Stein, DAML+OIL (March 2001) Reference Description, W3C Note 18 December 2001.

[Dean et al., 2002] M. Dean, D. Connolly, F. van Harmelen, J. Hendler, I. Horrocks, D.L. McGuinness, P.F. Patel-Schneider, L.A. Stein, eds., Web Ontology Language (OWL) Reference Version 1.0, 12 Nov 2002. This W3C Working Draft is available at http://www.w3.org/TR/2002/WD-owl-ref-20021112/.

[Fensel & Bussler, 2002] D. Fensel, C. Bussler, The Web Service Modeling Framework WSMF, In: White Paper and Internal Report Vrije Unversiteit Amsterdam, 2002, available at www.cs.vu.nl/ swws/download/wsmf.paper.pdf, 2002.

[Fensel et al., 2002(a)] D. Fensel, C. Bussler, A. Maedche, Semantic Web Enabled Web Services, In Proceedings of the International Semantic Web Conference 2002, LNCS, Springer, pages 1–2, 2002.

[Fensel et al., 2002(b)] D. Fensel, C. Bussler, Y. Ding, V. Kartseva, M. Klein, M. Korotkiy, B. Omelayenko, R. Siebes, Semantic Web Application Areas, In: Proceedings of the 7th International Workshop on Applications of Natural Language to Information Systems, Stockholm - Sweden, June 27–28, 2002.

[Fensel & Musen, 2001]   D. Fensel, M.A. Musen, The Semantic Web: A Brain for Humankind, Intelligent Systems, IEEE, March/April 2001.

[Mitra, 2003]   N. Mitra (ed.), SOAP: Version 1.2, W3C Recommendation, 7 May 2003, URL: http://www.w3.org/TR/soap12-part0/.

[Newcomer, 2002]   E. Newcomer, Introducing Web Services, Addison Wesley, May 31, 2002, URL: http://www.iona.com/devcenter/ NEWCOMER. ch01.qk.pdf.

[Ohlms, 2002]   C. Ohlms, A Perspective on the Market Adoption of Semantic Web Technologies, In Proceedings of AIK-Symposium, 2002.

[Paolucci et al., 2001]   M. Paolucci, T. Kawamura, T.R. Payne, K. Sycara, Importing the Semantic Web in UDDI, In: Proceedings of Web Services, E-business and Semantic Web Workshop, 2001.

[Sankar et al., 2003]   K. Sankar, K. Liu, D. Booth, eds., Web Services Description (WSDL) Version 1.2: Primer, World Wide Web Consortium, 3 March 2003. The editors' version of the Web Services Description Version 1.2: URL: http://www.w3.org/2002/ws/desc/.

[Sirin et al., 2002]   E. Sirin, J. Hendler, B. Parsia, Semi-Automatic Composition of Web Services Using Semantic Descriptions, *Accepted to "Web Services: Modeling, Architecture and Infrastructure" workshop in conjunction with ICEIS2003*, 2002.

[Sliwa, 2002]   C. Sliwa, From e-Speak to Web Services, Computerworld, December 2, 2002, URL:
http://www.computerworld.com/developmenttopics/development/webservices/story/0,10801,76207,00.html.

[Sollazzo et al., 2002]   T. Sollazzo, S. Handschuh, S. Staab, M. Frank, Semantic Web Service Architecture – Evolving Web Service Standards toward the Semantic Web, In: *Proceedings of the 15th International FLAIRS Conference*, Pensacola, Florida, May 16–18, 2002. AAAI Press.

[Sycara, 2003]   K. Sycara. Autonomous Semantic Web Services, In: Proceedings of the 15th Conference on Advanced Information Systems Engineering, Velden, Austria, 2003. URL: http://www-2.cs.cmu.edu/~softagents /presentations/parisseminarcolor.pdf

[Trastour et al., 2001]   D. Trastour, C. Bartolini, J. Gonzalez-Castillo, A Semantic Web Approach to Service Description for Matchmaking of Services, In: Proc. International Semantic Web Working Symposium (SWWS), Stanford, CA, USA, July 2001.

[UDDI]   UDDI: The UDDI technical white paper, 2000, URL: http://www.uddi.org/.

Uni-Grid P&T: A Toolkit for Building Customizable Grid Portals*

Jieyue He[1], Hongqiang Rong[2], Zongwei Luo[2], Joshua Zhexue Huang[2], and
Frank Tong[2]

[1] Department of Computer Science, Southeast University
Nanjing, China
jieyuehe@seu.edu.cn
[2] E-Business Technology Institute
The University of Hong Kong, China
{hrong,zwluo,jhuang,ftong}@eti.hku.hk

Abstract. This paper presents an architecture and functional design
of Uni-Grid P&T, a toolkit for building customizable Grid portals for
different application domains in a typical university environment in
China. Based on a layered architecture, the functions of the toolkit are
designed on top of the new Open Grid Services Architecture (OGSA)
and based on the standards of Web services. We particularly address
the issues of collaborative portals and portlet implementations of the
toolkit. The development of the toolkit is part of the initiative of the
ChinaGrid project launched in 2002 by the Ministry of Education of
China that is aimed to build a China national education Grid to link
more than 100 major universities across China.

Keywords: Grid computing, Grid portal, Grid portal toolkit,
Web services.

1 Introduction

After a decade of development and experiment, Grid Computing has gained a
wide acceptance as a new infrastructure for computing and information management [1,2]. The Grid is an innovative model of distributed computing focusing
on large-scale resource sharing for data processing, collaborative applications
and high performance computing[3]. The resource-sharing model promises researchers and scientists in all disciplines to access and use HPC (high performance computing) facilities to solve their research and engineering problems.

In China, the HPC development is facing a dilemma[4]. On one hand, many
researchers and engineers need HPC facilities but do not have the access due
to the centralized control of these facilities and the lack of specific skills to
program and operate. On the other hand, the computing facilities are often not

---

* The work was conducted when the author was visiting the E-Business Technology Institute of The University of Hong Kong, under the support of the IBM China Scholar
Visitorship Program and the China's National '863' project (#2002AA231071).

M. Jeckle and L.-J. Zhang (Eds.): ICWS-Europe 2003, LNCS 2853, pp. 198–212, 2003.
© Springer-Verlag Berlin Heidelberg 2003

fully utilized because of lack of users and job submissions. The valuable resources are idle and wasted. We see the Grid sharing model offers to fill the gap between the great demand from the large user community and the scarcely accessible high performance computing resources.

In this paper, we propose a platform and tools that can be used to build Grid portals for different disciplines in a typical university environment in China. We name it as Uni-Grid P&T. Building on top of the OGSA infrastructure[11][25], the Uni-Grid P&T provides an open architecture and a set of tools which allow rapid development of customizable portals in different application domains, such as physics, chemistry, biology and bio-informatics, etc.

The Uni-Grid P&T initiative is a part of the ChinaGrid project that was launched by The Ministry of Education (MoE) of China in 2002. The first phase of ChinaGrid is to connect 12 universities through the MoE's broadband network (CERNET). The final goal of ChinaGrid will connect 100 major universities across China and link ChinaGrid to Hong Kong. The project itself is a great challenge because of the vast geographical region and the diversity of various resources. As part of it, the Uni-Grid P&T will be implemented at the Southeast University (SEU), China. SEU is participating in the first phase of ChinaGrid project. Among the 45 departments and research centers in SEU, there are good many setups of high power servers and HPC systems. These facilities will be connected in the campus Grid which is planned to become a node in ChinaGrid.

To give a broader access to university students and researchers in different disciplines, the key solution is to build different Grid portals for them to use. To close the gap between the complicated Grid environments and the common users, provision of portals with easy-to-use interface and user familiar services is essential. Although there are toolkits available for building Grid portals[5], e.g. Cactus[6], Gateway[7], Unicore[8], Legion[9] and Gridlab[10], they are not entirely suitable to the diversity of users and application domains in China in the considerations that (i) most portals are domain-specific, and cannot be shared efficiently, (ii) cross-domain portals normally require high budget and large supporting staff, (iii) many projects have become outdated in face of the rapid development of Grid technologies, for instance the OGSA[11][25] and Web services[12], and (iv) most issues of deployment and administration in portals are not well addressed[13].

Our goal is to develop a campus Grid platform through which university students and staff can access the Grid from their own terminals and stations. We will provide them the users tools for rapid development of customized portals for different disciplines. New portals and services can be readily built on top of existing services offered in the campus Grid. Serving portal needs of different disciplines, our work will reference the techniques of user specific Grid portal[14] but adapt with focus on the provision of domain-specific portal functionality. In particular, our proposed platform and tools will fulfill to address the following issues:

(1) Rapid development of domain specific portals for university students and researchers. These portals will provide the basic Grid services, and will include

application specific services that are needed in solving domain problems in various disciplines such as in bio-informatics, GIS, physics, etc.

(2) Rapid development of new applications on top of the basic Grid services. We will develop a graphic tool that allows users to build high-level applications by integrating a process of the basic Grid services. For example, a data-clustering algorithm can be implemented as a basic Grid service, and domain specific portals can provide services accessing it.

(3) Portal aggregation that creates new portals by aggregating services from multiple portals to support cross-disciplinary applications.

(4) Client environment that is used to develop basic Grid services such as coding a parallel clustering algorithm, compiling and registering it with the service resources.

This paper is organized as follows: In Section 2, we present the major features and services to be provided in the Uni-Grid P&T. In Section 3, we describe the Uni-Grid P&T architecture. In Section 4, we discuss the technical issues. We illustrate on the topic of collaborative portal customization in Section 5. The related projects are discussed in Section 6. The conclusions and our future work are given in Section 7.

2   Portal Services

2.1   Services

We classify services accessed from the Grid portals into three categories: *basic generic services, basic domain specific services and super services.* The basic generic services are those services that provide common Grid operations. Examples are submissions service and data service. The basic domain specific services are those services that provide basic operations required in a particular domain. For example, geographical data conversion from vector presentation to raster presentation is a basic domain specific service in GIS. The super services are those services that are built of a set of basic services to provide high-level services. The super services can be either generic or domain-specific. Domain application developers use a graphical interface and a visual definition language to create domain specific super services.

The basic generic services are divided into the following three groups: *core services, development management and administration management.* Major services in each group include the following.

(1) Core Service

Security Service – Users logon to the portal with a secure Web form to gain access to services provided by the Grid. Each site can restrict and limit accessible resources at each target system, thus retaining the ultimate control on the resources.

Submission Service – The users can specify the host on which they run their jobs. For parallel jobs, we provide a graphic interface for the user to interactively create the execution process of mutually linked jobs and submit the process to the Grid. A task is divided into subtasks that form an execution tree. In the graphic interface the user can use a mouse to select different services for different subtasks and link them into a process. The Resource service first selects the most appropriate resource for a given job taking into account factors such as cost, CPU speed and availability. Then the File service is used to send jobs to different computers for execution.

File Service – This service is used to transfer the files in different resources. Monitoring service – To track and monitor the job execution, the job status function timely displays the job status with different colors of the subtask icons on the interface. The job states include waiting, executing, finished and failed. All the states are saved in the system logs for error checking.

Data Service – Users on the Grid not only share computing resources but also data resources. These resources are usually located in different geographical locations. The geographical locations of the resources are transparent to users. The data about the resources themselves and their usage include data about job executions needed and data created by the job upon its finish. Therefore, at job submission, the data service is used to select data for the job and specify the location to store the result.

Information Service – Because the user can only select the machines authorized to run his/her jobs, the resource availability status must be provided. This information includes the status of batch queuing system, load, and network performance between the resources.

Workflow Service – This service is used to define a procedure (workflow) comprised of one or multiple services. Thus, services in different domains could complete a task coordinately.

(2) Development Management

Application Service Customization – When a domain wants to share an application as a service, because of domain diversity, users can customize the service for their domains by application service customization.

Services Generation – Web services are designed to provide application integration via the use of a standard mechanism to be described, published, discovered, invoked, and composed automatically. Reusability and cooperation are trends of science technology development. A function should be converted into a Web service when it is shared in more domains. Services generation is an ability to convert functions of different domains into executable Web services so that they are accessed or called by other users with different languages.

Factory Service – Factory service is used to produce a service instance for a portlet. Portlet will be explained in section 5.

(3) Administration Management
Account Service – Manage users, including adding, deleting and modifying users.

Resource Service – Manage computers, large volume storage devices, data resource, etc.

2.2 Role Based Access to Services

The services can be used in portlets configured differently and aggregated into different portals for different application domains for different usages. We divide users who access to and use the Grid resources into four categories, each with a different role in the Grid service development and usage.

Grid Administrators manage users and resources including computing resources, data resources and service resources. Administrators are also responsible for maintenance, update and expansion of these resources, such as adding a new computing node to the Grid. The additions of new resources are reflected in the resource directory so the users can find and use them.

Service Developers include both basic generic service developers and basic domain specific service developers. As applications increase, more services are required. The basic generic service developers develop and add new basic services to the service directory for application developers to choose in implementing their applications. Frequently application developers need to convert non-Grid applications to Grid services. For example, when a computational biologist wants to share his algorithm code with other biologists on the Grid, he can make use of service generation to export it as a Web service and add it to the resource Grid service directory so other users can use this service.

Application Developers use the Grid services provided in the Grid portal to develop new applications using a graphic interface. A visual definition workflow language is used to connect a sequence of basic services to perform a computation operation. If the new application can be reused, it can be added to the portal as a super service. The requirements for the graphic interface are:

- A user friendly environment that can be accessed anywhere, anytime using different terminals such as PCs, PDAs and other mobile devices.

- It is critical to hide the complexity of both environment and applications from the operators. Application users should be free from (1)knowing the geographical locations of resources, (2) frequent separately logon and security checking of every resource used, (3)manually submitting jobs to particular computer systems and (4)keeping track of the status of computational tasks operating on the resources, or with reacting to failure.

Information Viewers only use portals to search for execution results of some jobs. For example, stock researchers who study a data model and develop programs construct the stock prediction application before it is submitted to a Grid to run. The execution result changes over time. Once it is configured and submitted, the Grid service can be provided to the users who use Internet browsers to view the results.

3 Architecture

Nowadays, Web services have become increasingly important in the enterprise community and many new standards and implementations are emerging. The Web Services Definition Language (WSDL)[16] permits services to be defined in a standard interface language and registered and discovered using the Universal Description, Discovery and Integration (UDDI)[17] technologies. The Simple Object Access Protocol (SOAP)[18] provides a standard for communicating structured information using XML. Building on such open foundations Web services have become an appealing technology for system and application integration. The OGSA, a recent trend for enabling the service oriented Grid has adopted web services technologies as well. In our Grid portal work, we also find it a right approach to building a Grid portal customization environment based on the service oriented architecture with a discovery and binding mechanism that can be used to deal with customizing and adding new functional services. This architecture provides abilities to connect several functional services that perform the tasks demanded by the application.

Fig. 1 illustrates the Uni-Grid P&T architecture. It is a layered structure. The lowest level is the Grid fabric resources distributed in the virtual organizations. The second lowest level is the Globus toolkit 3.0[19]compatible with OGSA. The Globus toolkit is the most widely used Grid middleware systems. It provides a small set of useful services, including authentication, remote access to resources, and information services to discover and query such remote resource. Unfortunately these services may not be compatible with the commodity technologies used for application development by software engineers and scientists, and do not provide much direct support for building Grid Computing Environment (GCE). Above Globus Toolkit is the Java Commodity Grid Kit (CoG)[20], which provides a Java Commodity Grid interface to the Gloubs toolkit. On the top of COG are the various services provided to users.

In order to provide the customization capabilities, services offered to end users will be provided in the form of portlets[21] contained in the portal. Portlets have become an increasingly popular concept used to describe visual user interfaces to a content or service provider. From a user's perspective, a portlet is

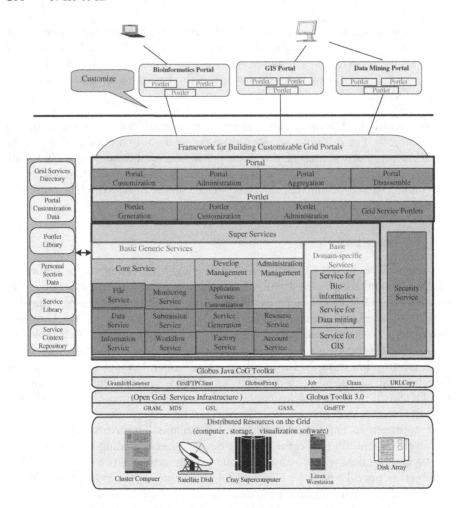

Fig. 1. Architecture of the Uni-Grid P&T.

a small window in the portal page that provides a specific service. From an application development perspective, portlets are pluggable modules that are designed to run inside the portlet container. Consequently, the portlet tier is on top of the services layer. Because all the Grid services will be used as portlet, the services will be converted into Grid service portlets by portlet generation. The portlet can be customized through the portlet customization process. The functions of portlet administration are used to publish, query portlets by UDDI, add and delete portlets.

Many portlets can be aggregated in a portal, so on the top of a portlet layer is the portal tier. It includes portal customization, portal administration, portal aggregation, and portal disassembling. Portal customization is used to customize a domain portal for a specific application. When the customization finishes, the portal configuration parameters will be saved in customization portal data. The portal administration service is used to select the portlets from the Grid services directory, search and delete portlets. Portal aggregation is used to aggregate portlets that have been selected into a portal. The portal as well as portlet information is published in the Grid services directory. When a user is customizing his/her portal, he may not only select the portlets, but also select the portal that has been aggregated. In this case, the original portal will be disassembled into portlets. Then these portlets will be aggregated to form a new portal.

The Uni-Grid P&T contains two types of portals. One is the portal formed when The Uni-Grid P&T is realized, i.e., the portal customization portal. The other type includes those portals customized through the customization portal.

Besides the usual mandatory metadata for describing resources, the Uni-Grid P&T also requires portal customization data, which is about the configuration parameters of a portal. The personal session data are also saved for each user to restore his last normal status when he logs in again to the portal. Since the Uni-Grid P&T is extendible, more services can be added and aggregated dynamically. These services are stored in the services library. The library itself can be distributed in the Grid nodes. The services are provided in the form of portlets to the service users. Each service has a corresponding portlet that is stored in the portlet library. Logically the portlet services will be published in the Grid service directory. Every service has a service context, which describes how this service is to be invoked. All the context information is saved in the service context repository. For example, when a new data mining cluster algorithm is encapsulated in a service, scientists must know the data format, parameters setting, and other configuration in order to use the algorithm to predict protein secondary structures.

The architecture is flexible. It has following advantages: (1)The functions provided by domains experts could be distributed geographically. Thus the authors of functions are able to maintain and deploy them with little cost.(2)Users can extend their services to the Uni-Grid P&T as necessary. (3)Users can easily replace a service, making it effective to expose a customized functionality to disparate user communities.

4   Technical Issues

As the Uni-Grid P&T is open, new functions can be easily converted into a service by service generation and added to the open system. Thereon, the Uni-Grid P&T will generate the portlets automatically for good efficiency and user convenience for the portlet creation. At the same time, the service context repository and the resource description are also inserted automatically. The process is illustrated in Fig. 2.

In Fig. 2, the service description gives an account of the service metadata and the interface information defined and published by the service generation. The services context repository tells about how to use the service such as the type of input data, the steps and so on. The resource description indicates where the service is located physically.

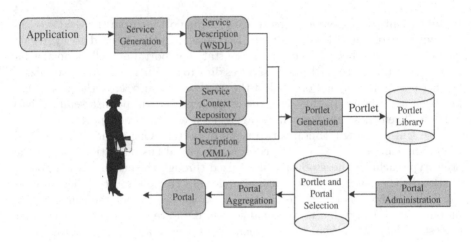

Fig. 2. The relations among an application, services, portlets and a portal.

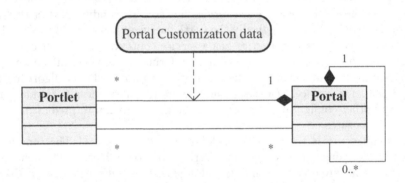

Fig. 3. The relation between a portal and a portlet.

In our framework, one can construct a portal by aggregating the existing portals as illustrated in Fig. 3. The process usually involves portal disassembling and aggregation. The underlining mechanism for portal aggregation is implemented through the communication scheme among portlets. For example, when a job is submitted through the submission portlet, the job id will be sent to the monitor portlet, so that the running status of the job can be shown and tracked. The process is conducted through the mechanism of the portlet event publication and consumption. As illustrated in Fig. 4, a portlet event coordinator is triggered when the portlet message/event arrives. The message/event listener detects the occurrence of the message, and the portlet handler provides the interface to handle the portlet event. For example, when the user generates a portlet event (he/she clicks a submission button), the portlet event message will be sent to the portlet event coordinator and then forwarded to the portlet handler.

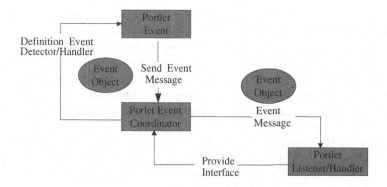

Fig. 4. The communication among portlets.

The current implementation of Uni-Grid P&T is based on the Apache projects Tomcat, Jetspeed and Axis[26]. Tomcat provides Web Application Server environment and a J2EE Web container. Jetspeed provides the flexible and reconfigurable portal environment. Axis running in a J2EE Web container provides a SOAP message listener (Axis Servlet) and is responsible for SOAP request/response serialization and de-serialization. WSDL2Java converter is used to generate the client side and server side code for the target Web service. There exist many services in the platform, each having a language associated with it. For example, in the security service, WS-Security protocol stack is used to describe the security policies and in the workflow service BPEL4WS[24] is chosen and remote portlets are enabled by Web Services for Remote Portals (WSRP)[23].

5   Collaborative Portal Customization

The Uni-Grid P&T can be used not only for customizing a portal for a specific domain, but also for a super collaborative portal across many application domaions. In this section we describe how to use the Uni-Grid P&T to make collaborative portal customization. We illustrate the steps using an example in bioinformatics application domain. The customization process can be generalized to other domains as well. Bioinformatics is a multi-discplinary field requiring collaboration efforts. Reserach activities like Gene Regulatory research, DNA sequence assembly, prediction of protein secondary structures invovles mathemtical, statistical and computer systems to analyze biological data. Bioinformatic applications use computer systems to the store and analyze genomic and proteomic sequences and structures. All of them require huge computing power and mass storage in which the Grid technology is an ideal candidate. At the same time, it is necessary to have a portal to facilitate such collabtiavtive activities. Such a portal usually requires customizations for the target usage.

For example, when an application developer wants to build a Grid portal for the users in bioinformatics, he first needs to logon to the customiation portal. Once he is authenticated, all the actions authorized for him will be made available. He will be permited to check the customization portal data to see if the desired portal has been built. Each service is encapsulated as a portlet and published in a Grid services directory. Thus, if the developer does not find the desired portal, he can query the Grid services directory and find out the ones he needs. The developer selects necessary portlets through portal administration service and then can customize them. The portal configration data will be added into the portal customization data as part of the user portal profile. The process is showed as the left part of Fig. 5.

Bioinformatics research requires the collaboration of experts in multiple domains. Uni-Grid P&T provides a collaborative protal to realize such mechanisms. For example, in the gene regulatory research, it is necessary to establish the mathematical evaluation model for the relativity of the gene representation models, through the aggregation analysis of the gene representation data. The procedure includes the Gene regulatory information retrieval, data cleaning, cluster analysis, relevant mathematic model building. If a new cluster analysis algorithm is provided, it must be converted into a service through the service generator and saved into the service library. At the same time, it will be converted into a portlet for other users to use. Because the functions provided by domains experts could be distributed geographically, obviously, it would be much more convenient if remote Web services would appear as remote portlets including presentation and application logic[22] by WSRP[23]. These portlets will be aggregated to a portal that can be invoked through a standard interface using generic portlet proxies on the portal side. This means that no special portlet code needs to be installed on the portal. Use of generic portlet proxies eliminates the need to develop specific portlets for each service to run on the portal. Through the use of portlet proxies, the remote portlets appearing on the portals just like local portlets and can be selected by users easily. The services provided by domains experts can be distributed geographically and published as remote porlet Grid services in the Grid services directory as shown in Fig. 5. For example, data mining experts can publish a clustering function as portlet in the Grid services directory. Once the remote portlet is published, the bioinformatics researcher can use the portal administration service to search the Grid services directory, select the portlets needed, add them into the portlet and portal selection library, and then generate a portlet proxy used for calling remote porlet Grid services. Therefore, for a specific application domain portal, it includes two portlets: local portlets and remote portlets, which run on the local portal server and the Grid as remote services respectively.

The Gene Regulatory research constitutes many steps, connected in a process flow that is supported with the workflow service provided by the customization portal. The flow can be described in Business Process Execution Language for Web services (BPEL4WS[24]). The BPEL4WS describes a flow as a sequence of activities performed by various service providers (partners) and tied together through sequential control links. The activities, like other services, can expose their interfaces described using the standard WSDL for external use. On execution, the sequential control links will trigger the correspondent portlets and the user can use these portlets to perform his computational tasks.

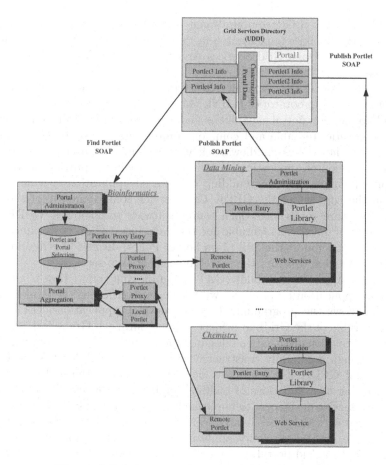

Fig. 5. Collaboration and remote portlet Web services.

6 Related Work

Development of suitable toolkits of higher-level Grid services is considered as an important catalyst to boost the use of the Grid technology and facilities[10]. In this section, we review three well-known pioneer toolkits that provide excellent references to our own work.

GridPort[15], a Grid portal toolkit for building Grid computing portal, was developed from the HotPage project carried out at the San Diego Supercomputer Center (SDSC) in late 90's. GridPort was generated from a subset of software that provides account management and resource usage functions for the HotPage portal. GridPort can support multiple application portals on a single Grid with a single login environment. Because it is simple, robust, and flexible, GridPort has been used to build several science portals such as the Laboratory for Applied Pharmacokinetics modeling portal at the University of Southern California, The Telescience portal at the National Center for Microscopy and Imaging Research at UCSD and the NBCR computational portal at SDSC. GridPort is one of the early portal toolkits implemented in Perl language. Its early design was not based on the new Open Grid Services Architecture (OSGA) and Web services standards.

The Grid Portal Development Kit (GPDK) was developed at Lawrence Berkeley National Laboratories (LBNL)[14]. GPDK is aimed to provide generic user and application portal capabilities and was designed with the following criteria: the generic, reusable and common components access the Grid services supported by the Globus middleware; it uses customizable user profiles to support easy creation of application portal specific profiles; it provides a complete development environment for building customized application specific portals based on the core set of the GPDK Grid service components; it provides an open architecture to leverage open source software technologies. GPDK provides a suite of JavaBeans suitable for the Java based GCE environment and was designed to support the JSP (Java Server Pages) display. The development of GPDK is moving to adopt the new standards of Web services.

The Grid Application Toolkit (GAT) is an on-going effort that is aimed to provide an application programmer with a single interface to the Grid environment and allows the programmer to easily develop applications. GAT is the main deliverable of the GridLab project, a joint European Grid effort[10]. GAT will provide functionality that enables an application to call the underlying Grid services through a carefully constructed set of generic high-level APIs. Unlike GridPort and GPDK, GAT is more focused on APIs to the underlying Grid services, rather than functions of building application portals. Therefore, GAT is a tool for service developers to implement domain specific basic Grid services.

Compared with the above related work, we are focused on collaborative portals to enable multi-disciplinary applications and inter-disciplinary collaborations. In this Uni-Grid portal framework, portal toolkits are provided to realize the wrapping of applications into web services. Then those services are aggregated in the form of portlets into a collaborative portal according to application requirements. Furthermore, individual collaborative portals can be aggregated into a new collaborative portal.

7   Conclusions and Future Work

The Grid is rapidly evolving in concepts, technologies and implementations. However, the ultimate success of this innovative computing model and infrastructure highly depends on its attraction of users in large numbers to use it and benefit from it. The Grid portal is moving the way to offer easy access to the Grid services. Development of the toolkits for building various portals in an economic way and offering opportunities to application developers to develop their own domain specific services is becoming a focal point in the Grid technology development. The Uni-Grid P&T design is our first step to develop a suitable tool for use of university research students and staff in developing Grid technologies and applications. We have built a test Grid environment consisting of an IBM

SP2 system, IBM pSeries 660 and 670 high-end servers, and a cluster of Linux PCs communicated with the Globus middleware. Since the framework is very huge, there are many services to be implemented. To accomplish all these purposes, we plan to partner with other ChinaGrid participating universities. The core services will be implemented first along with other development management services, like service generation and administrative management services to construct the basic Grid computing platform. More and more domain specific services including super services will be added accordingly when this platform is used to develop applications to enable more and more inter-disciplinary collaborations.

References

1. David De Roure, Mark A. Baker, Nicolas R. Jennings and Nigel R. Shadbolt, "The Evolution of the Grid", in Grid Computing – Making the Global Infrastructure a Reality, ed. by Fran Berman, Geoffery Fox and Tony Hey, John Wiley & Sons, 2003, pp. 65–100.
2. Fran Berman, Geoffrey Fox and Tony Hey "The Grid: past, present, future", in: Grid Computing – Making the Global Infrastructure a Reality, ed. by Fran Berman, Geoffery Fox and Tony Hey, John Wiley & Sons, 2003, pp. 9–50.
3. Ian Foster, C. Kesselman and S. Tuecke. "The Anatomy of the Grid: Enabling Scalable Virtual Organization", Int. J. of Supercomputing Application, 15(3), 2001.
4. Liu Peng, Li San-li, Huang Zhen-chun, Du Zhi-hui, He Chuan and Chen Yu, "xGrid: a Grid Prototype for Interdisciplinary Research", To appear in Minicomputer and Microcomputer System, 2003 (in Chinese).
5. Geoffrey Fox, Dennis Gannon and Mary Thomas "Overview of Grid Computing Environments", in: Grid Computing – Making the Global Infrastructure a Reality, ed. by Fran Berman, Geoffery Fox and Tony Hey, John Wiley & Sons, 2003. pp. 544–553
6. Cactus http://www.cactuscode.org/
7. Marlon E. Pierce, Chonhan Young, and Geoffrey C. Fox, "The Gateway Computational Web Portal", Concurrency and Computation: Practice and Experience Vol. 14, No. 13–15 (Grid Computing environments Special Issue), pp. 1411–1426, 2002.
8. Dietmar W. Erwin, "UNICORE-A Grid Computing Environment", Concurrency and Computation: Practice and Experience Vol. 14, No. 13-15 (Grid Computing environments Special Issue), pp. 1395–1410, 2002.
9. Anand Natrajan, Anh Nguyen-Tuong, Marty A. Humphrey, Michael Herrick, Brian P. Clarke and Andrew S. Grimshaw, "The Legion Grid Portal", Concurrency and Computation: Practice and Experience Vol. 14, No. 13–15 (Grid Computing environments Special Issue), pp. 1365–1394, 2002.
10. Gabrielle Allen, Kelly Davis, Konstantinos N. Dolkas, Nikolaos D. Doulamis, Tom Goodale, Thilo Kielmann, Andrè Merzky, Jarek Nabrzyski, Juliusz Pukacki, Thomas Radke, Michael Russell, Ed Seidel, John Shalf and Ian Taylor. "Enabling Applications on the Grid: A GridLab Overview", International Journal of High Performance Computing Applications: Special issue on Grid Computing: Infrastructure and Applications, to be published in August 2003.
11. Ian Foster, Carl Kesselman, Jeffrey M. Nick and Steven Tuecke, "The Physiology of the Grid: An Open Grid Services Architecture for Distributed Systems Integration." June 22, 2002. http://www.globus.org/research/papers.html

12. Web services http://www.w3.org/2002/ws/
13. Gregor von Laszewski, Eric Blau, Michael Bletzinger, Jarek Gawor, Peter Lane, Stuart Martin and Michael Russell, "Software, Component, and Service Deployment in Computational Grids", The First International IFIP/ACM Working Conference on Component Deployment, June 20–21, 2002 Berlin, Germany
14. Jason Novotny "The Grid portal development kit", in: Grid Computing - Making the Global Infrastructure a Reality, ed. by Fran Berman, Geoffery Fox and Tony Hey, John Wiley & Sons, 2003, pp. 657–673.
15. Mary P.Thomas and John R. Boisseau "Building Grid computing portals: NPACI Grid portal toolkit", in Grid Computing - Making the Global Infrastructure a Reality, ed. by Fran Berman, Geoffery Fox and Tony Hey, John Wiley & Sons, 2003, pp. 675–699
16. Web Services Definition Language http://www.w3.org/TR/wsdl
17. Universal Description, Discovery and Integration http://www.uddi.org
18. Simple Object Access Protocol. http://www.w3.org/TR/SOAP/
19. The Globus Grid Project http://www.globus.org
20. The Java Commodity Grid (Java CoG) Kit, http://www.globus.org/research/development-environments.html
21. What is a Portlet? http://www-3.ibm.com/software/webservers/portal/portlet.html
22. Thomas Schaeck "WebSphere Portal Server and Web Services White paper", http://www-3.ibm.com/software/solutions/webservices/pdf/WPS.pdf/
23. Web Services for Remote Portals http://www.oasis-open.org/committees/wsrp/
24. BPEL4WS Business Process Execution Language for Web Services http://www-106.ibm.com/developerworks/webservices/library/ws-bpel/
25. Ian Foster and D. Gannon, "The Open Grid Services Architecture Platform", Feb 16, 2003, http://www.ggf.org/ogsa-wg
26. http://www.apache.org/

On Extracting Link Information of Relationship Instances from a Web Site*

Myo-Myo Naing, Ee-Peng Lim, and Dion Hoe-Lian Goh

Centre for Advanced Information Systems
School of Computer Engineering
Nanyang Technological University, Nanyang
Avenue, N4-B3C-13, Singapore 639798, SINGAPORE
mmnaing@pmail.ntu.edu.sg, {aseplim,ashlgoh}@ntu.edu.sg

Abstract. Web pages from a web site can often be associated with concepts in an ontology, and pairs of web pages can also be associated with relationships between concepts. With such associations, web pages can be searched, browsed or even reorganized based on their concept and relationship labels. In this paper, we investigate the problem of extracting link information of relationship instances from a web site. We define the notion of link chain and formulate the link chain extraction problem. An extraction method based on sequential covering has been proposed to solve the problem. This paper presents the proposed method and the experiments to evaluate its performance. We have applied the method to extract link chain information from the Yahoo! Movie Web Site with very promising results.

Keywords: Ontology, Information extraction, Hyperlink structure.

1 Introduction

1.1 Background and Motivation

Web extraction refers to extracting data from web pages. Due to the heterogeneous nature of web information and the different application usage, many different types of web extraction problems can be defined. Nevertheless, these problems are important because there are enormous amount of web information waiting to be extracted.

In this paper, we assume that a set of ontology concepts and relationships are given to enhance the access to web pages from a web site. The web pages can be associated with the concepts while pairs of web pages can be associated with the relationships between concepts. For example, web pages from a university web site can be usually associated with concepts such as faculty, department, course, lecturer, etc.. These web pages can therefore be treated as concept instances. Relationships between concepts such as TeachCourse(lecturer,course) and OfferCourse(department,course) exist, and so are the relationship instances

---

* This work is partially supported by the SingAREN21 research grant M48020004.

M. Jeckle and L.-J. Zhang (Eds.): ICWS-Europe 2003, LNCS 2853, pp. 213–226, 2003.
© Springer-Verlag Berlin Heidelberg 2003

relating pairs of web pages. When concepts and relationships are associated with web pages, several new possibilities to access a web site become feasible [1]. For example, web pages can be queried by their concept labels, and can be navigated using the relationship labels.

In the previous web extraction research, most efforts have been devoted to the *attribute extraction* [2,6] and *relation extraction* [3,8,14] tasks that assume information to be extracted come from one single web page.

This paper, on the other hand, attempts to investigate the extraction of link information for pairs of web pages that are associated with some relationship. Since the link information may span across multiple web pages, both the training and extraction processes must scan different web pages before a piece of link information can be uncovered.

For example, at the Yahoo! Movies Web Site [1], we may be interested to know the instances of the ActorOf(movie, actor) relationship which are actually the web pages of movies together with the links to their actors' web pages. To efficiently find the link information connecting from the movie web pages to their actor/actress's web pages, we need a fully automated web extraction method.

The main objective of this paper is to formally introduce the link chain extraction problem. We propose that relationship instances can be obtained by extracting the link chains between the source and target web pages of the relationship instances. We also present an extraction method that semi-automatically extracts link chain information using very few training examples from a well-structured web site.

To measure the performance of a link chain extraction method, we further define the precision and recall measures for the extracted link chain information. A series of experiments are also conducted to evaluate our proposed method.

This link chain extraction research is closely related to several applications using web content. In our context, we are interested in automated ontology-based web annotation (OWA) [12] and would like to treat link chain extraction an essential step in automated web annotation.

1.2   Paper Outline

The rest of the paper is organised as follows. In Section 2, we describe the related work. We formally define the link chain extraction problem in Section 3. Our proposed method to learn extraction rules for link chain extraction is given in Section 4. The evaluation of learnt extraction rules on web pages to extract link chain information is given in Section 5. Performance evaluation of our prosed method is presented in Section 6. We finally conclude the paper and present future research directions in Section 7.

---

[1] http://movies.yahoo.com/

2   Related Work

There are a lot of extraction systems attempted to extract information from the Web [2]. Depending on the nature of the underlying sources, these systems can be generally categorized into two types: the systems for extracting information from natural language documents and those for extracting information from semi-structured documents. The general survey of different information systems has been presented in [10,5]. As our web extraction problem involves semi-structured web pages, we survey some related extraction systems focusing on semi-structured information sources.

To extract information from a single web page, text extraction rules are often used to identify the relevant information in the page using some knowledge about the way the page is formatted or structured. In the case of web pages, this knowledge includes the way HTML tags are used to markup their semantic content.

WHISK [13] presented a rule induction approach to generate patterns for the relation instances contained in a semi-structured and free text web page. By using the users' markup training web pages, the WHISK algorithm generates the rules that utilize regular expression patterns to identify the relevant phrases and extract the delimiters of these phrases. WHISK is suitable for situations where multiple records are found in a single web page.

In the SRV project [7], information from HTML sources are extracted by using a set of training examples. The rules in SRV rely on a set of token-oriented features identifying the simple or relational properties of the tokens. These simple properties include *word*, *numeric*, and *punctuation* and the relational properties include *prev-token*, *next-token*, etc. By examining the features found in the training examples, SRV rules are able to extract a single record from a given HTML page. SRV rules are used in the WEB→KB [4] project to extract attribute instances of an ontology.

The system that is closely related to our work is the STALKER [11]. By giving a sequence of tokens around the item to be extracted and an Embedded Catalog Tree, STALKER generates the rules that can handle the hierarchical nature of the items to be extracted. STALKER rules are general enough for the documents with different formats by allowing the rules to have disjunctive properties. Rules generated by WIEN [9] are similar to STALKER but they cannot handle the nested structure or other variation of semi-structured documents.

3   Problem Statement

In this section, we formally define the hyperlink information extraction problem. Before that, we define a few important terms as follows:

Let w be a web page. The URL of w is denoted by $w.url$. Let l be an anchor element in a web page. The target URL and anchor text of l are denoted by $l.target$ and $l.atext$ respectively.

---

[2] http://www.isi.edu/info-agents/RISE/

Definition 1. (Relationship Instance)
Let C_s and C_t be the concepts and $R(C_s, C_t)$ be a relationship in an ontology, a pair of web pages (w_1, w_2) from a web site is an **instance of** $R(C_s, C_t)$ *if w_1 is an instance of C_s, w_2 is an instance of C_t, and w_1 is semantically related to w_2 by the relationship R. We call w_1 and w_2 the* **source concept instance** *and* **target concept instance** *respectively.*

Definition 2. (Link Chain)
Let (w_1, w_2) be an instance of a relationship $R(C_s, C_t)$. The **link chain** *of (w_1, w_2) with respect to $R(C_s, C_t)$ is a list of* **link elements** *denoted by $((p_1, l_1), (p_2, l_2) \ldots, (p_n, l_n))$ where $p_1 = w_1$, $l_n.target = w_2.url$, l_i is an anchor element in p_i and $l_i.target = p_{i+1}.url$ $\forall 1 \leq i \leq n (n \geq 2)$, .*

The source concept instances may or may not be directly linked to the target concept instances. When they are indirectly linked, one or more intermediate pages will be included in the link chain to provide the list of link elements. To uniquely locate each anchor element, say l_i, in a page, we can represent each anchor element by its page offset denoted by $l_i.pos$.

Example:
Consider the web page pair (w_i, w_j) shown in Figure1. The URLs of w_i and w_j are $w_i.url=$
"http://movies.yahoo.com/shop?d=hv&cf=info&id=1808415480&intl=us",
and
$w_j.url=$
"http://movies.yahoo.com/shop?d=hc&id=1802753883&cf=gen&intl=us"
respectively. The (w_i, w_j) pair is an instance of the relationship $ActorOf(Movie, Actor)$.

The link chain of (w_i, w_j) with respect to $ActorOf(Movie, Actor)$ is $((p_1, l_1), (p_2, l_2))$, where $p_1 = w_i$, l_1 is an anchor element in w_i such that $l_1.target = p_2.url =$"
http://movies.yahoo.com/shop?d=hv&id=1808415480&cf=cast"
$l_1.target = w_k.url$ for some intermediate web page w_k
l_2 is an anchor element in w_k such that $l_2.target = w_j.url$

3.1   Anchor Element Path and Patterns

To extract link chain for a given web page pair, we borrow the notion of embedded catalog(EC) description defined in the STALKER project [11] for describing the structure of *selected* anchor elements within a web page known as *anchor element path*. The original embedded catalog has been defined to represent a web page by a tree-like structure consisting of basic values as leaf nodes and composition constructs as internal nodes. Instead of using an embedded catalog to describe all components found in a web page, we use anchor element path to describe the anchor element to be extracted from a web page in order to form a part of a link chain.

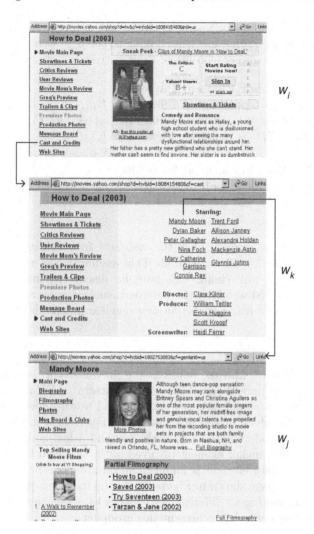

Fig. 1. (w_i, w_j) as an instance of ActorOf(Movie, Actor) Relationship

Definition 3. (Anchor Element Path)

Let w be a source target instance (source web page) or an intermediate web page of a link chain $((p_1, l_1), (p_2, l_2), \ldots, (p_n, l_n))$. *That is, there exists* $i, 1 \leq i \leq n$ *such that* $p_i = w$. *The* **anchor element path** *of w is defined as a tuple* (N, E) *where N and E denote a set of nodes and a set of directed edges respectively, such that the nodes in N are connected by edges from E to form a directed chain. Each non-root internal node is either a repetitive list of another internal node or a leaf node. The leaf node represents the anchor element* l_i *in w.*

In the above definition, the root node represents the entire web page. Each internal node in the anchor element path represents some grouping of anchor elements of the same type. This arises when the link chains of different instances of the same relationship share some common web page (often the hub page of the website), and the anchor elements linking to the next web page of these link chains are grouped together as a list or table entries.

Definition 4. (Anchor Element Pattern)
*The **anchor element pattern** of a link chain $((p_1, l_1), (p_2, l_2), \ldots, (p_n, l_n))$ is defined as an ordered list of **anchor element paths**, $(AEP_1, \ldots, AEP_n)$ such that each p_i has AEP_i as its anchor element path.*

Definition 5. (Well Structured Web Site)
*A web site is known to be **well structured** if all instances of any given relationship found at the web site have their link chains sharing the same anchor element pattern.*

In this paper, we assume that the web site from which the link chains are to be extracted is well structured. This assumption is necessary because rules for extracting link chains can only be discovered for structured web sites. For unstructured websites, the heterogeneous representation of link chain information will make it impossible for any rule learning method to derive some useful patterns.

Example:
Consider the Yahoo! Movies website, the instances of relationship *ActorOf(Movie, Actor)* share the anchor element pattern (AEP_1, AEP_2) shown in Figure 2. AEP_1 consists of only a root node and a leaf node representing the anchor element involved in the link chain starting from a movie page. AEP_2 consists of a root node, another internal node and a leaf node. While the leaf node represents the anchor element involved in the link chains that leads to an actor page, the anchor element is found in an intermediate page (known as the Casts and Credits page shown in Figure 3). As the intermediate page groups all anchor elements linking to different actor pages as a list, the internal node in AEP_2 is therefore defined to represent this grouping.

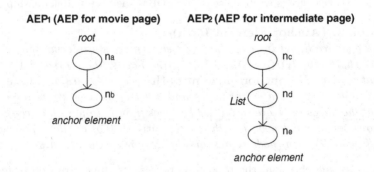

Fig. 2. Anchor Element Pattern of ActorOf(Movie, Actor) Relationship

3.2   Extraction Rules Definition

Anchor element paths and anchor element patterns are designed to model the structure of web pages containing the anchor elements involved in link chains. They alone, however, cannot be used for extracting anchor elements from web pages. We therefore have to introduce the notion of **extraction rule**.

Given an anchor element path, $AEP = (N, E)$, we associate an extraction rule with each non-root node in N.

Definition 6. (Extraction Rule)
An extraction rule is defined as a triple $< sr, tr, er >$ where sr, tr and er represent the start, target and end rules respectively.

Given a non-root node n in AEP, the start, target and end rules of n are denoted by $n.sr$, $n.tr$ and $n.er$ respectively.

Definition 7. (Start/End Rule)
*A **start/end rule** is defined as a $Skipto(\langle landmark \rangle)$ predicate or a disjunction of conjuncts of $Skipto(\langle landmark \rangle)$ predicates. The argument $\langle landmark \rangle$ represents a sequence of tokens.*

Definition 8. (Target Rule)
*A **target rule** is defined as a $HasAnchorTextPattern(\langle regularExpression \rangle)$ predicate.*

The purpose of a start (or end) rule is to skip the content that appears before (or after) portion of content represented by a node. The target rule, only applies to a leaf node, is used to verify the content within the portion of web page represented by a leaf node. The $\langle landmark \rangle$ of a start (or end) rule is a sequence of tokens which can be string tokens or token classes. There are 7 different token classes, namely, HTMLTag, Punctuation, Alphabetic, Alphanumeric, Numeric, AllCaps, and Symbol.

A $Skipto()$ predicate skips everything in the web page content until it has consumed a sequence of string tokens matching its landmark. The $Skipto()$ predicate returns True if a match is found, and False otherwise.

The $HasAnchorTextPattern()$ predicate matches the anchor text of an anchor element with its regular expression ($\langle regularExpression \rangle$) argument. If the anchor text satisfies the regular expression argument, the predicate returns True. Otherwise, a False value is returned.

3.3   Extraction Rule Evaluation on a Web Page

Given the AEP of a web page, we would like to be able to evaluate the extraction rules of the AEP nodes and extract anchor elements from the web page. The extraction rule evaluation algorithm is given in Algorithm 1.

In the EvaluateRule algorithm, *page* and AEP_{page} are the given web page and its AEP respectively. The *anchor-elements* variable stores the list of anchor elements from the web page. The algorithm evaluates the non-root nodes in a top-down manner. The variable *content* is used to store the portion of web content extracted using the start and end rules of the parent node.

Algorithm 1 EvaluateRule(*page*,AEP_{page})

1: Let *anchor-elements* be empty
2: Let *content* be *page*
3: **for each** non-root node n in AEP_{page} from the topmost level to the leaf level **do**
4:    **if** n is a leaf node **then**
5:        Extract an anchor element *ae* by applying *n.sr* and *n.er* on *content*
6:        **if** *ae* satisfies *n.tr* **then**
7:            Add *ae* to *anchor-elements*
8:        **end if**
9:    **else**
10:       Extract a new *content* by applying *n.sr* and *n.er* on *content*
11:   **end if**
12: **end for**
13: Return *anchor-elements*

---

4   Extraction Rule Learning Problem

4.1   Formal Definition

Having define the extraction rules for AEPs, we now formally state the extraction rule learning problem as follows:

Definition 9. (Extraction Rule Learning Problem)
Given a set of link chains $\{lc_1, \ldots, lc_m\}$ of instances belong to a relationship $R(C_s, C_t)$ where $lc_i = ((p_{1i}, l_{1i}), \ldots, (p_{ni}, l_{ni}))$, the anchor element pattern of web pages in the link chains $(AEP_1, \ldots, AEP_n)$, the **extraction rule learning problem** *is to derive the extraction rule for each non-root node in $AEP_1, \ldots, AEP_n$.*

As shown the above problem definition, we assume that the AEPs of web pages are given. A set of link chains is also used as input to generate rules. Since the extraction rules consist of start, end and target rules, we will describe how the given link chains are used to derive training data for learning different types of rules. We will also present our proposed rule learning method.

4.2   Training Data

Let a web page w be a sequence of tokens S. A token is a number, a word or a HTML tag. When a web page w follows the structure of a particular AEP, we say that w as an instance of AEP. The content of a root node in AEP is the entire sequence S, and the content of a child node in AEP is a subsequence of the content of its parent node.

We divide the training data for rule learning into two components, the training data for generating start and end rules denoted by TR, and that for generating target rules denoted by EX. Given a non-root node n in AEP, the two kinds of training data are denoted by $n.TR$ and $n.EX$. Hence, from the input link chains, it is necessary for us to derive $n.TR$ and $n.EX$ for every non-root node n in AEP.

Given a non-root node n from a AEP, $n.TR$ consists of a set of ($content, prefix^+, prefix^-, suffix^+, suffix^-$) tuples, one for each web page having AEP as the anchor element path. The $content$ component represents the web page content extracted by the start and end rules of its parent node of n. The $prefix^+$ and $prefix^-$ components are the positive and negative training sequences for $n.sr$ respectively. The $suffix^+$ and $suffix^-$ components are the positive and negative training sequences for $n.er$ respectively. Suppose the content to be extracted from a training web page for n is a subsequence ($content[k], content[k+1], \cdots, content[m-1]$) and $content$ has a length of p. A positive training sequence in $prefix^+$ is ($content[1], \cdots, content[k-1]$). A positive training sequence in $suffix^+$ is ($content[m], \cdots, content[p]$). Once $prefix^+$ is derived, equal number of negative training sequences are derived from $content$ and included in $prefix^-$. The same applies to $suffix^-$.

If n is a leaf node, $n.EX$ is also required. It consists of a set of anchor text of the anchor elements from the training web pages for AEP and is to be used as training data to generate the target rule.

4.3 Extraction Rule Learning Algorithm

With the training data, we learn the start and end rules using the **GetSERule()** algorithm, and the target rules using the **GetTargetRule()** algorithm shown in Algorithms 2 and 4.

We demonstrate how to generate these rules using the anchor element path AEP_2 in Figure 2 and a web page satisfying AEP_2. Figure 3 illustrates the part in the web page containing the *list* of anchor elements leading to the different actor/actress pages.

The start and end rule to be learnt for the non-root internal node in AEP_2 are:

$n_d.sr =$ Skipto(`<b>Starring:</b></font></td>`)Skipto(`<font>`)
$n_d.er =$ Skipto(`</table>`) Skipto(`</font></td>`)

The start rule, $n1.sr$, skips everything from the beginning of the web page until reaching the landmark "(`<b>Starring:</b></font></td>`)" and again skips the remaining content until the landmark "(`<font>`)". The end rule $n1.er$ starts from the end of the web page, skips everything until reaching the landmark "(`</table>`) " and again skips the remaining content until reaching the landmark "(`</font></td>`)". The following start, end and target rules are to be learnt for the leaf node of the AEP_2:

$n_e.sr =$ Skipto(`<font>`)
$n_e.er =$ Skipto(`</font></td>`)
$n_e.tr =$ HasAnchorTextPattern(*namepattern*)

The rules $n_e.sr$ and $n_e.er$ are quite straightforward. The target rule $n_e.tr$ verifies if the anchor text within the anchor element extracted using $n_e.sr$ and $n_e.er$ matches the *namepattern* pattern which is defined as follows:

$namepattern =$
```
[A-Z][a-z]{1,15}[-]?\s?[A-Z]?\.?\x?[[A-Z][a-z]{1,15}]*
```

The above pattern looks for name string that begins with a uppercase character. Several other patterns in the form of regular expressions, e.g. date pattern, can also be defined and used in target rules.

The **GetSERule()** algorithm (see Algorithm 2) is a sequential covering algorithm adapted from [11]. It learns the start or end rule of the given *examples* in $n.TR$ for a non-root node n of the AEP. To generate a start rule, *examples* consists of a set of (*content, prefix$^+$, prefix$^-$*). To generate an end rule, *examples* consists of a set of (*content, suffix$^+$, suffix$^-$*) tuples. The covered positive examples are removed while the negative examples unchanged throughout the learning process. As long as there exists an uncovered positive examples (prefixes or suffixes), it tries to generate the perfect rule. The perfect rule is the rule that accepts only the true positive examples and rejects the negative ones. Once all the positive examples are covered, the best start or end rule is returned. The **GetSERule()** algorithm calls **LearnRule()** function to learn a perfect rule. This latter first generates the initial set of candidates by using the shortest prefix (or suffix) in the training prefixes (or suffixes). It repetitively selects and refines the best candidate until the candidates are empty or the rule is perfect. The GetBestRefiner() and GetBestSolution() functions are based on some pre-defined heuristics to refine the rules and they return the best solution by applying different sets of criteria.

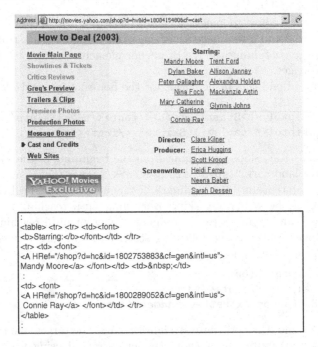

Fig. 3. Example intermediate web page and it's partial source

---

Algorithm 2 GetSERule(*examples*)

1: *SERule* ← empty
2: **while** *examples* ≠ empty **do**
3:    *rule* ← LearnRule(*examples*)
4:    *examples* ←(*examples* − *examples* covered by *rule*)
5:    *SERule* ← *SERule* + *rule*
6: **end while**
7: Return *SERule*

Algorithm 3 LearnRule(*examples*)

1: *Seed* ← *example_i* with shortest length in *examples*
2: *Candidates* ← GetInitialCandidates(*Seed*)
3: **repeat**
4:    BestRefiner ← GetBestRefiner(Candidates, *examples*)
5:    BestSolution ← GetBestSolution(Candidates ∪ BestSolution, *examples*)
6:    Candidates ← Refine(BestRefiner, *Seed*)
7: **until** IsPerfect(BestSolution) **or** BestRefiner is *empty*
8: return PostProcess(BestSolution)

Algorithm 4 GetTargetRule(EX)

1: Let P be a array of predefined pattern strings
2: **for each** $P[i]$ in P **do**
3:    *match-count*$[i]$ ←0
4: **end for**
5: $max = match\text{-}count[1]$
6: **for each** A_{textj} in EX **do**
7:    **for each** $P[i]$ in P **do**
8:       **if** A_{textj} match $P[i]$ **then**
9:          *match-count*$[i]$ ← *match-count*$[i]$+1
10:          **if** *match-count*$[i]$ > *max* **then**
11:             max ← *match-count*$[i]$
12:             $position$ ← i
13:          **end if**
14:       **end if**
15:    **end for**
16: **end for**
17: $a - pattern = P[position]$
18: $TargetRule$ ← $HasAnchorTextPattern(a\text{-}pattern)$
19: return $TargetRule$

The **GetTargetRule()** generates a target rule by examining the training anchor texts in $n.EX$. Each training anchor text is compared with the pre-defined patterns. The pre-defined pattern with maximum match count is determined and used as the argument of the $HasAnchorTextPattern$ predicate which is in turns returned it as the target rule.

5   Link Chain Construction

In this section, we describe how the link chains of a particular relationship are to be constructed by using **ConstructLinkChain()** algorithm shown in Algorithm 5. Inputs to the ConstructLinkChain() algorithm are the Anchor Element Pattern and a set of source web pages.

The algorithm firstly extracts anchor elements from the source pages and assign them to $anchor\text{-}element_1$. From these anchor elements, it obtains the next set of pages P_2 by applying the $GetPages()$ function. The extraction of anchor elements from pages in P_2 will be performed. This process repeats until all the required anchor elements are extracted. The algorithm then constructs the link chains using different combinations of link elements.

Algorithm 5 ConstructLinkChain(P_1, $AEPPattern$)

1: Let $linkchain \leftarrow$ empty
2: Let $AEPPattern$ be $(AEP_1, \cdots, AEP_m)$
3: **for each** p_1 in P_1 **do**
4:     $anchor\text{-}elements_1 \leftarrow$ EvaluateRule(p_1, AEP_1)
5:     **for** (i = 2 to m) **do**
6:         $P_i \leftarrow$ GetPages($anchor\text{-}elements_{i-1}$)
7:         $anchor\text{-}elements_i \leftarrow$ EvaluateRule(P_i, AEP_i)
8:     **end for**
9:     **for each** combination of $(< p_1, a_1 >, \cdots, < p_m, a_m >)$ where $p_j \in P_j, a_j \in$ $anchor\text{-}element_j, 1 \le j \le m$ **do**
10:         Add $(< p_1, a_1 >, \cdots, < p_m, a_m >)$ to $linkchains$
11:     **end for**
12: **end for**
13: Return $linkchains$

---

6   Performance Evaluation

We evaluate our proposed algorithms on Yahoo! movie web site. The movie home pages are taken as the source pages for four kinds of relationships: Actor-Of, Directed-by, Produced-by and Written-by. The target pages are the home pages of Actors, Directors, Producers and Writers. Giving at most 4 training link chains and anchor element pattern of the given link chains, the rules of nodes from the anchor element paths are generated for extracting the series of anchor elements from the given pages.

We then apply the learned rules on (1000) movie homepages from the movie web site, and observe whether the extracted link chains actually lead to the correct target pages.

Given a relationship, let the number of link chains existed in the test data set be N_{lr}, the number of extracted link chains be N_{le} and the number of correctly extracted link chains be N_{lc} . The recall R and precision P is defined as follows:

$$R = \frac{N_{lc}}{N_{lr}} \tag{1}$$

$$P = \frac{N_{lc}}{N_{le}} \tag{2}$$

The number of example link chains, precision and recall for each relationship are described in Table 1.

Table 1. Link Chain Extraction Results of Yahoo! Movie Web Site

Relationship	# training link chains	# extracted link chains	Precision	Recall
Actor-Of	4	7918	100%	100%
Directed-by	3	970	100%	100%
Produced-by	2	1312	100%	100%
Written-by	1	48	100%	100%

The results was very encouraging as we obtained 100% precision and recall for all relationships for even very small number of training link chains. This results is achieved mainly because the Yahoo! Movie web site is a well structured web site. The extraction rules generated by our algorithms are able to accurately select the anchor elements to be extracted.

7   Conclusion and Future Work

In this paper, we propose to extract link chains, an important piece of information linking pairs of web pages with some relationships. The link chain information can be very useful in several web applications including ontology-based web annotation [12]. By including link chain information in an annotation of relationship instance, users can use it to guide the browsing process for a web site. The experimental results show that our method of extracting link chain information achieves high precision and recall for the web pages in a well structured web site.

We plan to conduct our method on loosely structure web site of other domains. Currently, our method is only suitable for link chains sharing the same anchor element patterns. As part of our future work, we will continue our research in the following directions:

- Enhance our method to extract relationship instances that involve different anchor element patterns.
- Investigate methods for deriving more information from the extracted link chains to facilitate ontological web annotations.

References

1. T. B.-Lee, J. Hendler, and O. Lassila.   The Semantic Web, May 2001. URL:http://www.scientificamerican.com/2001/0501issue/0501berners-lee.html.
2. S. Baluja, V. Mittal, and R. Sukthankar. Applying machine learning for high performance named-entity extraction. *Computational Intelligence*, 16, Nov. 2000.
3. Sergey Brin. Extracting patterns and relations from the world wide web. In *WebDB Workshop at 6th International Conference on Extending Database Technology*, 1998.
4. M. Craven, D. DiPasquo, D. Freitag, A. McCallum, T. M. Mitchell, K. Nigam, and S. Slattery. Learning to Construct Knowledge Bases from the World Wide Web. *Artificial Intelligence*, 118(1-2): 69–113, 2000.
5. Line Eikvil. Information Extraction from World Wide Web-A Survey. Technical Report 945, Norweigan Computing Center, 1999.
6. F.Ciravegna. Adaptive Information Extraction from Text by Rule Induction and Generalisation. In *Prodeedings of the 17th International Conference on Artificial Intelligence*, Seattle, USA, August 2001.
7. D. Freitag. Information extraction from HTML: Application of a general machine learning approach. In *Proc. of the 15th Conf. on Artificial Intelligence (AAAI-98)*, pages 517–523, 1998.
8. Benjamin Habegger. Multi-pattern wrappers for relation extraction from the Web. In *Proceedings of the Europeen Conference on Artificial Intelligence*, 2002.
9. N. Kushmerick. Wrapper induction: Efficiency and expressiveness. *Artificial Intelligence*, 118(1-2): 15–68, 2000.
10. Ion Muslea. Extraction patterns for information extraction tasks: A survey. In *In AAAI-99 Workshop on Machine Learning for Information Extraction*, 1999.
11. Ion Muslea, Steven Minton, and Craig A. Knoblock. Hierarchical wrapper induction for semistructured information sources. *Autonomous Agents and Multi-Agent Systems*, 4(1/2): 93–114, 2001.
12. M. M. Naing, E.-P. Lim, and D. H.-L. Goh. Ontology-based Web Annotation Framework for HyperLink Structures. In *Proceedings of the International Workshop on Data Semantics in Web Information Systems*, Singapore, December 2002.
13. S. Soderland. Learning Information Extraction Rules for Semi-structured and Free Text. *Journal of Machine Learning*, 34(1-3): 233–272, 1999.
14. N. Sundaresan and J. Yi. Mining the Web for Relations. In *Proceedings of the WWW9 Conference*, pages 699–711, 2000.

Author Index